RUSSIAN THEMES

By Mihajlo Mihajlov

*

RUSSIAN THEMES
MOSCOW SUMMER

MIHAJLO MIHAJLOV

RUSSIAN THEMES

TRANSLATED BY *Marija Mihajlov*

MACDONALD : LONDON

SBN 356 02492 X

First published in the United States and Canada

Copyright © 1968 by Farrar, Straus & Giroux, Inc.

The original foreign language versions
Copyright © by Schweizerisches Ost-Institut, Bern

Extracts from *The Trial Begins*, by Abram Tertz and translated by Max Hayward and from *The Icicle*, translated by Max Hayward and Ronald Hingley (published in the United States under the title *Fantastic Stories*), published by Harvill Press.

Extracts from *Virgin Soil Upturned*, by Mikhail Sholokhov and translated by Stephen Garry (published in the United States under the title *Seeds of Tomorrow*), published by Putnam & Company (London).

First published in Great Britain in 1968 by
Macdonald & Co. (Publishers) Ltd.,
49 Poland Street, London, W1

Printed in Great Britain by
Thomas Nelson (Printers) Ltd, London and Edinburgh

I would like to express my particular gratitude to Mrs. Miriam Dow for her moral support and her help with this translation. Acknowledgment is also due to Christopher Bird, Helen Janin, Kosara Gavrilovich, Ludmila Toman, Marcia Rucker, and Lana Gromoff.

Marija Mihajlov

CONTENTS

*   *   *

RUSSIAN
THEMES

ABRAM TERTZ: FLIGHT FROM THE TEST TUBE

There was enough talk about Man.
It is time to think about God.

ABRAM TERTZ

*   *   *

I WAS in prison when I heard of Tertz for the first time.[1] A package of books had been sent to me from Paris among which was a thin volume entitled *Fantastic Stories*. Since I was in prison awaiting interrogation, the package was given to me.

It contained a miracle. Comparative literature is my specialty and reading books is my profession. I had spent years reading world literature and had become increasingly convinced that no new book could offer me anything really interesting or novel. The name Abram Tertz meant nothing to me. I learned from a magazine included in the packet that it was the pseudonym of a young Russian writer who had sent his manuscripts abroad illegally. This did not seem promising. From previous experience, I knew that these kinds of manuscripts usually turn out to be fairly dull anti-Communist tracts.

1 In 1965, after the publication of the first two parts of *Moscow Summer* in Belgrade, Mihajlov was arrested for "damaging the reputation of a foreign state." After spending thirty-seven days in jail, he was given a suspended sentence and released. At that time it was not generally known that "Abram Tertz" was in fact Andrei Sinyavsky, now serving a prison term in Russia for having published abroad works considered to be anti-Soviet. [Trans.]

So a miracle occurred. In the interval between two daily interrogations, while I was walking on the fenced roof of the prison, I discovered a great, in fact a unique, talent. I saw a vision of the world, well-known yet new, whose significance for contemporary literature, particularly Russian literature, is immeasurable.

I sensed immediately that Tertz was important and that his potential influence on the so-called "socialist period" of Russian literature might be equal only to that of Franz Kafka on European literature in the middle of this century. What puzzled me was that I had not previously heard of Tertz, whose writings tend to make those of Dudintsev, Yevtushenko, Ehrenburg, Voznesensky seem infinitely less noteworthy by comparison.

Tertz's writing seemed so fresh and new that I felt I was reading something from an unknown period. His settings and certain of his characters were of the present: streets, houses, cliché heroes, the leader of the state, an old revolutionary, a young writer, a colonel of the secret police. But though they were part of the environment of today, they were at the same time different. There is nothing narrowly political, no specific social protest, in Tertz. His vision of our horror-laden time is not social but metaphysical. He compares with Sholokhov as Mayakovsky compares with Turgenev. It is their spiritual quality rather than style, form, or language that distinguishes each pair of writers. Turgenev and Sholokhov live on one planet; Mayakovsky and Tertz on another. Sholokhov is the past, Tertz the future.

Shortly after reading Tertz, I read George Orwell's *1984*, a novel which also astonished and impressed me. It is surely one of the most significant books of our time, as it reveals the origins and the causes and effects giving rise to and produced by the spirit of the world we live in. Tertz and Orwell are obviously spiritual brothers; the difference between them is that Orwell is tragic and Tertz is ironic. Neither man knew about the other's work and it is fascinating that a common attitude should appear in the two books, one written in England, the other in socialist Russia.

Most amazing of all is the fact that Yugoslavs have heard little or nothing about these two men. Why has so little been written about them? Hemingway, for example, is superficial and pale compared to Orwell. And who is Leonid Leonov in comparison with Tertz? A conservative, aging author. Yet every year innumerable essays and books about Hemingway and Leonov appear—but scarcely anyone, in the socialist countries at least, has heard of Orwell or Tertz, chiefly because it is impossible to obtain any of their works. In the West, where people can read anything they wish, there are few who would respond, at gut level, to the high degree of realism in Tertz and Orwell.

To anyone who understands the spirit and customs of Soviet society, it is clear why Tertz had to write under a pseudonym and publish in the West. Though politically he is less contemporary than Dudintsev or Solzhenitsyn, the latter have been published in the Soviet Union but Tertz has not. Nor is there any hope that he will be published—which can also be said of Pasternak's *Doctor Zhivago*. This is not because Tertz is politically hostile—an anti-Communist or a social reformer. He simply does not move on that plane. But the spirit of his work is so foreign to the whole scale of existential values touted by Soviet officialdom since the October Revolution that no one need ask why a writer of Tertz's stature, a master, is not published in his own country. As long as a Tertz exists, mundane considerations such as the volcanic noise of the building up of new social relations, or the whole ghastly machinery of Stalinist collectivization and forced labor, remain relatively unimportant, somewhere on the periphery of life. In this sense, Tertz is more of a realist than Sholokhov: Sholokhov sees externals as the ultimate, absolute reality; Tertz, like Dostoevsky, reveals the basis of existence itself.

Tertz's settings and environments are unmistakably Soviet; such details as communal kitchens in which housewives padlock their cooking pots, the enthusiasm with which trousers of "real Czech half-wool" are received, and countless others that could not have been invented testify to Tertz's having lived on Russian soil since birth, probably never having visited the West.

One could point to links between Tertz and earlier Russian writers such as Evgeny Zamyatin, with whom he shares a common technique, and Alexander Grin, whose mysticism he equals. His closest "kin" in the West are Kafka and Orwell.

THE TRIAL BEGINS

> The court is in session, it is in session throughout the world. And not only Rabinovich, unmasked by the City Prosecutor, but all of us, however many we may be, are being daily, nightly, tried and questioned. This is called history.
> The doorbell rings. Surname? Christian name? Date of birth?
> This is when you begin to write.
>
> A. TERTZ, The Trial Begins

This novel, written in 1956, is one of Tertz's early works. Its structure, on the whole, is that of classic fiction. Except in the extraordinary Prologue and in a few passing digressions, it holds throughout to a certain characteristic realist-expressionist view of Stalinism.

The author involves himself in the plot. In the Prologue, he tells us that he has been entrusted by the "highest authority" to characterize and exalt several examples of the "heroic epic." In the Epilogue, Tertz tells us:

I had come to the camp later than the others, in the summer of '56.

The amnesty had virtually emptied the camp of its inmates. Only some ten thousand of us, dangerous criminals, were left.

In the course of the interrogation it was established that everything I had written was pure invention, the product of a morbid and ill-intentioned mind.

At the end of the novel the author is left in the concentration camp digging ditches with the two heroes of his novel.

The protagonist of the novel is the Public Prosecutor, Vladimir Globov, a fanatical Stalinist, whose son, Seriozha, a secondary-school student, attempts to create a "revolutionary organization" and ends up in prison, and whose wife, Seriozha's stepmother, is unfaithful to her husband with the Counsel for the Defense, Karlinsky.

Using a masterful technique of writing in which the elimination of everything irrelevant makes the prose unusually condensed, Tertz describes Globov and his wife, Seriozha and the counsel Karlinsky, the schoolgirl Katya and the Interrogator from the NKVD with a great deal of grotesquery and irony.

Central to the novel is the conflict between the father, Globov, who defends the position that "the end justifies the means," and his son, Seriozha, who does not agree. At one point Globov upbraids his son:

"Get one thing into your head. What matters is our Glorious Aim. And it's by this you have to measure every other thing—everything, from Shamyl to Korea. The aim sanctifies the means, it justifies every sort of sacrifice. Millions of people—just think—millions have died for it. Think of the cost of the last war alone!

And now you come along and quibble about details—'this is wrong and that's unfair'!"

Globov's attitude is shared by Seriozha's grandmother, an old revolutionary, who quarrels with Globov after Seriozha's arrest.

"Do you know what happens, Mother, when tanks go into attack?" asked Globov hoarsely and got up. "Whatever's in their way, they crush it. Sometimes even their own wounded. A tank simply cannot turn aside. If it went out of its way for every wounded man it would be shot to pieces by antitank guns blazing at it point-blank. It just has to crush and crush!"

The prosecutor stood, his unhealthy face grave and sad. Ekaterina Petrovna got up too—she couldn't help it.

"You don't have to teach me my ABC's, Vladimir. Our aim justifies any sacrifice. But nothing else would justify it, you see that? Nothing else."

The strange thing is that Seriozha too believes that the end justifies the means, but he is not conscious of this. Unwittingly, we remember the vow of Orwell's hero in *1984* to use any means, even the dirtiest, to fight the party dictatorship, because the dictatorship will use any and all means to oppress the people under it.

During an "illegal meeting" with the schoolgirl Katya at the zoo, Seriozha expounds his philosophy:

Seryozha got into his stride. He had taken off his cap, heedless of the risk of catching cold, and was waving it about as he spoke with growing eloquence. A new world, Communist and radiant, unfolded before Katya.

Top wages would be paid to cleaningwomen. Cabinet Ministers would be kept on short rations to make sure of their disinterested motives. Money, torture, and thievery would be abolished. Perfect liberty would dawn, and it would be so wonderful that no one would put anyone in jail and everybody would receive according to his needs. The slogans in the streets would be mostly by Mayakovsky; there would also be some by Seryozha, such as "Beware! You might hurt the feelings of your fellow man!" This was just as a reminder, in case people got above themselves. Those who did would be shot.

Actually, Seryozha put it very much better than this, and the only detail that remained unclear to Katya was whether the Government should be overthrown at once by force of arms, or whether it was better to wait a little, until other countries had done away with their capitalist systems. Seryozha proposed that they should wait for the world revolution, but admitted sadly that after it there would still have to be a *coup d'état*.

It is comical that these are the same words and the same methods that the Prosecutor Globov and Seriozha's revolutionary grandmother would have used in their youth. In this respect, Abram Tertz differs from Soviet rebels and social reformers such as Dudintsev and Yevtushenko. Tertz believes that any reform of society and any "development of friendly relations" which are limited to the social realm must inevitably end in terror. This is brought out in a conversation between Seriozha's friend Katya and the cynical counsel, Karlinsky, whom Katya consults about Seriozha's "revolutionary vision":

"Revolution, party-maximalism, democracy in peasant shirt sleeves, vintage 1920's." He waved the notebook. "The Trotskyists argued along much the same lines. . . ."

Katya was shocked. What did enemies of the people, spies and saboteurs, have to do with it? Such men had to be destroyed, mercilessly, as was being done by Berya. But Seryozha's organization, so far nameless, existed for the struggle for freedom and for a genuinely Soviet regime. She shuddered with disgust as a newspaper cartoon came into her mind: Trotsky, or Tito, or some such mercenary killer, pictured as a long-tailed rat and surrounded by his hangers-on, sat enthroned upon a hill of human bones.

Yury did not, however, go into the details of Trotskyism. He had a more amusing task on hand. He, the lifelong counsel for the defense of thieves and speculators, would now defend the world's foremost Power.

"How can you admit . . . Everybody knows . . . Either or . . . Never mind about . . . Marxism, nihilism, skepticism . . . Action, fraction . . . Left deviation, Right deviation . . . Essentially . . . Necessary sacrifices . . . Glorious aim . . . In the name of . . . Aim, aim, aim . . ."

"A noble end ought to be served by noble means," Katya protested weakly.

Karlinsky's blood was up. Trust a goody-goody who doesn't know where babies come from to fancy herself a Sophia Perovskaya.

"Noble means indeed! Just wait and see what will happen to you and your noble means . . . If you were in power, you would yourself . . . Suppose I took it into my head to become an emperor . . . or even to blow up the Pushkin Monument on Tverskoy Boulevard . . . Would you pat me on the back for that? And what difference will it make to me which lot puts me in the clink? You reformers! I suppose you'd like to see a kindly socialism, a free form of slavery . . . ?"

The novel transforms the social vision of Stalinism into a cosmic, metaphysical vision of the world and of life. Here Tertz comes close to Kafka. As in Kafka's *The Trial* and Alexei Remizov's *The Pond*, mysterious twin policemen appear. Thus Stalinism becomes not just a social but a universal, cosmic evil. Tertz shows why in his Prologue:

Whenever I was at the end of my strength, I would climb up on the window-sill and poke my head out through the narrow window. Down below, galoshes squelched and cats cried like children. Thus, for a few moments, I hung over the city, gulping its raw, damp air; then I jumped back onto the floor and lit another cigarette. That was how I wrote this story.

I hadn't heard them knock. There were two of them in plain clothes standing in the doorway. They had modest, thoughtful faces and they looked like twins.

One of them went through my pockets. Then he made a small neat pile of the sheets of paper scattered on the table and, moistening his fingers, counted them; there were seven all together. He ran his hand over the first page and, presumably by way of censorship, scooped up all the characters and punctuation marks. One flick of the hand and there on the blank paper was a writhing heap of purple marks. The young man put them in his pocket.

One letter—I think it was an *s*—flicked its tail and tried to wriggle out, but he deftly caught it, tore off its legs, and squashed it with his fingernail.

In the meantime his companion was listing in his notebook all the details of my private life. He tapped the walls, went through my linen, and even turned the socks inside out. I felt embarrassed as if I were before a medical board.

"Are you arresting me?"

The two plain-clothes men shyly hung their heads in silence. I was not aware of having done anything wrong but I realized that those above knew better and I humbly waited for my fate.

When they had finished, one of them glanced at his watch and said:

"You are being trusted."

One wall of my room thinned, grew lighter, and became transparent. Through it, as through a sheet of glass, I saw the town.

Temples and Ministries rose like coral reefs. Orders and decorations, shields and emblems, clung to spires of multistoried buildings. Ornaments of pure gold, molded, cast, or fretted, covered the façades of huge stone piles. Granite dressed in lace, reinforced concrete painted with frescoes of monograms and garlands, stainless steel coated in cream for beauty, all told of the wealth of those who lived in the Great City.

While above the roofs, amid the ragged clouds crimsoned by the rising sun, I saw a hand. Such was the invincible strength of the bloodshot fingers clenched into a fist and motionless above the earth, that I shivered with delight. Closing my eyes, I fell upon my knees and heard the Master speak. His voice came straight from heaven, at moments thundering like an artillery barrage, at others purring gently like an airplane. The two young men stood stiffly to attention.

He spoke:

"Mortal, arise. Behold the hand of God. Wherever you may steal away and hide, it will reach and find you, merciful and chastising. Behold!"

The hand in the sky cast a huge shadow. Where it fell the streets and houses opened out; the city was sliced open like a cake and you could see its stuffing: cozy apartments and people sleeping singly or in pairs. Big hairy men smacked their lips like babies and their plump wives smiled mysteriously in their sleep. Their even breathing rose toward the reddening sky.

Only one man was awake at this early hour. Standing at his window, he was looking at the town.

"Do you recognize him, writer?" the divine voice murmured in my ear. "He is the hero of your tale: Vladimir, my beloved and faithful servant. Follow him, dog his footsteps, defend him with your life. Exalt him!

"Be my prophet. Let the light prevail and may the emeny tremble at your word."

The voice ceased. But the wall remained transparent like a sheet of glass, and I could still see the clenched fist poised above me in the sky. Its violence increased and the knuckles whitened with the tension. The man still stood at his window looking at the sleeping town.

Now he buttoned up his uniform and raised his hand. It looked small and puny when compared to the right hand of the deity, but its gesture was as menacing and as magnificent.

And again, in a poetic description of Stalin's death which recalls a passage in Zamyatin's *The Eyes:*

The Master was dead.

The town seemed empty as a desert. You felt like sitting on your haunches, lifting up your head, and howling like a homeless dog.

Dogs who have lost their masters stray about the earth and

sniff the air in anguish. They never bark, they only growl. They keep their tails between their legs, or if they do wag them they look as if they were crying.

When they see a human being coming, they run aside and gaze at him longingly—is it *he* at last?—but they don't come near.

They wait, they are forever waiting, gazing, longing: "Come! Come and feed me! Come and kick me! Beat me as much as you like (but not too hard, if you please). Only come!"

And I believe that he will come, just and chastising. He will make you squeal with pain, and leap, tugging at your chain. And you will crawl to him on your belly, and gaze into his eyes, and lay your tousled head on his knees. And he will pat it and laugh, and growl reassuringly in his cryptic master's dialect. And when he falls asleep, you'll guard his house and bark at the passers-by.

Already, you can hear a whine here and there:

"Let's live in freedom and enjoy ourselves, like wolves."

But I know, I know only too well, how they guzzled in the past, these mercenary creatures—poodles, spaniels, pugs. And I don't want freedom. I want a Master.

Oh, the misery of a dog's life! How shall I ever satisfy my sharp hunger, for years denied?

How many lost, homeless dogs wandering about the world?

THE BREAKDOWN OF REALITY

Tertz's cosmic vision, presented in *The Trial Begins,* is developed in two stories, "Tenants" (1959) and "Graphomaniacs" (1960). In these stories, increasingly irrational and supernatural forces hover somewhere behind the "real" world. In "You and I" (1959), Tertz discovers the existence of a personal God. Finally, in "The Icicle" (1961), he attains a totally mystic vision of the world and of life.

In "Tenants," in addition to grotesquery and irony, in addition to the banal reality of the tale's communal-apart-ment setting, Tertz brings in the many spirits which inhabit our world. We are not sure if he is serious or spoofing:

And soon only water nymphs were left. And even they—well, you know yourself the industrialization of natural resources. Make way for technology! Streams, rivers, and lakes began to smell of chemical substances. Methylhydrate, toluene. Fish simply died and floated belly upward. As for the water nymphs, they'd pop out and somehow cough up all that river water, and there'd be tears (believe it or not) of grief and despair in their eyes. Seen it myself. The whole of their voluptuous bosoms covered with ringworm, eczema, and (if you'll forgive my saying so) signs of recurrent venereal disease.

Where could they hide?

They didn't pause long for thought, but took the same route as the wood spirits and witches—to the town, to the capital city. Along the Moscow-Volga Canal, over those—what do you call 'em?—lock gates into the water-supply network where it's cleaner and there's more to eat. Farewell, O native land, our primordial element!

What a lot of them perished! Countless numbers. Not entirely, of course—after all, they are immortal beings. Nothing to be done about that. But the brawnier specimens got stuck in the water mains. You've probably heard it yourself. You turn on the kitchen tap, and out of it come sobs, various splashings, and curses. Have you thought whose antics these are? The voices are those of water nymphs. They get stuck in a washbasin and it's murder the way they sneeze!

The mermaids dwell in the water faucets, and Russian housewives appear as witches:

Can you imagine the scene? A fearful commotion in the kitchen. In the smoke these witches are swaying to and fro, gripping each other's disheveled locks. They spit in each other's faces at close quarters. They call each other rude names very succinctly.

"Witch! Whore!"

"Same to you! Where did you ride off to tonight on the lavatory pan?"

If the real world is only an illusion beyond which lies a mysterious world of spirits, if supernatural forces exist, then one omniscient and omnipotent force, God, can exist too. The tragically realistic story "Graphomaniacs," dealing with the life of an unsuccessful Soviet writer, refers to an unseen hand:

Being tired and upset, I was lurching on my feet, tottering and swaying. My difficult path along the street was whimsical and zigzag-shaped. It suddenly seemed to me that I wasn't walking along the street myself, but being guided by someone's fingers as a pencil is guided over paper. I was walking in small uneven script, following as hurriedly as I could the movement of the hand that was composing and noting down on the asphalt these deserted streets, these houses with windows here and there in which the lights had not been extinguished, and me myself, my whole long, long, unsuccessful life.

Then I snapped out of it, braked fiercely, and halted in full flight. I almost fell over and looked frowningly at the dark sky that hung low above my forehead. Addressing myself in that direction, I said softly but weightily enough, "Hey, you there—the graphomaniac! Stop work! All your writings are worthless. How feeble all your compositions are. You're unreadable . . ."

"You and I" gets its inspiration from the Biblical Jacob and his night-long struggle with the adversary. It is not an accident that the title of this story is similar to that of Martin Buber's philosophical work *I and Thou*.

The story is told partly by an insignificant Soviet clerk, Nikolai Vasilyevich, partly by omniscient God. The clerk suddenly acquires the power of clairvoyance, like Dostoevsky's "Double." During a family celebration at the house of a colleague:

As if this wasn't enough, you suddenly felt as though somebody invisible and all-seeing was looking at you at this moment (was it through the window, from or through the wall?) and at all those present, who were sitting bolt upright in front of their plates, as though they were posing for a group photograph.

Quite tragicomic is the fact that the hero thinks the "some-body" who is looking at him has something to do with the NKVD:

He had a hunch that he was being watched, and I *was* watching him, but he thought it was *they*. I found this very funny. I concentrated on him and took a closeup of him in the bright focus of my eye. He was like a germ under a microscope and I examined him down to the last pathetic detail.

The hero tries unsuccessfully to evade the attention of the "All-knowing." He hides. He flees. But more mysteriously, the "Onlooker" himself cannot stop watching the hero:

I've been watching him now for four days and nights. For him I am like the python whose cold-blooded stare can mesmerize a rabbit. His ideas about me are utter nonsense, but, even if one takes his absurd fantasies as a starting point, I am not sure which one of us has the whip hand. We are both prisoners; we are unable to take our glazed eyes off each other. And although he can't see me, the beam of fear and hatred trained on me from under those reddish eyelashes is so strong that I want to shout, "Stop it, or I'll swallow you! I only have to shut my eyes and you'll vanish like a fly!" The contest is beginning to weary me.

"Get it into your fat head that you are alive and breathing only while I look at you. You are only you, because that is how I address you. You are only a man because you have been seen by God . . . Oh, you!"

This wretched sight hurt my eyes. They were smarting pretty badly. I had a feeling that my eyelids were propped open with matchsticks and that both eyeballs were bleeding from scratches . . .

To give myself some relief, and also to soothe the pain caused by my observation of the man, I tried to look in a different direction and went walking along such distant streets as Maryina Roshcha and Bolshaya Olenya near Sokolniki Park. But it didn't help. Wherever I went—on foot or by trolley—the same angry eyes and the same fingers, covered with freckles and red hairs, were always there in front of me . . .

I knew well enough that the whole business might end badly. When I couldn't stand it any longer, I took a taxi and drove straight to the scene of the events.

My idea was to entice Lida from her post and thus to ease the situation. I thought I might reduce the number of eyes that he had concentrated on himself by dint of imagination. But this was not my only motive: I wanted to take my mind off things. I needed a third person to amuse me and protect me from my persecutor.

A catastrophe becomes inevitable. The clerk cannot escape the piercing gaze which looks at him even from within:

He thought that if he disengaged his brain by means of obvious gibberish, he would rid himself of the snoopers who were spying on him from within. Not content with setting the whole outside world against himself, he had noted within himself the signs of my secret investigation and had decided to start a battle of minds with me.

In the end, he cuts his throat with a razor blade. At the last moment the "Onlooker" turns into a man and in an effort to avoid staring at his victim, copulates with the unfortunate clerk's mistress:

I was in a hurry. I had to plunge at once into what I was doing, so that you would at last cease to notice me and give up the struggle with all your furtive dreams of vengeance.

All in vain. As the "Onlooker" takes the woman, Nikolai Vasilyevich kills himself. The story ends:

Nothing had changed. It was snowing and the time of day was just as vague. The two engineers—his former colleagues, Lobzikov and Polyansky—were playing Chopin. Four hundred women were still giving birth every minute. Vera Ivanovna was applying a compress to Graube's black eye. An auburn-haired girl was putting on trousers. The brunette, bent over a basin, was preparing for her meeting with Nikolay Vasilyevich, who, as had happened before, was running, slightly drunk, through the cold. The body of Nikolay Vasilyevich was lying in the locked room. Lida paced up and down like a sentry under his window. I saw all this and could not get him out of my mind. I was rather sad.

You have gone and I am left. I do not regret your death. I am sorry I can't forget you.

The vision of the world we see through the eyes of the "All-knowing" in "You and I" is most interesting. Many different events are brought together into a unified picture that is shown over and over, never changing in its essence. The "eye" takes it all in at a glance:

Gradually, through the snowdrifts and the walls, and also through Nikolay Vasilyevich's back, which, pierced by electric light, receded down an incline toward the brunette, a panorama unfolded before me.

It was snowing. A fat woman was picking her teeth. Another fat woman was gutting a fish. A third was eating meat. Two engineers were playing a Chopin duet. Four hundred women were simultaneously giving birth in the maternity wards.

An old woman was dying.

A coin fell under a bed. A father said, laughing, "Oh, Kolya, Kolya!"

Nikolay Vasilyevich was racing through the cold. The brunette was douching in a basin in readiness for their meeting. A woman with auburn hair was putting on trousers. Three miles away, her lover—also called Nikolay Vasilyevich, for some reason—was sneaking through a bloodstained flat with a suitcase in his hands.

An old woman was dying—a different one this time.

Goodness me, the things they were doing! Cooking sago

pudding. Shooting guns and missing. Unscrewing bolts and weeping. Zhenya was rubbing his cheeks, his skates pressed under his arm. A shop window was smashed. A woman with auburn hair was putting on trousers. A doorkeeper spat with disgust and said, "Here they are! They've come!"

Racing with a suitcase in a basin in readiness for the meeting. Unscrewing cheeks from a gun, giving birth to an old woman and laughing: "Here they are! They've come!" A brunette was dying. Zhenya was dying and being born. A girl with auburn hair was playing Chopin. And another girl with auburn hair—the seventeenth in succession—was putting on trousers.

The whole point was the synchronization of these acts, each one of which had no meaning by itself. All these people were unaware of each other and, what is more, they did not know that they were details in a picture composed by me as I looked at them. Little did they know that their every move was under observation and liable to careful investigation at any moment.

It's true that some of them were troubled by conscience, but they had no way of sensing that I was watching them all the time, directly, penetratingly, and vigilantly, never taking my eyes off them. In their ignorance they behaved very naturally, perhaps, but also most shortsightedly . . .

THE ICICLE

I remember a similar talk with the professor about the "undeveloped mind."

"The undeveloped mind," I thought, "it sees, it is not blind, but how powerless it is. And discipline is necessary —a bridle for its development, strengthening, Euclid's geometry is needed; and the "developed mind" if it is squeezed into Euclid's irons, is blind, it sees not. And then when it becomes too confining, all axioms are broken like chains, whether you want it or not. And you will see spirits and witches, the bewitched and vampires, and apparitions, and ghosts, and all sorts of dwarfs, "devils," but in a different way, not with empty hands.

A. REMIZOV

Tertz's great story "The Icicle" (1961) is undoubtedly one of the most original narratives in contemporary Russian literature. What makes it so unusual, compared to everything else written in the last few decades (not just in Russian), is its novel view of reality as a metaphysical phenomenon. It relates to contemporary literature as Einstein's theory of relativity relates to Newton's mechanics.

Let us not forget that Tertz is not a philosopher but an artist. "The Icicle" is an artistic work, not a philosophical thesis; the story is arresting, full of suspense. At the same time, though superbly written, it makes no concession to the thought processes of the "normal" world of today. In its new world, the confines of reality are expanded. Time becomes as conquerable as space. In this world, unreal to us, Tertz is a realist. Yet this is a new realism, the realism of a man of a new spiritual era, or, as Nikolai Berdyaev would say, "a new Middle Age."

The story is told in the first person and is addressed to a future reader who (as we learn later) is in fact the narrator, but has been reborn after several metamorphoses. The narrator describes an unusual experience he had one winter's day as he was sitting on a Moscow boulevard with his sweetheart, reminiscing about his childhood:

And I rummaged in my childhood memories, hoping to turn up something long since forgotten. This was probably the psychological cause of the physical changes which came over me that evening and which were shortly to alter the whole of our lives.

Now, many years later, I find it difficult to say exactly how it happened. Perhaps I had been prepared for it by the course of my previous development, and had been predestined, as they say, to go through all the things that I subsequently underwent. I don't know, I don't know . . . At that moment, at any rate, I was not thinking about this at all, but was simply battering at the gates of memory, trying to force them open and remember the past. Then some fateful barrier suddenly gave way and I hurtled headlong into an abyss with an almost physical—and unpleasant—sensation of falling. I fell down and down and down, at a loss to understand what was going on, and when I came to, all my surroundings were different and I was not quite the same.

I was in a long ravine which was hemmed in by ranges of bare mountains and flat-topped hills. The bottom was covered with a crust of ice. Trees, also bare, grew along the edge of the ice at the foot of the sheer cliffs. There were not many of them, but the hollow moan of the wind showed that the forest was not far away. There was a smell of corpses. Rotten branches glowed in large numbers—though they probably were not rotten branches but bits of the moon which had been torn to pieces by wolves and which was now waiting for the moment when its bones would again grow white, luminous flesh and it would rise into the sky to the envious baying of the wolves . . .

But before I had a chance to wonder about the meaning of all this, I was charged by a monster with a gaping mouth. It moved its unseen legs at enormous speed and I guessed that it had not four, or even five, legs but at least as many as the fingers and toes on my hands and feet. Smaller than a mammoth, it was nevertheless as hefty as the largest bear, and when it was close up, I could see that it had a transparent belly, like a fish's bladder, in which tiny humans, swallowed alive, were tossing up and down in the most terrible way. The monster must have been so greedy that it swallowed its victims without chewing them and they went straight to its stomach, still writhing and jumping.

Of course, I am only giving a rough idea, in my own words, of what I felt. At the time, there were no words at all in my head, only conditioned reflexes and various religious throwbacks, as they are now called, and, in my terror, I muttered vows of such a nature that I can't bring myself to put them down on paper.

But I remember that, at that moment, these nonsensical vows had a definite effect, and the monster relented, moving off along the cliffs without touching me, and throwing up, by way of warning, a shower of electric sparks. I suppose it is only because these sparks appeared to my clouded mind as "electric" that I realized I had been passed by a harmless trolley car and I was restored to my lost sense of the actual moment.

This momentary vision disappears and a normal description of events continues. The narrator and his friend Natasha are spending New Year's Eve with friends. He offers to entertain them by telling them about "the future and the past." When he begins, he suddenly finds that he can look into the future and the past of all the people in the room:

After the Georgian, all the other guests began to change. The outlines of their bodies and faces began to waver, reminding one of the oscillating blips on a radar screen. Each line broke up and became blurred, giving birth to dozens of breathing shapes. Many of the women grew beards; people with fair hair went dark and then bald, again grew a new crop of hair; they became covered with wrinkles and then grew young again—so young that they were like children with bandy legs, large heads, and vacant eyes. These, in their turn, began to grow; their bones set, and they became fat or thin.

Just the same, each of them kept some likeness to the original form, so it was not too difficult for me to identify them and talk with them, though I could no longer be certain about their past or future.

Up to now I had known which one of them was a thief, a bigamist, or the secret daughter of a runaway White Guardist, but at present everything was all mixed up and in flux and I had no means of knowing where one person ended and another began. When a young engineer by the name of Belchikov turned to me politely and asked me to guess the year of his birth, I almost blurted out on the spur of the moment the preposterous reply—contradicting all the laws of nature—237 B.C.!

This reply came to me involuntarily and automatically, under the influence, evidently, of the changes which had taken place in Belchikov. An ancient fireman's helmet gleamed fleetingly on his head, and under his loose-fitting worsted suit there were white sheets in which he had very unskillfully draped his large torso, leaving his legs bare under the trousers. But of course it was not the trousers but the helmet and some other more elusive features which suggested to me that Belchikov had been born in 237 B.C.

Fortunately I didn't say this aloud. The helmet dissolved into thin air, the sheets billowed, and out stepped a woman of great beauty, no longer all that young, but still completely serviceable —and without drapes. I saw immediately that she was a prostitute and also, probably, of fairly ancient origin. She moved her whole body invitingly, but I had no time to feast my eyes before the frivolous creature disappeared, giving way to a priest—or it may have been a eunuch. He quivered for a couple of seconds and turned back into a prostitute, but a different one this time and less attractive than the first one. And so it went on—monks and prostitutes changing places and trying to outdo each other, different every time in price and quality, until at last they achieved the status of engineer Belchikov again.

He attempts to explain to himself and to the others this breakdown of the "reality of the moment":

I hasten to say that I am not trying to make a theory of this or to take sly digs at anybody. I am perfectly well aware that every man, even a Leonardo da Vinci, is the product of economic forces which are responsible for everything in the world. To this I would only add that the individual, the character, the personality—or even, if you like, the soul—also have no part in life and are only reflexes of our vision, like the spots we see when we press our eyeballs or look at the bright sun for a long time without blinking.

We are used to seeing people against a background of air, which looks empty and transparent, while the human figure appears to be of great firmness and density. Now, we are wrong to attribute the unvarying density and sharpness of outline of the human silhouette, which comes out particularly well in the bright light of day, to man's inner world and to call this his "character" or "soul." In fact there is no soul, but only a gap in the air through which mutually unconnected psychic substances rush in nervous gusts, changing according to the age and the circumstances.

When I say that whores and priests occupied a prominent place in Belchikov's life, I am far from wanting to hurt the good man's feelings. I am simply pointing out a situation common to all. It wasn't the engineer Belchikov himself, but the person using his name at the moment, or rather the indefinable empty space at present filled with his substance, which at other times gave refuge to completely different and constantly changing substances. Why this happens, I don't know—perhaps to preserve some historical balance.

Anyone who looks closely into himself will easily detect the most unexpected lapses into past and future states, the urge to steal, for instance, or to kill, or to sell oneself for money. I must say that I have sometimes felt even worse impulses in this thing called the soul, and so will you, unless you cheat and abjectly shy off. The main thing is not to be hypocritical, and then you will see that you have no right to say, "He is a thief," and "I am an engineer," because, in fact, there is no such thing as "I" and "he," and we are all thieves and prostitutes, or even worse, perhaps. If you think you are not, then you are just lucky for the time being, but we all were in the past, even if it was a thousand years ago, or we all certainly shall be in the future, as our sweet memories and bitter presentiments never cease to tell us . . .

I later got the upper hand of my art of seeing further than our nature permits. I learned to check and control myself and to treat people as if they really were confined to the strict limits of their own personalities and biographies.

One of his visions is imminently threatening. He sees his sweetheart, Natasha, with her head pierced by an icicle which falls at a given moment in the very near future from the roof of a Moscow building. He tries to dispel this vision but it reappears every time he looks at Natasha. He goes on to analyze himself and finds that he has lived past lives in various guises, as an Indian, a soldier, a woman, and so on. More important, he realizes that, even now, all these past personages still live within him.

I sat at home for several days, absorbed in these visions. They came in snatches, without rhyme or reason, and I was unable to sort out my different existences and arrange them in their proper sequence, in order of time. I was also intrigued, from the scientific point of view, by the absence of any connecting links between death and birth. But apparently it was not given to me to know these subterranean stages, and so the whole logic of my transformations escaped me and I couldn't see who was so intent on making a laughingstock of me. At one moment, you see, I was a Red Indian, then an Italian, and then just poor, innocent Mitya Dyatlov who for some unknown reason died at the age of eight toward the end of the thirties in the last century . . .

At one point he is present at and watches his own funeral, or rather the funeral of one of his former selves, and notes how this is like the feeling one has when looking into a mirror:

Men are so made that they never find their appearance quite convincing. When we look in a mirror, we never cease to be amazed. "Is that ghastly reflection really mine?" we ask. "It can't be!" This inability to dissociate ourselves completely from ourselves is one of the most deadly things in life, and, as one who has witnessed his own funeral and just described what it is like, I may say that my feelings at the time were just like the common experience in front of a mirror, but ten times worse. It is the feeling of protest at being carried out somewhere, when all the time you are here inside. I imagine that there is someone inside us who violently objects at every attempt to persuade him that the person he sees in front of him is none other but himself. Hold up to his nose as many mirrors as you like and, however flawless they are, the person locked up inside you will look and wave his arms.

"You must be out of your mind! Do you really think that's me?"

"Well, who is it, then?"

"No, no, no! It's not me! It's not me!" he will squeal, in the face of all the evidence.

This theme is expanded in a passage in which his present self looks into the mirror and sees a past self gazing into a crystal ball:

He was a small, brown man, old and wizened, like a bat with folded wings. To obtain a reflection of himself he was using a lump of crystal, which fragmented his tiny figure—as though it wasn't fractured enough already—into many pieces. But then I got a closeup of his head, which was bald and bony with a tight membrane of dark, tanned skin, and the lean, malignant face peered so sharply into mine that I realized he was here and could see me. Yes, I could see him and he could see me, and we froze before each other in fright and astonishment, for he too had suddenly noticed that I was looking at him, and he was no less startled than I. "My God! Was I once *that!*" was the thought that flashed through my mind, and my wet, cold forehead was touched by a burning memory of the very distant past . . .

I was in a desert with quartz all around, holding a crystal in my hand. What shall I be like in the seventy-fifth incarnation? Shall I ask? You mustn't! I will! No one will ever know . . . And I see myself—a fine, intelligent head with skin like leather . . . But what's this—white and slimy and bathed in sweat? Just like a snail. How utterly vile! A carcass dressed in rags with a rope around its neck; must have hanged himself. A monster. He's seen me. He's looking! He's looking *from there!* Can he really see me? He can, he can . . . His lips are trembling . . . and this is me, this is me! Is *that* what I shall be like?

And almost at the same time as I saw him, I saw myself in the mirror against his dark brown background. I saw myself as he had seen me in his crystal, and the memory of the impression I had then had of my present state came back in a flash—the outlandish jacket, the tie around the neck of a white, misshapen head . . . I, with my fine, leathery head, had choked with rage at this jelly-fish in a jacket. I rushed away from the crystal (the mirror?) across the desert (the room?) and, falling down on the sand (the bed?) , covered my face with my hands. I think he did the same with his face—whether the one like leather or the one like jelly, I just wouldn't know any more . . .

He tries to explain the new reality in which he lives, and he does it with a note of irony and skepticism, so that the reader is never sure whether or not he is joking:

In other words, if one thinks of it logically, nothing perishes in nature; all things are interconnected and leave their mark on each other, solidifying in different forms. Thus, we humans also preserve in our mobile features, in our various habits, in our mannerisms and smiles, the fixed characteristics of all those who once lived, as though in catacombs or warrens, in our convoluted souls, leaving behind the debris of their occupation.

It is amazing that science has not yet discovered and given a complete logical proof of the transmigration of souls. Yet there are examples all around us.

Then there are lunatics. What a gift of second sight they have! A fellow walks around with his nose in the air and says, "I am Julius Caesar." And nobody believes him—nobody, that is, except me. I believe him because I know that he was Julius Caesar. Well, perhaps not Caesar himself, but he has been a great military leader of some sort—only he's forgotten who, when, and in which branch of the forces.

After history, I thought of other subjects we did at school: geography, zoology . . . They say that the human embryo goes through various stages. First, it's a fish, then apparently an amphibian, and after that it gradually grows into something like an ape. What do you make of that?! So fish, and even frogs, were given some chance of jumping around and showing off their paces in my body. Only I can see that our old teacher didn't get around to telling me that these are not just abstract stages that my organism went through while it was an imbecile embryo gradually forming in my mother's womb. In those golden days I was twin and partner, as it were, to some quite specific living carp which had perhaps swum in the river Amazon eighteen million years ago. And all other fish, every one of them, found a home in my contemporaries.

For now I was firmly convinced that none of us will ever disappear and, in the words of the song, "will never and nowhere go under." We shall simply move to other, and perhaps even more comfortable quarters.

We shall settle inside some roomy citizen of the future and I think that he will not be indifferent to us. He will be a polite man of tact and advanced views, and the science of these progressive times to come will have told him the whole story. . . .

Hey! You there, man of the future! Listen to what I say! Don't forget to remember me on that quiet summer evening. Look, I'm smiling at you, I'm smiling in you, I'm smiling through you. How can I be dead if I breathe in every quiver of your hand?

Here I am! You think I don't exist? You think I've disappeared forever? Wait! The dead are singing in your body; dead souls are droning in your nerves. Just listen! It's like bees buzzing in a hive or the hum of telegraph wires carrying news around the world. We were people too; we also laughed and cried. So look back at us!

I want to warn you, not out of malice or envy, but only out of friendship and fellow feeling, that you too will die. And you will come to us as an equal to equals, and we shall fly on and on into unknown reaches of time and space! This I promise you.

Finally, this metaphysical knowledge of the indestructibility of the human soul and of its infinite metamorphoses leads him to a paradoxical conclusion:

No! Do as you please, but until things change for the better, I shall stand by the dead. One can't leave a person in this destitute state, in this final and ultimate degradation. For who is more degraded than a dead man?

It's disgraceful to go on living when all the others are dead. But there's nothing I can do about it . . . And then—a quite different situation—I'm standing on a balcony and beating on the lighted window, along with the moths. But again I can't get through the transparent screen to the brightly lit room inside. Natasha is alive and sits there reading a book—the very book that I have written, perhaps. And I am writing from here and trying to break in there, not knowing whether this forlorn tapping will ever be heard . . .

Will you hear it, Natasha? Will you read to the end, or will you give up halfway through and never know that I was so close? If I only knew! I don't know and I don't remember. I ought to tell her everything from the beginning. But it's no good. Any moment now she'll close the book. Wait just one second! The story isn't finished yet. I want to tell you one more thing, the last thing I have the strength for . . . Natasha, I love you. I love you, Natasha. I love you so much, so much . . .

These reflections of the narrator are only a minor part of the story, which otherwise develops according to all the rules of "realistic" novels, but set in a new reality. All the past selves are realistically drawn and take an active part in the story.

The narrator tries to save Natasha by getting her as far as he can from Moscow, where on some eave or beam the icicle that will kill her is already forming. He and Natasha go by train into central Russia but are followed by NKVD agents, who have been alerted by Natasha's first husband. The agents overtake them on the train:

There was no time to explain things to her. I was somehow confused and my mind wouldn't work. All my conflicting feelings —all the parasites traveling on my ticket—got into a flutter and pulled me in different directions. Some—probably those who had been women—told me to leave Natasha immediately ("Why get involved with trash like her?") and clear off while the going was good. Others were worried about the money, spent all for nothing, which had to be returned in a month. Somebody else advised me to offer armed resistance.

I couldn't make out who this was. Was it Stepan Alekseyevich with his aristocratic bravado? Or the Red Indian who had gone under with the scalp in his teeth? Or was it some soldier, as yet unidentified, buried inside me together with the cowards and the pennypinchers? Dear old unknown soldier!

Armed with his moral and physical support, I immediately choked off the shabby mob: "Shut up, you bastards, I'll hang the lot of you!" I muttered through my teeth, and when they had quieted down and stopped hissing, one could hear the rattle of the wheels and the creak of the wooden partitions which muffled the creak of boots and the distant murmur of the people who were coming through looking for me.

Natasha returns to Moscow. The narrator is left in prison, where the NKVD attempts to utilize his telepathic abilities to uncover "a plot" against the regime.

Just before their arrest, the narrator tells Natasha under no circumstances to go to a certain street in Moscow on the day and hour when the icicle is to fall. But this very warning compels her to go, and she dies. This confirms the narrator's realization that it is precisely when people try to escape their fate that they bring about the fulfillment of the preordained.

One may ask whether I understood at the time how utterly hopeless the situation was, whether I realized that our efforts were scarcely less futile than those of the caretakers and that we were only preparing the way for events and helping them to keep strictly to their timetable.

No sooner had I told her about this thing that had been on my mind for so long than I realized I shouldn't have said it. If I hadn't told her not to, perhaps it would never have occurred to her to go there, but now I had prepared the way myself and it was too late to do anything about it.

One has only to start talking or thinking about something for it to happen. I had noticed this a long time before. Perhaps my predictions come true only because there's no escaping what is known beforehand, and if we didn't know beforehand what's going to happen to us, then it simply wouldn't happen.

The moment this thought crossed my mind I understood that unavoidable disaster was lurking somewhere close by and that I had known about it all the time, and that I had only been fooling myself by pretending that everything was all right.

Don't you see that anything accidental is quite inevitable once it's been foretold? It's like passing sentence. You know what it's like with your tribunals: no appeal. Some people are killed by germs and others by icicles. And some while trying to escape. It varies from case to case. Strictly between you and me, we're all under sentence of death. Only we don't know the day and the hour or the other details of the execution. But I do know, I know and I'm worried sick. If only I didn't know!

Thus, a gift of prescience cannot change anything.

If I was in some degree omniscient, there was no question of my being omnipotent as well. What can I do? I know everything and can do nothing. And the more I know, the worse it is, and the fewer legitimate reasons I have for doing anything or putting my faith in anybody.

The narrator knows things in advance just as Raskolnikov, in Dostoevsky's *Crime and Punishment,* recognizes that he *knew* in advance that certain things had to happen.

. . . but I could not rid myself of a feeling that as soon as she reached the next but one lamppost, which she was now approaching, the ballerina would have an accident. To be more precise, I felt that she would slip at the very spot foreseen by me, and I even wondered whether to warn her, but curiosity prevented me and I watched her progress with baited breath. And when she reached the place and fell down, throwing her short arms up in the air, I felt a twitch of conscience somewhere deep down, as though I myself had given her a push.

He put my identity papers in his breast pocket and handed me a document which I didn't bother to read. I had a feeling all this had happened to me before, and even Sysoyev's cape, a splendid fur-lined officer's cape, seemed familiar. I had never seen Sysoyev, or his white cape, in my life, but I just knew that the whole thing would be like this; this was how I pictured it from the start.

After Natasha's death, the narrator loses his power to see into the future and becomes a normal person—albeit with some ill effects:

My illness was due to a feeling of insecurity. I was afraid to move my legs in case I stumbled and fell. As one who had got used to knowing everything beforehand, I found it difficult to return to normal life with all its unforeseen events. If a doctor in a white cap came near me, my heart would beat violently. You see, I just didn't know whether he was going to take my pulse or hit me on the nose. Who could tell what was at the back of his mind?

One day he meets a little boy accompanied by his nurse-maid. He believes the little boy to be a reincarnation of his father.

But his little blue eyes said very much more. They were the same blue, twinkling eyes that looked into my face in early childhood. The gaze of a wise old friend, who knows what's what. I even had the impression that he was winking at me.

"Daddy!" I whispered so that the nurse couldn't hear. "Daddy dear! How are you getting along? Are you all right in your new home?"

Tertz's stories are difficult to interpret because they are pithy and full of fictional devices. I repeat, Tertz is not a philosopher but an artist, and his vision of the world is not philosophically rationalized but depicted artistically. See how he describes how the hero's mind jumps back into the past and how events in the hero's conscience are played back in reverse as if in a film track that is being reversed.

The woodcock plummeted from the birch tree as though pulled on a string. I pressed the trigger and, taking aim, saw that it was sitting on a branch, a great black cock, looking at Diana. We climbed from our horses and galloped off. Katya, in her pink bonnet, waves good-by from the veranda. "Come back safe!" Jumping into the saddle, I run down the steps and pull on my boots.

"It's time to get up, master, it'll soon be daybreak!" Nikiphor shouts into my ear.

I clasp his fat calves in my hands. "Don't leave us, for God's sake; I implore you for the sake of your son . . ."

He looks away, white with anger. "Someone might see us, ma'am." I take the scalp between my teeth and start swimming. In the middle of the river I feel sick. With my teeth still clenched, I begin to sink . . .

"Tell me, Vasily, who is Pushkin?" my wife asks at dinner.

"He was one of those ancient Russian writers, my dear. He was shot five hundred years ago."

"And who is Boldyrev?"

"Another great writer, my dear. He wrote a play called *In the Dark* and a lot of poems. He was shot two hundred years ago."

"You know everything, Vasily," says my wife with a sigh.

I fire a cannon, I shoot with a crossbow, I shoot with a catapult. They run away. We run and run, on into the town.

"Let's go to the cellar," says Bernardo. "We've got a girl. Unfortunately she's dead, but she's not gone stiff yet."

TERTZ'S GENERAL SIGNIFICANCE

Up to this point we have tried to analyze in some measure the creativity of Abram Tertz. He is so original, however, that to speak of him to someone who is not at least minimally acquainted with his work is as futile as talking about Mozart to someone who has never heard his music.

It is difficult to exaggerate the importance of a talent like

Tertz's. And this has nothing to do with Stalinism, socialism, or any other socio-historical movement. Rather it involves something much more powerful and far-reaching. Tertz rebels with his whole being against the era which began with the Renaissance, and thus joins the ranks of such figures as Pascal, Kierkegaard, Dostoevsky, and Shestov. If he is an opponent of so-called "scientific socialism," this is only because it was precisely in the time of human history which he repudiates, which in Russia dates from 1917, that men recognized the power of "the reality of the moment" over the eternal soul, the power of death over man.

What Kierkegaard and Shestov achieve in their philosophical writings, Dostoevsky and Tertz achieve in their art: the toppling of raw power, the power of the obvious, and the destruction of the *dogma of reality,* and, thereby, the liberation of man from the power of the moment. In this sense, the conflict between Dostoevsky, Tertz, Kierkegaard, and Shestov on one hand and Spinoza, Hegel, Marx, and Lenin on the other is incomparably fiercer and more irreconcilable than the struggle of anti-Stalinists against the Soviet regime. Tertz rebels against a dogma which shackled the human soul and which is called, in modern language, "scientific cognition." He is indeed a representative of a new era, as Lenin was the last great man of the preceding era. The October Revolution is not the last revolution preceding a "new age" but the first in a series of revolutions to come.

It is symptomatic that men like Tertz and Orwell emerge in a period in which science, surging to victories in space, is enjoying its finest hour. Tertz is not nonscientific, but he is anti-scientific if one understands by "science" a contemporary dogma about absolute reality, the reality of momentary illusion. Scientific dogma strengthens faith in a belief that a visible and measurable world is the sole final reality and that man's goal is to adjust to this reality as best he can in order to make his life pleasant, to lengthen human life, to "conquer nature," and ultimately perhaps to make man physically immortal in this world.

But one need only question the "irrefutable truth" that this world is the only one, that the reality in which we live is final, that the human soul dies together with the body, to make the importance of science in its present form doubtful and purposeless.

Why should medicine prolong man's life if man is not mortal? Why conquer nature if it is only a momentary illusion in time and not the ultimate reality? Why try to build an earthly paradise if life on this earth is but a fleeting moment?

In these questions is rooted the irreconcilable and insurmountable antagonism between Tertz and the scientific community. As for Marxism, Tertz is an incomparably greater enemy than any capitalist ideologist.

At the same time the appearance of Tertz and others like him confirms Spengler's prediction in *The Decline of the West:*

Assuming the possibility that the most talented men of the future generations will prefer the salvation of their souls to all the powers of this world, that the most gifted minds will become more and more aware of the satanic nature of the mechanistic under the influence of metaphysics and mysticism which presently substitutes for rationalism (the step from Roger Bacon to Bernard of Clairvaux, then nothing will be able to forestall the end of this great spectacle, the game of spirits, a game in which hands are supposed only to help.

One thing is clear: Tertz is a first swallow in the world of socialism, the first in a generation brought up on a doctrine of "new social relations." It is also clear that a new generation is being born—a direct product of socialist "scientific spirit"—which will send Hegel, Marx, science, technology, and socialism, in the forms in which they now exist, to the devil. This generation is being born in the East, not the West.

THE TEST TUBE

> They forget that critical activity must be based on one method, which is seemingly also arrived at only in a critical way but as a matter of fact originates solely from the way the thinking concerned is inclined, so that the result of the critique is defined by the method which lays in its foundation. The latter, however, is defined by the current carrying and penetrating the aware, conscious being. Faith in cognition not based on hypothesis characterizes the great naïveté of the rationalistic era. The theory of natural science is no more than the dogma which historically precedes it, though in altered form.
>
> OSWALD SPENGLER

The Soviet journal *Novy Mir* in 1965 published a long article by Henrik Volkov entitled "Man and the Future of Science." The author describes the future of humanity as he sees it:

. . . The whole population of the globe will be concerned with science . . . everybody, in one way or another, will be able *to serve* science.

. . . Science aspires to be a *controlling*, if not all-encompassing, sphere of human activity. [Italics mine. M.M.]

Referring to Academician N. N. Semynov, Volkov notes that he

. . . visualizes the future as a universal network of people's laboratories in which the population will be occupied with free scientific research.

Here we have the real essence of the "scientific spirit." Science, cognition of life, is not a means but an exclusive end. In a word, cognition is the purpose of life. Life is only a means for this cognition. Cognition means power over life, or over that part of reality which is visible and measurable. Science negates the existence of other realities because reason, conscience, the glass test tube, as Goethe called it in the second part of *Faust*, does not permit man to see other worlds. The existence or nonexistence of an immortal soul or of other worlds and of realities other than our own is not defined by art but by reason, and reason's laws are only superficially based on visible reality. When a human body dies, everything about a human being that can be touched or seen disappears. Death is final because there is no soul. By extension, only the visible, material, "real" world exists. Since knowledge about it can be obtained and through this knowledge the world itself can be controlled, it follows that the world is the sole reality and "matter is indestructible and eternal." As the Russian philosopher Levitzky puts it: "The denial of the Absolute leads to the absolutization of the Relative."

Lev Shestov wrote that science is life confronted by reason. Above life are cognition, reason, the glass test tube. But the closed, finite world, the only one that science knows, is and can be (whether we like it or not) no more than a prison without exits, no matter how it is perfected technically or how adequate it becomes. And we are all only prisoners to be judged and sentenced to death in advance.

By what criterion is this world guaranteed to be the only one? What proof exists that the soul dies with the body or that there is a soul? Experience? No. We cannot know of the dead. But the experience of innumerable people throughout history shows—mystically, it is true—that this world is not the only one.

The fact is that all science is based on dogma, on a priori faith in a finite, sole, and exitless reality of this world. Like every dogma, scientific conscience wages a fierce fight against doubts of its absolute infallibility and attempts in every way possible to immortalize the prison of the "real material world." However, this is possible only if the goal of human life on this earth is proclaimed to be cognition of life. Science cannot state why this cognition is the goal and can put it forward only as an a priori assumption. The answer offered is usually that cognition gives us *power* over nature and therefore gives *man freedom* as well. This is a lie that can deceive only the naïve. The true scientific spirit will never acknowledge that science and cognition are *only the means* for a freer, better life. This claim reduces science to something second-rate, like, say, a trade. Shoemakers make shoes so that human feet will not freeze. Science has other advantages and it does *serve* human freedom. But, according to Volkov, in the "people's laboratories" of the future *man will serve science.* Thus, man is a means to an end, the end being cognition, science, power.

Therein lies the essence of the conflict between religion, which holds that this life is not the only one, that the soul is immortal, and that natural "laws" are neither unconquerable nor eternal, and science, which in order to justify itself as *the absolute goal* must insist that this is the only world, that it is a finite, ultimate reality followed only by death. If science acknowledged the possibility of the soul's immortality, of other worlds, of its own reality, a reality concerned with learning and with dominating which is only a passing illusion, and of the existence of a personal God who interferes with our lives and by *His authoritative free will* changes natural laws, then all science and cognition (including Engels, Marx, and Freud) would become not the *master* but the *servant* of life. This is precisely what science cannot permit, and this—and only this—is the conflict between religion and science. Science as an end or science as a means, a means which, when it ceases to *serve* man, can be thrown away like a kitchen rag!

There is no conflict between science as a tool of life (like the shoemaker's trade; yes, Einstein was only a highly qualified shoemaker!) and religion, i.e., the direct connection between the individual human soul and immortality, absolute freedom, God. When it is cold, we put on shoes; yet the shoes are not the end and meaning of life. But between science as investigation of "natural laws" and as power over life, on the one hand, and, on the other, religion as eternal life which does not recognize natural laws, the conflict is irreconcilable!

As long as it is only a means, science (cognition) can be rejected at any moment. When we are no longer cold, we take off our winter shoes. When I am no longer interested in the structure of the atom, I don't need physics.

To prevent this rejection from taking place, science (cognition) and the people *who serve it* must banish every thought that this world is not finite, that man is an immortal and free being, free even from the laws of nature. In order to remain the *eternal master* over human souls in this world, in order not to be *rejected* one day together with other *household objects,* science and reason must be dogmatic in asserting that man is mortal, that this world is a prison without exit, that man can aspire to no greater achievement than to dominate this finite world. The power to rule over life is given by cognition, that is, by *serving* science and reason. Therefore, to conquer the world, you must humble yourself.

Inasmuch as the goal of science is totalitarian, doubtless there exists a close relationship between social totalitarianism and the spirit of science. Science immortalizes the prison of material reality, thus barring man's way to freedom. The higher the pedestal cognition is put on and the more men are required to *serve* it, the more is mankind enslaved.

This spirit is maintained in totalitarian societies in which individuals must *serve* "society," the secret police, all-out espionage, and all other instruments of modern totalitarianism. As shown in Orwell's *1984*, these are only the means available to an authority seeking to rule human souls, because if one admits the possibility that science itself, society itself equals the *means* that must serve the freedom of an individual human soul, as finite, immortal, and extreme reality, the domination of science over life and over the soul comes to an end. But power, cognition, science, reason, or, to put it more archaically, the devil, death, nonbeing, seeks to be eternally supported by its servants, who, like all slaves, become its ablest executioners. This is why it is important for science to uphold the dogma that cognition is the *aim* of life and to predict "people's laboratories" in which all humanity will *serve* science.

If power, science, reason are eternal, what about man's soul? It simply dies. It is mortal. It may not even exist. It is only an illusion. Because, if this were not so, power and science would become *mortal*.

The human soul is mortal, so we are all condemned. But science, reason, and power will last forever. The goal of science, then, is science itself, not the liberation of man. Or, as Orwell puts it:

Power is not a means; it is the end. One does not establish a dictatorship in order to safeguard a revolution; one makes the revolution in order to establish the dictatorship. The object of persecution is persecution. The object of torture is torture. The object of power is power.

If you want a picture of the future, imagine a boot stamping on a human face—forever.

This is also Kafka's "Trial" of human souls. This is also Tertz's *The Trial Begins*. This is the nightmare which the *dogma* about the sole reality of this world wishes to immortalize. And if what reason holds to be true is indeed so—that only this world is real, that man is mortal, that natural laws are insuperable, and that Christ did not rise from the dead—then we are all dead a priori, like heroes in Orwell's *1984*.

Even if this social paradise were realized on earth, we would still be dead, because man's metaphysical predicament cannot be solved on a socio-economic-historical plane while death exists. It is precisely because reason seeks to immortalize the lack not just of a social but of a cosmic way out that Ivan Karamazov "returns the entrance ticket to God," and that Tertz writes in "The Icicle":

No! Do as you please, but until things change for the better, I shall stand by the dead. One can't leave a person in this destitute state, in this final and ultimate degradation. For who is more degraded than a dead man?

Ivan Karamazov, then, is right in saying that the final truth about life and death is in the hands of reason and science: man really dies and is left in destitution. But Ivan is right only because science wishes to perpetuate this idea. His rebellion is nonexistent if we assume that it is not reason which speaks the truth, but Alyosha Karamazov, who maintains that the dead will rise and joyfully recount to one another the events of their past lives.

The controversy continues to rage. Which is greater, worthier: the individual human soul or cognition and science; and which must serve the other? If man is to serve science and cognition, and if reason is immortal and man is mortal, then death has conquered, death dominates the world. But if the soul is immortal, and reason, cognition, and science are transitory and mortal, eternal life exists, and this world is no longer a prison without exit. The reality of the "Trial" is a transitory, surmountable illusion, and power over reality becomes second-rate, its worth not much more than the products of tradesmen.

The struggle begun by Abram Tertz standing in for Dostoevsky and Lev Shestov is indeed much more important than any anti-Stalinist or anti-Communist rebellion. It is the struggle with death: cosmic, universal.

ON THE "SCIENTIFIC PARADISE" OF THE FUTURE

> There are attempts to equate death with birth. But why, for instance, can we not equate birth with death? When man is born, he really dies: the womb is the grave and my conception was my passage to death.
>
> V. ROZANOV

Scientific knowledge, whether or not it wishes to do so, assumes that all nature, all life is a remarkably well-organized mechanism.

Were this otherwise, it would not be possible to establish "laws" of nature or to "master" life. Let us grant that life, from its lowest to its highest forms, is an organism and not a mechanism. Let us grant that even the tiniest manifestation of life is a free (not lawful) bid for existence, that in the reality of nature there are no laws, and that existence is freedom while the absence of freedom is death. Let us grant further that in the movement of a mechanism there is no more freedom than in an immobile stone and that a mechanism is dead.

That granted, all scientific knowledge, reason, logic (Shestov: "Logic is a reflection of the law of inertia") become not only suspect as values but positively damaging because they blind man and prevent his coming into contact with the genuine, live, objective reality of freedom. In this respect, all cognition, scientific knowledge, and reason, instead of leading us to an unlimited reality in which there is no death, create their own world, a finite, mortal world. With their own laws they create a schizophrenic world of an eternal mechanism and derive these laws, it seems, from nature itself.

All knowledge is in essence like a Tower of Babel because, in place of an immortal, free present, it creates a mortal, finite future according to "developmental laws." Instead of creativity, which is always a free and unrestricted drive toward the center of existence, we have work. Instead of love, which is always freely offered (man cannot love and stop loving at will and the Biblical Jews knew that "marriages are made in heaven"), we have the institution of marriage, rational choice of partners, and sex education.

And so we come to a world organized to the ultimate degree. In this world, disciplines such as cybernetics, genetics, mathematics, semantics, linguistics, etc., have developed apace. People serve scientific knowledge in "national laboratories" and all their lives "freely" study (master) the universe.

We are close to achieving perfect peace of soul and physical health, ubiquitous automation and the exclusion from life of danger and suffering. There is no tragedy, even if we have only the muffled hum of planets constantly, rhythmically *working,* the perfect movement of a mechanism, a life in which it is possible to know and calculate each step since birth and from which the unknown and the terrifying has been excluded. Mastery over life is complete. Heaven on earth is here.

Liberated from disease, natural disaster, poverty, backbreaking labor, and exploitation, man can now devote himself to knowledge, to the arts, and to life's ennoblement.

It is in this vision of earthly paradise that Dostoevsky discerned a strange and terrifying character, a man with "an

ignoble or rather with a reactionary and ironical countenance" who says, with hands in pockets: ". . . Hadn't we
better kick over the whole show and scatter rationalism to the
winds? Why? . . . to enable us to live once more at our own
sweet foolish will!" [*Notes from the Underground*]. With
unconcealed satisfaction and glee, Dostoevsky writes that
these characters of reactionary and ironical mien are bound
to win followers and will finally achieve their goal.

The mere thought of the appearance of men of "reactionary and ironical countenance" is repugnant to the votaries of
the earthly "scientific paradise." For one thing, they say, such
a thought is absurd because it is in the "scientific paradise"
that man will be free to occupy himself as he wishes, having
been liberated by technology from the necessity of working
for his daily bread. Moreover, there will be exceedingly
efficacious, scientifically based means of "persuasion" of a
very forceful character indeed, to convince everyone that the
best possible world has arrived. It is therefore essential, I
believe, to recognize that society organized on "scientific"
principles, as, for instance, "scientific socialism," must be a
police-ruled, totalitarian society. After all, it is impossible to
govern nature without governing "human nature" (that is,
the soul), since human nature is so undisciplined and capricious. "If my theory doesn't correspond to the facts, so much
the worse for the facts," said Hegel, the most important
ideologist of totalitarianism.

Just as the basis of all scientific knowledge is spying on
nature and life, so in all totalitarian, "scientific" societies the
core elements, without which society cannot be held together, are the secret police and spying.

That last word in technology, the "telescreen," is an apparatus that sees and hears all and transmits it to police head-
quarters, in Orwell's *1984*. The "psychoscope," in Tertz's
The Trial Begins, is one of the fantasies in the minds of the
twin police agents. Interestingly, police twins also appear in

Alexei Remizov's *The Pond* and in Kafka's *The Trial*. In Tertz's novel they walk through the deserted streets of a silent Moscow (which also recalls the title of Yuri Bondaryev's novel: *Silence*) :

Silence. Two men in plain clothes stroll through the city streets. Two men in plain clothes. Slowly, decorously, they advance along the sleeping streets, peering into lifeless windows, gateways, doors. There's nobody. One is named Vitya, the other Tolya. And I am frightened.

In other words, means of "persuasion" must exist despite the fact that "man will have no reason to be dissatisfied with anything." He will not have to work; he will suffer neither pain nor lack of material comforts; women will bear children painlessly, if they bear them at all, since it will be possible to create a fetus in a test tube. Thus, man will be totally free. True, it might be a bit boring: not everyone enjoys painting, visiting museums, attending concerts, doing scientific research in "national laboratories," or investigating the universe. However, science will solve the problem of boredom too, it is claimed—and in a scientific manner, of course. A vision of incredible splendor!

But what if man wants to work? Not pursuing a hobby, but real work, the work assigned him when he was thrown out of paradise, the work of creating and building, the work on which his life truly depends, work done "by the sweat of his brow" for daily bread; indeed, the pain of childbirth. It is this kind of work that will not be permitted him. Persuasion will be used to set this world up so that everyone may do just what he wants, as long as it is a hobby. Machines will have taken over the work.

It does not occur to anyone that *forced nonlabor* (which already exists in technologically advanced countries) is as horrible as *forced labor* in a concentration camp; they are two sides of the same coin. The important difference is not between work and nonwork, but between forced labor and forced nonlabor on the one hand and free labor, which, precisely because it is free (and not because it is done) in the realm of the arts or the sciences, can create and build. The difference between work (slavery) and creation (freedom) is not *what* man does—whether painting, playing a musical instrument, digging ditches, plowing the earth, giving birth, or doing nothing—but *whether* he does these things of his own free will, without external or internal pressure. This is the criterion for determining whether creation is authentic or not. The same difference exists between a marriage contracted out of love ("made in heaven") and one contracted without love (in itself a kind of prostitution). The difference is not that, in the first, two people sleep together and, in the second, they are "liberated" from that need, but that in the first, outwardly identical with the second, there is freedom, happiness, and creativity, and in the second there is only slavery.

Speaking metaphorically, science assumes that all marriages are loveless and man therefore should be liberated from marriage, from slavery, from exploitation, from physical suffering. Marriage partners who do not like each other must be liberated from sleeping together, while, at the same time, woman is liberated from the pangs of childbirth. And yet, liberated people will not be much happier than slaves. All that remains for them is the pursuit of hobbies in "national laboratories."

Love in marriage is happiness, freedom, life; and the pangs of childbirth are transformed into a happiness which a woman in love will never surrender. In such a marriage, sleeping together is not slavery but the greatest joy. In real life, it is ludicrous to speak of hobbies and "national laboratories" and to say that science will deal with boredom. What boredom? All is happiness, eternal life.

Just as science and reason cannot bestow love, they are also incapable of discerning "laws of love," because love is bestowed and man cannot produce it, however perfect his science and technology. Yet science aspires to total control of life, which forces it to claim that happiness comes with being liberated from marriage and from all kinds of work except that which can be called a hobby (one of the "scientific" attempts to solve the problem of boredom). Because science cannot produce true life, which is bestowed, the spirit of science seeks to perfect the prison of unauthentic life, to offer material comforts, to liberate man from physical suffering, anguish, fear, and danger. It seeks to substitute for a poor, dangerous, mutable, and imperfect life one that is new, scientific, immutable, eternal.

However, like the happy woman who truly lives and who does not experiment with socio-scientific activities, all men who live a true life, who create freely by the sweat of their brows, never even think of liberating themselves from their circumstances. And for any woman who loves, being "liberated" from marriage to the man she loves is the greatest tragedy. The substitution of machines for man, machines that perform the functions of the free creator, brings death to the soul. The existence of even a single true creative work or one true love casts suspicion on the entire artificially created, scientific, technological Babel because it shows that everything that is most valuable is freely bestowed, whereas what is produced by reason and science is of lesser value. The spirit of science and totalitarian society, which, if only to survive, must persecute those who truly live, those who are free, is what Orwell portrayed so brilliantly in *1984*. Because science cannot liberate man from physical death, it *liberates him from life itself*.

We see, then, that instead of eliminating the inauthenticity of the past, we increase it in geometric progression. Paradoxical as it may seem, the world of science, the Tower of Babel, has its roots in the traditions of the church. The world is evil;

let us build our own, better one, let us shut ourselves in the monastery. Marriage is not authentic; let us be celibate. Nature is imperfect; let us perfect it and master it scientifically. The beginnings of science have their roots in medieval monasteries.

Dostoevsky, in his brilliant *Grand Inquisitor,* points out that "scientific socialism" is the darling of church tradition and that the conflict between the Christian and other religions on the one hand and socialism and science on the other is the result of a misunderstanding. Sooner or later, "scientific socialism" and Christianity will join forces.

We must be careful not to identify the socio-historical organization of the church with the teachings of Christ. As Spengler says, the church came into being "when the teachings of Christ became the study of Christ." This happened in the first generation of Christians.

Even if we grant that science will alter life sufficiently to offer a kind of paradise on earth, the question of death remains. If sooner or later the life of the individual ceases, even if he should live ten thousand years, this world is a sealed prison.

Such a thought affects Yuri Karlinsky, Public Prosecutor in *The Trial Begins:*

Yury could not sleep. It often happened to him nowadays: he remembered that he must die and he lay awake. . . Self-deception was the only way out. This was the remedy in common use: anything to take your mind off this nothingness, which could easily drive you mad. Some went in for politics, like that oaf Globov. . . ."

Fear of death stimulates the need for self-deception. Paradoxically, belief in the immortality of the soul, which liberates us from the fear of death and thus provides an exit from this finite life, is, according to the "accepted findings of contemporary science," "self-deception," an opiate, etc. A *belief* that this life is finite, irredeemably finite, that death exists, and that therefore this life is to be lived painlessly (with science attacking boredom, and people occupying themselves with political activity and "scientific investigation") is proclaimed to be the truth!

Since science, even after infinite progress, cannot liberate man from death, it liberates him from life, for life is unknown, terrifying, and painful. The task of science is to free the world from the terror of the unknown, from pain, from wonder and mystery. However, life in a world where all is known, a world without wonder and mystery, a "mechanistic" world, is indeed the death of the soul. There is nothing new in this world if we refer only to perception, reason, and knowledge. Perception of pain is the same now as it was ten thousand years ago. Perception of love is eternal and has not changed significantly since the time of the *Song of Songs*. The concept of pain, the concept of love—that is, words, thoughts, $2 \times 2 = 4$—are eternal. Even so, my own *individual* pain, my wound, is ever new, even if before me billions of people have been wounded. My love is ever new, even if billions of others have loved. But the perception of love, the perception of pain are always the same.

If science should succeed in liberating man from death, what would happen? Such a thing would be possible only in a world without wonder, a world that is completely understood, in which there is nothing unexpected, a totally mechanized and "lawful" universe. Nikolai Berdyaev, in *Freedom and the Spirit*, gives the following opinion about such a situation:

A life in the flesh in this sinful and wicked world if it had no end would be too terrible to contemplate, for such an existence would be nothing more nor less than spiritual death.

We are not against material well-being produced through scientific discovery, or against a struggle to bring happiness to mankind. We recognize that scientific progress has value, however limited (a value rated quite differently by science itself). We believe that man must struggle for earthly happiness and fully agree with Lev Shestov when he says: "There are no unhappy people, only unhappy swine." We also believe that only people who are completely happy in this life save themselves for eternity. We second Kierkegaard in saying: "The knight of faith is the truly happy man, the man who completely masters the finite, not just the infinite." And we support Berdyaev when he says:

The kingdom of God is not of this world, it is not the kingdom of nature and cannot be manifested within its limits, for there only the symbols of other worlds are possible.

And yet the kingdom of God is being realized at every instant of our lives!

Therefore we side with Tertz, because he sees that the solution to man's happiness or unhappiness does not lie with science and cognition, technology and automation; that, quite the contrary, these things make happiness impossible. We agree with Berdyaev that:

Mystery is not a negative category, but the positive fullness of life's infinite depths.

He is also right in saying:

The free life is the most complex, while the easy life is that which is subject to restraint and necessity. Freedom entails suffering and tragedy. The abandonment of freedom brings with it an apparent relief from the sufferings and tragedy of life.

Because of this, the efforts of the "spirit of science" lead to the greatest possible enslavement of man, to death in this world and in eternity.

THE JUSTIFICATION OF SCIENCE

In taking away life, in destroying freedom and creating a mechanism, science and so-called "scientific socialism" fulfill their missions. The results of course will be negative in terms of the goals scientific knowledge and socialism have set themselves, but that does not alter the fact that in some way science and reason will participate in the creation of an eternal life for man, though in a negative sense. As Berdyaev wrote:

It is true that revolutions have certain positive results besides and that they determine new epochs in history, but the good which they do is the result not of revolutionary but of post-revolutionary activity. It is due to the understanding of what has been lived through. Evil can be overcome only inwardly and spiritually.

Every experience is an enrichment, even if enrichment involves the negation of this experience. [*Freedom and the Spirit*]

To pass through the experience of atheism may be a purification of the human idea of God, and emancipation from a base sociomorphism. [*The Human and the Divine*]

The appearance of Tertz, Pasternak, Solzhenitsyn (let us recall his recently published, profoundly religious short stories) proves this. In this sense we can say that Spinoza, Hegel, Marx, and Lenin were fulfilling God's mission. This idea is further supported by their own faith in themselves as the elect and their belief that their opponents were pharisees. The rationalist Hegel had *infinite faith in reason,* while his contemporary, Kierkegaard, who was opposed to Hegel, admitted that he himself was not a "knight of faith" because he did not have the courage needed for faith ("I know all but can do nothing").

Hegel, Marx, and Lenin took up their role in response to God's call: "Go and blind that people, that they may look but not see, listen but not hear." And precisely because they so fervently *believed,* they have blinded the world. They themselves are saved because they believed in what they did and because they were happy in their success. At the beginning of this century, Lev Shestov, in a brilliant metaphor, showed the relationship between those committed to the "changing and developing of this realistic life" and those committed to eternal life:

A caterpillar transforms itself into a cocoon and lives for a long time in a warm and tranquil world. If it had human consciousness, it might claim that this is the best of all worlds, even the only one possible. But the time comes when an unknown power makes it begin acting to destroy. If other caterpillars could see the horrible activity it is engaged in, they would call this immoral, impious, they would talk about pessimism, skepticism, nihilism and similar things. Why destroy something that has required such efforts! And then what is wrong with this warm, comfortable, finite world! To protect it, it is necessary to invent a sacred morality and a theory of cognition. And the fact that wings have grown on the caterpillar and that, having eaten through its old nest, it will fly out into the free world in the form of a gorgeous and light butterfly is of no concern to anybody. The wings are mysticism, and conscience is reality. The people who create it deserve suffering and punishment. And in this wide world there are enough prisons and voluntary hangmen: the majority of books are also prisons, and great writers were often hangmen.

Hegel, Marx, and Lenin built a tight cocoon and they were right. Dostoevsky, Kierkegaard, Shestov, Berdyaev, and Tertz want to destroy the cocoon and fly out into the open and they are right. It is true that without a well-constructed cocoon a caterpillar would never become a butterfly; it would remain a caterpillar forever. It is also true that a butterfly dies if it cannot bite through the cocoon and discard it.

The caterpillar builds, "as if for eternity," his warm, closed, perfected, comfortable world; the butterfly discards it and flies into majestic, unknown, dangerous, and infinite space. Both are right. Because the isolation of life in Russia (a life not as comfortable as in the wealthy West) lasted so long, we see today the appearance of the first butterflies, who, very often, still have not the strength to bite through and discard the cocoon and fly into sunlit space.

Tertz is one of the first to bite through the cocoon, to shatter the test tube. True, he is not flying yet. But more of that later.

The visionaries of the "national laboratories" would like to keep the butterfly in the cocoon forever. The cocoon ceases to be a means and becomes an aim. This is why a bloody battle rages. Is the cocoon, science and scientific knowledge, a means or an end? If it is a means, then it is necessary today but tomorrow it will be discarded and all will be well. But if it is an end, then the butterfly will die and the cocoon will remain, forever, whole. This is a life-and-death struggle: everlasting cocoon or eternal butterfly. Only the butterfly which breaks out can live on in his progeny.

Is life on this earth the end or the means? Tertz submits that life on this earth is a means to eternal life and that eternal life begins to be realized right here on earth only if man really lives, only if he struggles for happiness, i.e., for freedom and authenticity. This holds whether we're speaking of the happiness of a Lenin who builds a cocoon or of Dostoevsky's man of the "reactionary and ironical countenance," the man who would destroy the cocoon.

Eternity is lost only to those who are not happy, who will not struggle for happiness, the slaves. They are in the majority. They say: "We will not build the cocoon, we will not be happy in this world because death in any case will destroy life. We must turn from life to eternity, we must reject earthly bliss and only 'save our souls.' " Others say: "The only thing that really exists is the cocoon and nothing follows after. There is no other life, there is no eternal life, let us make life pleasing by mastering reality, etc. . . ." The first are the priests, and the second, the socialists. Contradictory though it may seem, the two stand on the same ground. The elimination of belief in the immortality of the soul and the hope of final mastery over this world destroys in man the thirst for life in this world because it puts him into a prison from which there is no escape. Likewise, the rejection of individual love because it passes and the acceptance of celibacy, penance, and asceticism destroy the possibility of eternal life, which man must begin to realize in this life by working to make the cocoon (impermanent as it may be) by the building of earthly happiness.

Between the two, they do away with both eternal life (eliminated by those who reject this life) and life on earth (eliminated by those who deny eternal life). Those who believe that this life is a grave and a world of the dead, that death alone is resurrection (historical Christianity), and those who believe that only this life and this world are real and that death is the final end (Marxism) reflect two different images of the same thing. Death does not exist in the real, free, organic, godly world. All is life. The tree of knowledge brings death.

The conflict between Tertz and the Soviets is not based on the struggle between Marxist-socialist concepts of social organization and the concepts of the democratic, liberal West. Rather it is based on a struggle between the free spirit and the spirit enslaved by this world, whether in a "capitalist" or a "socialist" system. It is not a question of substituting one type of social organization, one type of socio-political doctrine, for another. Nor is it a question of making the world a freer, richer place. The question is existence itself, the reality of this world and "that" world, life and eternal death, now and forever.

The question is the existence or nonexistence of man's immortal soul: the image and likeness of God, or highly organized matter? Which is more real: $2 \times 2 = 4$ or the soul of Abram Tertz? Death or life?

SOLA FIDE

> *You see what's happening all around us? A man lives on and on, but suddenly—bang!—and he's dead, then other people walk around in his place until they too are senselessly destroyed. All you hear around is: bang, bang, bang!*
>
> "The Icicle"

> *Maybe all that is legitimate—I thought—and on a certain level in the development of the human spirit it is quite healthy for that same spirit to draw away from superstition, myths and prejudices, from all that is labeled superstition, which weakens man's will, chains him and keeps him in constant fear. Yes, it is necessary sometimes to untie hands so that all ghosts and wizards might disappear and leave man free with his own head, and in so doing, wake up the energy in him. To push him by arithmetic to act, arithmetic which will lead him to mathematics, higher mathematics, and the storm of integrals will overflow and then the ghosts and wizards will appear again, but you are no longer terrified or obdurate. No, you have a rooster's comb on your head, a three-pronged fork in your right hand, a little garland in your left hand, and your feet are like snakes; it is not without reason that there among the most mathematically gifted people in the world (in the Riche Institute in Paris) they take pictures of ghosts.*
>
> ALEXEI REMIZOV, "On the Cornices"

> *And now we are looking through a glass, darkly.*
>
> SAINT PAUL

To serve science is to master life. Give yourself to reason and you will govern. Here we see exposed the fact that all governing requires the enslavement of those who govern, that all who govern are slaves, and that a free man cannot govern. The end, governing, and the means, giving oneself or obeying recognized "laws," are shown to be identical. The means and the end are always identical. The means are the end, always and everywhere, however much man is deceived by the end. Education, forced education—all education is forced—has for its purpose, its end, the withdrawal of freedom, since the earliest years. One-party dictatorship whose end is the establishment of an "empire of freedom" turns out to be an end in itself. The peasants of Russia during the time of forced collectivization were not eliminated so that a so-called "material base" could be created for a rich and productive agriculture. They were eliminated so that dictatorship might survive.

Knowledge gives freedom. But what of the words of Dostoevsky in *Notes from Underground,* or of Kierkegaard, or of the main character in "The Icicle": "I know all but can do nothing"? Perhaps someone might answer: "But you must admit that technical development frees man of the need to labor for his daily bread and therefore gives freedom." If all work is creative and true, however, even the most grueling ditch digging or plowing, then it is not necessary to be freed from it. On the contrary, this "liberation" is the greatest enslavement, just as the greatest punishment for a woman who loves a man would be to deprive her of the chance of bearing and raising children in pain and worry.

We are concerned, therefore, not with "liberating" man from pain and suffering but rather with finding a way for man to live the true life. Yet all scientific progress, all scientific knowledge, automation, etc., cannot give man authentic life. Inner freedom—which alone opens the door to true life, creativity, love—cannot be *given* to man or to society; one cannot free a slave if he is not inwardly free. That is why scientific knowledge and "scientific socialism," however they attempt to free man from the agony of nonauthentic life, cannot give him authentic life. Nonauthenticity, nonbeing—in ordinary terms, boredom—is not only not disappearing but is proliferating to infinity and leading backward to self-destruction. I have all and wish for nothing. As Shestov says:

There was a moment in the history of the world when somebody took freedom away from men and gave them knowledge instead. And he even succeeded in persuading them that only knowledge can give freedom.

And further:

To perceive means to make known the unknown, but man has seen, tasted and examined all the known and has fled, as if mad, from it. If there is any hope for man, it is only a hypothesis that the unknown has and can have nothing in common with the known, and that the "known" is even not as well known as we are prone to think.

Man is destroyed by and man flees, even to death, from a nonauthentic, familiar, unchanging life. Real, authentic life, however hard it may be, is always a joy for which man struggles. This is why in time of war or natural catastrophe suicide rates drop. Yet in Sweden, where man has realized the ideals of "scientific society," the suicide rate is the highest in the world.

How are we to free ourselves of the dreadful prison, the test tube of the final, familiar, unchanging world? Is it possible that human cognition, scientific knowledge itself, will relinquish its role of teacher and liberator and admit that life is, after all, a mystery, that it cannot be known, that all explanation of reality is merely a blinding of people, and that, as Shestov says, "the work of philosophy is not to soothe but to disturb man"?

Where in history can one find authority which would willingly relinquish itself? Where is the wise man who would willingly relinquish his reason? True, the too-wise Socrates said: "I know that I know nothing," but he nevertheless continued to think himself the wisest of men and to teach his pupils to the last instant of his life.

Only one thing remains, the destruction of the prison and the test tube: what has been called *"sacrificium intellectus,"* very inappropriately, because, to cite Shestov again:

Reason is necessary, very necessary to us. In the ordinary circumstances of our existence it helps us overcome difficulties, even the great difficulties, which we encounter in our lives. But it happens also that reason brings man the greatest misfortunes, that it turns from benefactor and liberator into prison guard and hangman. To renounce it does not mean to sacrifice anything. There is only one question: how to free oneself from this hated power.

And further:

And that cannot, in any case, be considered *sacrificium intellectus*. It is not *sacrificium,* not a sacrifice at all. Is it a sacrifice when somebody kills his prison guard or his hangman?

We cannot free ourselves and society from authority in this way because invariably a new social system and a new authority are created (as a means to an end, however noble). It is impossible to free oneself from the authority of reason by substituting one theory of life for another. But fortunately, as Spengler puts it, "people do not discard this or that theory but faith in theory in general." They do not discard faith in a particular social system to accept faith in another social system; they discard *faith* in all social systems.

Emmanuel Mounier correctly considered the conflict be-

tween religious people and atheists as a conflict of *faiths*. If
the essence of all pure religion is Tertullian's *credo quia
impossibile,* meaning faith in a wonder external to the "laws"
of nature and logic, then the essence of the scientific spirit is
credo ut intelligam, meaning faith, a priori faith, in reason.
This faith is a blood tie, the binding together of man's soul
and the object believed in. Religious people (referring, of
course, to authentic religion, not clericalism) are bound to
God, eternal life, freedom. Believers in scientific knowledge
are bound to reason and, in the language of the Bible, to the
devil. For the religious man freedom, God, and eternal life
are the greatest realities. For those who substitute reason for
religion, consciousness, cognition, logic are not merely reflections of reality but reality itself, a test tube more real than
life because human souls are imprisoned in it and life is
outside it. Or to quote the opinion of old, naïve Bertrand Rus-
sell on this antagonism between two faiths: "The power of
prayer always has known boundaries; it was blasphemous to
ask for too much. The power of scientific knowledge has no
boundaries, according to some. They told us that *faith* can
move mountains, but *no one believed it.* Now they tell us
that atomic bombs can overturn mountains, and all believe
it."

For this reason we move and live in various worlds, depending on what the objects of our faiths are.

To destroy the test tube of finite, mortal, mechanistic life
means to liberate oneself. It is impossible to liberate man
from the outside. That is, force only strengthens the walls of
the test tube. That is precisely why the Catholic Church
deserved atheism's challenge. The failures of all social "corrections" of society and "scientific heavens" of whatever stamp
are similar. It is impossible to give man freedom from the
outside. Scientific knowledge has nothing to say on this. As
Berdyaev puts it:

The sciences concerned with the physical world do not succeed in penetrating to the real nucleus of being, for their researches are directed toward ascertaining the causes underlying the phenomena of the external world.

Man is determined from within, from the inmost depths of his being . . .

Only from within, out of an infinite thirst for life, for freedom, does man's soul shatter the test tube. In this respect, all exertion of force over people can be highly useful in a negative sense because it can stimulate the soul's indomitable thirst for life. Similarly, the comfortable, cozy "scientific paradise" can in reality be more terrible than the open, bloody "trials" of Hitler's totalitarian Germany or Stalin's Russia. It can be more terrible because it lulls man to sleep. A comfortable prison is much more dangerous than an ordinary concentration camp. And here we come to the puzzling words of Berdyaev:

True freedom is that which God demands from us and not that which we demand from God.

It is not man but God who cannot get on without human freedom. God demands from man the freedom of the spirit, for He only wants the man who is spiritually free.

and to those of Shestov:

Freedom does not consist of the possibility of choosing between good and evil. Freedom is the strength and authority which do not permit evil into the world . . .

Berdyaev continues:

. . . Freedom is not the result of necessity . . . but rather it is necessity which results from freedom, as a consequence of its own peculiar orientation.

The natural order is not eternal and immutable. It is but the expression of a moment which symbolizes the life of the spirit. Consequently, forces can arise in the depths of the spirit capable of transfiguring it and freeing it from the power which holds it in bondage.

Strength to destroy the test tube of "natural laws" can be found only in the depths of the human soul, strength not to substitute for this world the external ways of scientific knowledge and technology but to break the test tube, which conceals from man the greatest reality, that the world is an eternal wonder in which there are no "laws" but in which there is creative freedom; that the soul is immortal; that man is indeed created "in the image and likeness of God"; that faith, only faith, gives real freedom, a freedom which cognition cannot give. Authority is always authority over an object; authority and cognition cannot be directed at a subject and that is why cognition and authority turn everything into an object, enslaving and killing.

Only boundless hatred of death and slavery and unquenchable thirst for freedom, which is eternal life, can lead man to that supernatural wonder and blessed state: the liberation of oneself from *faith in reason,* from faith in the final reality of the test tube. When Tertz and Rozanov say that "God loves them," they mean only that they loved God, freedom, more than others. As Shestov says:

Faith is indeed the very freedom which the Creator's breath infused in a man together with life.

Freedom comes to man not from knowledge but from faith, which destroys all fear.

Faith is freedom.

Faith and faith alone gives a man strength and courage to face madness and death.

And Kierkegaard:

Everything that is not of faith is a sin. Therein lies one of the basic principles of Christianity: the opposite of sin is not morality but faith.

Hegel is right when he says that miracles are "forces overcoming natural ties to phenomena." Only it must be added that the so-called "natural ties to phenomena" ("laws of nature," reason, logic, the test tube) are the greatest blocks to miracles (God, the human soul, and life itself).

Man does not exist without a miracle, without a *personal God*, in the absence of which there is only "a product of socio-historical conditions" who must be disciplined through force to accept the "social paradise." A personal God because every miracle, all free urge, all freedom in general is personal, not abstract. It is not "laws" but "the personal" that makes man "in the image and likeness of God," if that is what he is. Personal, individual man is free even of natural laws and death.

This seems to reflect a certain contradiction: Dostoevsky and Tertz, Shestov and Berdyaev lead the battle for God, not for man, while Marx and Lenin and so-called "humanists" struggle against God for man. But Berdyaev says: "The existence of God is the existence of my independence of the world, of society, of the state."

Precisely for this reason, Peter Verkhovensky in Dostoevsky's *The Possessed* is the precursor and real ideologist of the totalitarian spirit of the twentieth century. He understood that it is necessary first to destroy man's faith in a personal God, a God who actively participates in man's life, a God who wrestles with Job and in the end lets him win and gives him back his wife and children, his herds; to destroy faith in a personal God who gives us both the blessings of this life and eternal life as well. After that it is easy to convince people that they must use their own strength to create a world better

than the existing scientific, technical, police-totalitarian, final
and mortal one, a world not bestowed but *prescribed*. Verkhovensky's success and the success of similar "humanists" is
understandable because, as Berdyaev puts it:

. . . It is God who demands that man should be free, not man
himself. Man himself loves servitude and easily comes to terms
with it. Freedom is not a right of man but a duty of man before
God.

And at the end of that road, which begins with the "death
of God"—more accurately, with the "murder" of God (Shestov says "Spinoza is the man who killed God") —we come to
an absolute standstill, the human end, the final object, as in
Orwell's *1984*. That is why there is no man if there is no
God. Imagine that God exists, and all the horrors of Orwell's
world, all the horrors of Ivan Denisovich's camp, pale as
phantoms into the dawn.

Spiritual revolution is a revelation of God. But every
revolution is primarily a convulsion. And when the test tube
is shattered, the convulsion will be particularly severe. As
Berdyaev says:

When thought forces itself to penetrate into the final mysteries of
the divine life it necessarily involves a drastic revolution in our
consciousness, which brings with it a spiritual illumination transforming the very nature of reason itself.

The destruction of the test tubes, the discarding of the
cocoon with its more or less comfortable furnishings in which
all is light, known, and familiar, confronts us with the limitless spaces of life about which we admittedly know nothing,
in which there is no lawfulness because there is no police, and
which seem to us now so dreadful and incomprehensible, so
dark and, most importantly, uncertain and endless. Today we
can rightly repeat what Lev Shestov prophetically wrote in
1905:

We are searching now for words and sounds to describe our former enemy poetically. Night, dark and soundless, opaque night crowded with horrors, doesn't it seem to us sometimes infinitely beautiful? And does it not appeal to us with its soft but mysterious, fathomless beauty more than limited and vulgar day? Before long, it would appear, man will realize that the same mysterious but all-knowing power which cast us into this world and taught us to reach for the light like plants, preparing us gradually for a free life, that same power leads us into a new realm where a new life with new blessings awaits us. *Ducunt volentem fata, nolentem trahunt.* And perhaps the day is not far off when an inspired poet, casting a last farewell look on the past, will boldly and joyfully exclaim: "Let the sun disappear, long live the dark!"

That this process has begun is evident in the emergence of Tertz, Solzhenitsyn, Pasternak—and no police, however "scientific," can stop us. Do we know our destination? No. All we know about the world we strive for is that it is infinitely free and that it is impossible to map our line of march beforehand. And we believe Shestov's words: "Only he who does not know where he is going can arrive at the Promised Land."

THE THIRD REVOLUTION

> *"The God of Abraham, the God of Isaac, the God of Jacob," but not the god of philosophers.*
>
> PASCAL

Death will not conquer life, however much the cyberneticists and geneticists struggle, however much they implant in children's minds the "truths" of scientific knowledge. A new, third revolution is coming. It is reversed, diametrically opposed to the French Revolution, to the Paris Commune, to the October "socialist" Revolution, to the National Socialist revolution of 1933. It is the revolution of the spirit in the name of life. It is a revolution that will shatter not only the "spirit of scientific knowledge" but also historical Christianity, which has done so much to bring mankind to the "reign of science." After atheism's fiery purge, mankind is returning to God. But not to the God of Catholicism or of any other religion, not to the God of the "holy Mass" and the "Virgin Mary," not to the God of death and the quiet killing of all life which marked historical Christianity, but to the God who said: "I am the living God."

The third revolution is incomparably closer in the socialist than in the nonsocialist world. Men everywhere are now perhaps closer to God than they have ever been. Socialism, as an ultimate totalitarianism, has served an important purpose, albeit in a negative sense. The world is returning to religion, but not to the moralistic and cloistered religion of the past, not to the institutionalized religion of yesterday, not to Sunday schools and Salvation Armies, but to a religion of laughter, life, vitality, a religion embattled and perhaps even bloody, as was Christianity when it began.

The bearers of religion today are spiritual kin to the men who, out of the deepest conviction, followed Lenin in 1917. Their opponents will be even as those who opposed Lenin and who in the socialist world of today burn incense and say Mass before Lenin's tomb.

The new religion will have very little in common with today's religions. And I can already see the churches uniting with the Marxist church to do battle against the new spring of eternal life, a river which will gush from a stone that everyone thinks is not even damp. I am firmly convinced that in the future the West will help the cybernetic Russian society to stem the new flow.

Great events are at hand. The day is not distant when

people will appear who will say right out that all nonauthentic work is not the dignified human occupation it is called today, but shame and slavery; that God, a personal God, exists and sometimes even participates in such jobs as the repairing of a burnt-out fuse; that the soul is immortal, whereas "cognition"—scientific knowledge and reason—is mortal; that love is incomparably greater than cognition of love; and, finally, that never before has man lived as great and complete a lie as he lives in our time. These people will assert that miracles, genuine miracles, have happened and miracles will happen again. These people will repeat to all scientific wise men and to all high priests of the cult of reason the old words from the ancient book: "The wisdom of man is madness before God."

Abram Tertz is blazing the trail.

Of course, one might ask why Shestov, Rozanov, Dostoevsky, and Tertz write at all, why they rationalize and bring into our consciousness the knowledge that all knowledge is inimical to life, that each articulated word is in itself a lie. After all, they are engaged in contradictory labors which negate precisely what they assert.

A number of people in history have already answered this question. Heinrich von Kleist said: "We must eat once again of the Tree of Knowledge in order once again to reach a state of innocence." Pascal said: "The final conclusion of reason points to the fact that there is something infinitely greater than reason." And Berdyaev: "Reason can grasp the existence of something above reason."

However contradictorily, reason remains and the knowledge that life is higher than reason remains also. And so does the knowledge that that particular knowledge, like all others, is false.

Shestov was reproached for calling all knowledge the death of the soul while imparting knowledge itself. He replied to the contradiction by saying:

When a man in his dreams is attacked by a monster that is going to crush and destroy both him and the world—at the very moment when he feels paralyzed and unable to defend himself, even to move his limbs, his salvation comes, along with the contradictory awareness that this nightmare is not reality but a passing fantasy. This awareness is contradictory because it requires that the sleeper know that the condition of consciousness in sleep is not real, a fact which negates itself. To escape from this nightmare, one must banish the "law" of contradictions on which in reality all evidence is based: one has to make an enormous effort and wake up.

Tertz, Shestov, and Berdyaev bring into the consciousness of man sleeping in the walled reality of an earthly, material, finite world the contradictory awareness that all consciousness is a dream. This awareness is dormant but its very being does away with the fear of the nightmare of reality and creates the possibility of liberation and awakening. Awakened man will not just write, read, rationalize, perceive life, and serve scientific knowledge. He will live. But for man to awaken, an enormous effort is needed, an effort which in no sense pertains to the sphere of cognition and scientific knowledge—the kind of effort a man has described who made such an effort: "Rejoice, today I conquered the world . . . O death, where is thy sting? O grave, where is thy victory?"

MORE ON THE SIGNIFICANCE OF TERTZ

In his time Shestov wrote the following of Martin Buber:

His endless passion for challenge was indispensable to express anew, in present-day language, the searchings and truths of the distant past when men themselves were not creating truth but having it revealed to them.

We can say something similar about Tertz, although Tertz conceals himself behind a screen of irony even when revealing his deepest convictions. We can even say that the more ironic Tertz is, the more serious is his intention:

If I was in some degree omniscient, there was no question of my being omnipotent as well. What can I do? I know everything and can do nothing. And the more I know, the worse it is, and the fewer legitimate reasons I have for doing anything or putting my faith in anybody.

If Feuerbach and Marx discovered "only" natural phenomena such as thunder and lightning (from which, as we know, primitive peoples created gods because they could not explain what they feared) behind the "idea" of God, then Tertz discovers the supernatural behind natural phenomena, even the most banal, such as electrical energy in common fuses.

If Spinoza identified God with nature and thus depersonalized God and made nature absolute, Tertz does exactly the opposite. In the tale "You and I," God is an identity, a most individual identity, and man is literally, not metaphorically, made "in the image and likeness of God" as an identity. The tragedy of Nikolai Vasilyevich, the main character in "You and I," lies in his inability to believe in the existence of God. When God takes an active part in his life, Vasilyevich responds with fear and hatred, thinking it is the NKVD.

The dreadful reality of Orwell's *1984,* Kafka's *The Trial,* and Tertz's *The Trial Begins* is relieved only by the possibility of some supernatural event, a miracle. And so Tertz repeats the words which were the leitmotif of Dostoevsky's creative achievement: "If there is no God, there is no man." As Tertz puts it: "We've had enough talk of man. It is time to think of God."

Only belief in the supernatural, in God, a personal God, gives man the strength to look death in the face, knowing that with death nothing ends, as man passes into the other reality of a new life. Tertz, in the excellent aphorisms collected in *Thought Unaware,* says:

Death separates the soul from the body like a butcher tearing off the meat from the bones. It is just as painful. But thus and only thus comes liberation.

One should die in such a way as to be able to cry out (or whisper) before the end: "Hurrah! We are sailing away!"

Conscious that his faith, which liberates him from the horror of final reality, is bestowed, Tertz speaks as Vasily Rozanov once did:

The Lord favors me.

It was given to Tertz to escape from the fetters of "normal reason," the test tube of Homunculus, as Goethe called him, and to return to the consciousness of those of our ancestors who, in Plato's words, "lived closer to God" than later peoples. In this respect Tertz "returns to nature," in the right sense of the expression and not in the sense of Rousseau's masquerade. Indeed, it is possible to live in a world of high technical achievement and remain in existence because the whole realistic world in which science and technology have made themselves so at home is nothing but an illusion, a "reality of the moment."

"However much atheists prove that there is no God and that only nature and laws of nature exist, they will always be talking about something else," said Dostoevsky. On this point Dostoevsky was a "primitive," like Tertz. In this sense, he lived "closer to nature," to existence, to God.

In his book on the mythology of primitive tribes, Levy Bruhl writes about the consciousness of "primitive men" in exactly the same way we can write about Tertz, Dostoevsky, Shestov, or Kierkegaard, people who broke through the test tube of reason:

In their mystical orientation they are always ready to admit the existence, behind the visible things and facts of our world, of invisible powers. Each time they are surprised by something unusual and strange, they are aware of those powers. In their eyes the supernatural surrounds and penetrates into the natural, which it imitates. Hence the viscosity of nature. Myths do not explain nature; they only reflect it. This supernatural is precisely what gives myths their content.

These "primitive men" contemplate all life, all reality, and not only that small part of momentary reality which reason and scientific knowledge allow us to glimpse.

To contemplate life as a whole, one must stand beyond it. To contemplate time as a whole, one must stand beyond it. Tertz in some way is always "outside the reality of the moment," like Camus's "Stranger," like the Jews. Shestov and Berdyaev, who come closest to Tertz in spirit, are émigrés, people also thrown out of everyday reality; Dostoevsky was wrenched out of life into ten years of hard labor. Thrown out of time, out of the "reality of the moment," they discovered things which Shestov and Berdyaev described in terms of philosophy and Dostoevsky and Tertz through their art: that this is not the final, last world, that another reality and another life exist, and that man had no reason to fear death or the horror of material reality because faith liberates the human soul and opens the path to eternal life.

The difference between Tertz on the one hand and Kafka and Orwell on the other is great. Kafka's *The Trial*, Orwell's *1984*, Tertz's *The Trial Begins* are the children of one spirit, but Kafka, like Orwell, was unable to shatter the test tube and to the end of his life remained in the clutches of an inescapable reality. *The Trial Begins* was only the beginning for Tertz. He broke through the test tube and fled into life. Kafka did not succeed in saving himself from the horror of reality in this life, not even in spirit, as Tertz did.

The "new realism" of Tertz can be compared with the creative achievement of Dostoevsky, with the paintings of Hieronymus Bosch, with European surrealist painting, with the philosophy of the "absurd," with the writings of Shestov, Rozanov, Berdyaev, and especially with the work of the young and gifted Belgrade painter Leonidas Sejka, whose paintings might well illustrate Tertz's stories. Tertz is a man of the new era, the era soon to come, the "new Middle Ages." He is close, of course, only to those who were driven by the reality of *The Trial, The Trial Begins,* and *1984* and by their unlimited thirst for life to break out of the test tube of reason, out of the walled world of "final reality," into the limitless space of eternal life.

To those who do not yet recognize reality as an exitless prison (as all of us must recognize, though perhaps not until the moment of our death) Tertz will appear odd, alien. Because he is moving the ground from under them, they will shout that he is abnormal, psychopathic. Just as yesterday he was under arrest, today he will be exiled and tomorrow proscribed.

All in vain. We who look at the world through Tertz's eyes are increasing in numbers, particularly in the socialist countries, where thousands have lived in ceaseless horror of enslavement to this world, more particularly in Russia, where the thirst for life is strongest and therefore the "Trial" is most difficult to endure.

Lev Shestov wrote prophetically:

I do not know what will bring man to flee: the knowledge that behind him is the head of Medusa with the terrible snakes and the power to turn him to stone, or the certainty that behind him is the inflexible security and immutability provided by the law of causality and by contemporary science. Judging by what is happening today and by the degree of tension which human thought has presently reached, it is correct to consider Medusa's head less awe-inspiring than the law of causality. Fleeing the latter, man is ready for anything: it seems that he would more willingly accept insanity—not the poetic variety, full of ardent words, but the real thing, for which they put a man into an asylum—anything but a return to the sphere of lawful cognition of reality.

Russian literature today has two poles, which, however far apart they lie, nevertheless meet. One pole is Tertz, the man who breaks through the test tube. The other is Solzhenitsyn, for whom the test tube is the greatest reality. But because Solzhenitsyn describes the test tube so truthfully, he prepares its destruction. The relationship between Solzhenitsyn and Tertz exactly parallels that between Tolstoy and Dostoevsky.

It is not worth bringing up those literati who claim that the test tube, the "Trial," does not exist, who say that all is beautiful in this world, and therefore strengthen the walls of the test tube. Those who seek to break the test tube do not listen to them.

STYLE AND TECHNIQUE

Here is how Tertz describes saluting guns and fireworks:

The earth shook. Steel pipes reared into the upturned sky. This was the aorta of the city, bursting somewhere behind the Universal Stores. They should put on a tourniquet, but it was too late. Other vessels had already burst, and fountains of multi-colored blood splashed into the sky.

It is obvious that Tertz is an original, gifted stylist, a mature master with his own technique of expression. His portraits are plastically alive. Before him, only Zamyatin and, to a certain extent, Andrei Bely wrote in this way. Certain descriptions show great virtuosity and could be published and read outside of the text of the stories themselves, as, for example, this description of a radio broadcast:

Arab wailing took the place of a French commercial. And here were two programs incongruously tangled up: a service relayed from a Scandinavian church, and an account, in a rich Ukrainian contralto washed with disinfectant, of the achievements of the distinguished lathe-turner Nalivayka who had fulfilled his year's plan in time for the Anniversary.

Yury's fingers throbbed. They vibrated with the ether. Sound-waves looped and looped about his neck. And echoing in his belly and his hollow chest, the black magnetic sky hummed and shuddered, riddled now and then with Morse like tracer bullets.

Yury was an aerial. But he wanted to be a transmitter sending out powerful waves of any length he chose. "Hello! Hello! Karlinsky calling! Listen to me and to me alone!"

The stations, each busy with its own affairs, were shouting one another down. They surrounded him like market women. He spun around, twiddling the knob, turning to each in turn almost without a pause.

He hummed psalms; his feet under the table tapped to a Brazilian samba. But what had *he* to offer to the world in his own name? Some potpourri of Freud and a Hawaiian guitar? Who and where was he, the one and only Yury, if the time had come for everyone to speak?

Finally he found the wave length of Radio Free Europe. Very confidentially—he must have been a little frightened himself—the announcer promised something spicy in honor of the October celebration, and passed the microphone to a former lieutenant-colonel of the air force, turned gray with bitterness and hardship in the Soviet service. But his other-worldly voice got no further than "My dear brothers and sis . . ." when it was interrupted by an angry roar. Our jammers were in action. A rattle of machine guns and artillery, loud enough to split the eardrums, swept American jazz, Paris commercials, and Radio Free Europe and wiped them out. On boundless electronic fields, the battle was engaged.

Yury skipped across no man's land and drew breath. The gunfire was dying down and giving way to parade-ground music and shouts of hurrah. The first unit of the marchers was passing the main tribune.

This was the last straw. He switched off, wrenching the knob as if he were wringing the neck of a netted bird. He even fancied he heard the crunch of bones.

Or this description of a concert:

The music flowed. It oozed like oily, rainbow-patterned puddles. It rose. It roared and stormed off the stage into the body of the hall. Seryozha thought about the cloudburst in the streets outside and wriggled with pleasure. The music reproduced his private image of the Revolution. The flood drowned the whole of the bourgeoisie in a most convincing way.

A general's wife in evening dress floundered, tried to scramble up a pillar, and was washed away. The old general swam with a vigorous breast stroke but soon sank. Even the musicians were, by now, up to their necks in water. Eyes bulging, lips spitting foam, they fiddled frenziedly, at random, below the surface of the waves.

One more onslaught. A lone usher, riding on a chair, swept past. The waves beat against the walls and lapped the portraits of the great composers. Ladies' handbags and torn tickets floated among the jetsam. Now and then, a bald head, white like an unripe watermelon, slowly floated up out of the sonorous green depth and bobbed back out of sight.

"What music!" exclaimed Globov. "That's not Prokofiev or Khachaturian for you. That's real classical stuff."

He too was fascinated by the flood but he understood it better than Seryozha. What struck him was that the flowing music wasn't left to its own devices, it was controlled by the conductor.

The conductor built dams, ditches, aqueducts, canalizing the capricious elements in accordance with his exact blueprint. He directed the flow; at the sweep of his arm one stream froze, another surged forward in its bed and turned a turbine.

Globov slipped into the front row. Never had he been so close to the conductor, never had he realized how hard was the conductor's work. No wonder! Think of having to keep an eye on all of them, from flute to drum, and force them all to play the same tune.

The conductor streamed with sweat, his jowls shook, his chest heaved hoarsely at each pause. From a distance he looked as graceful as a dancer who used arms instead of legs to dance. But here, close up, he was a butcher hacking carcasses and chopping ice, grunting out his short, thick breath at every stroke.

Louder and louder rose the music. Streams and waterfalls were no longer flowing—they had long since frozen: icebergs floated down, as if the ice age had come back, and crashed and ground against each other.

At various moments Tertz interrupts his narrative with small digressions, like the famous lyrical poem in Gogol's *Dead Souls* about the troika which symbolizes Russia. For Tertz it is no longer a troika, but a train:

Train! Train with the wings of a bird! Who invented you? None but a quickwitted people could have given you birth! Although no artful craftsman of Tula or Yaroslavl, but the cunning English Stephenson, they say, contrived you for the good of the cause, you are yet mightily well fitted to our rolling Russian plain and you speed on your way, up hill and down dale, hurtling past the telegraph poles, now faster now slower, till the head spins and the eyes hurt! Yet if one looks more closely, what is it but a stove on wheels or a peasant samovar with a line of wagons in tow? An angry creature at first sight, it's really generous and kindhearted. It puffs and blows and labors up any hill you like, grunting now and then by way of warning, but when it gives that piercing, devil-may-care whistle, you know you'd better watch out, if you don't want to be flattened.

Tertz's most interesting technical feat is his depiction of character through dialogue. We hear the words of only one of the speakers, but—and this is extraordinary—we see even more vividly the other speaker whose words we cannot hear.

Let us read a conversation between the Prosecutor Globov and an elderly revolutionary, the mother of his first wife and the grandmother of his son Seriozha, who has just been arrested as a "Trotskyite":

"No Mother," said Globov, his eyes on her wet felt boots. "There's a big roundup going on. . . . I can't . . .

"What did you say? Afraid? Have I ever been afraid of anyone? They were all afraid of me. . . . No, but I am a prosecutor and my conscience won't let me. Think of all the people I see every day, people who are still less guilty and whom I have to . . .

"What future? Whose heirs? Mine? I'll manage without. No traitor can be a son of mine.

"What nonsense! Really, what has the word of honor of a revolutionary woman to do with it? It sounds a bit old-fashioned, Ekaterina Petrovna. And we have certain information.

"Oh, no! You're wrong there. It's no joke to lose a son. . . .

"That's enough! What about yourself . . . What about your brother, your own brother, do you happen to remember? He skipped abroad and I suppose you . . .

"It didn't surprise me. I had an idea . . . But if I'd known to what length . . .

"Have you gone clean out of your mind, you crazy old woman? I did *not* denounce him. Do you hear? I did *not*.

"Leave me alone. Stop clutching at me. Will you keep your hands to yourself . . .

"I told you who gave him away. A girl who belonged to his own group. One of the teachers told me. The fellow who teaches history. She went to the principal . . . as if to ask his advice . . . He wanted to hush it up, but . . .

"But it was a girl, I tell you. Don't you understand plain Russian? A schoolgirl.

"Well, you know, that's going a bit too far. I've never yet strangled any little girls or boys. But when it comes to enemies, of course, that's another matter. . . .

"Shut up, you old witch, before you are put away yourself! After this I never want to . . .

"Very good, and what then? So you did look after me for twenty-five years? I've had quite enough of your bullying.

"You needn't. I'll be very glad if you never come again."

Though we hear only Globov, we see the revolutionary grandmother even more clearly because she is not limited by her own words and is left entirely to our imaginations.

Unfortunately, I have not had the opportunity to read Tertz's latest novel, *The Makepeace Experiment*. Since my first imprisonment, books no longer reach me very regularly.

One day, undoubtedly, Tertz's influence on Russian prose, in the technical sense as well, will be as great as the influence of Andrei Bely, Alexei Remizov, Evgeny Zamyatin, and other great Russian modernists.

[1965]

DOSTOEVSKY'S AND SOLZHENITSYN'S
HOUSE OF THE DEAD

* * *

i

In its eleventh number for 1962, the Soviet journal *Novy mir* published Solzhenitsyn's *One Day in the Life of Ivan Denisovich,* which deals with Stalin's concentration camps. Thanks primarily to the fact that this topic had previously been forbidden, and also to the undoubted artistic merits of the work, it attracted the attention of the whole world and brought its author well-deserved fame. Within record time it was translated into many of the languages of the civilized world, and the polemic it aroused continues both in the West and in its author's homeland, where in 1964 the story was nominated for a Lenin Prize and was one of seven works listed for final consideration.

Exactly one hundred years before, in 1862, another work appeared which also brought its author, Dostoevsky, world fame and which dealt with penal servitude in Siberia. This was *The House of the Dead.* There are many similarities and also differences in the historical background and the subject of the two books. Yet the fact that they are the works of two great artists (today it may be taken that Solzhenitsyn is in this category) , who have given us a more profound picture of people and their times than could any statistical data or socio-economic analysis, makes it possible for us, by examining the living reality of the two books, to establish the similarities and differences between two worlds—that of the nineteenth and that of the twentieth century.

Both writers emerged at a turning point in their country's history. Serfdom had been abolished in the Russian Empire in 1861; the years 1956–57 had seen the dissolution of most of the Stalinist concentration camps in the U.S.S.R. Both writers had themselves experienced the life they set out to describe: Dostoevsky had served four years at hard labor at Omsk; Solzhenitsyn had spent ten years in a Siberian concentration camp. Both writers, moreover, felt obliged to apologize somewhat for the unusual and delicate subject they chose to write about. Dostoevsky more than once indicates that penal servitude no longer exists in the form he describes:

I am describing olden times, therefore, things that have long since passed away . . .

. . . in the past, of course, in that recent past the tradition of which is fresh, though difficult to believe. . . .

Everything that I write here about punishments and beatings refers to my day. Now, I hear, all this has changed or is changing.

The same thing is in effect done for Solzhenitsyn by Tvardovsky, editor of *Novy mir,* in the opening lines of his introduction to the novel:

The raw material of life which serves as a basis for A. Solzhenitsyn's story is unusual in Soviet literature. It carries within itself an echo of the painful features in our development related to the cult of personality, which has been debunked and repudiated by the Party, features that, though they are not so far off in time, yet seem to be in the distant past. But the past, no matter what it was like, never becomes a matter of indifference to the present. The assurance of a complete and irrevocable break with everything which beclouds the past lies in a true and courageous comprehension of its full consequences.

The heroes of both works, Alexander Petrovich Goryanchikov and Ivan Denisovich Shukhov, are condemned to ten years' hard labor, but whereas *The House of the Dead* gives Goryanchikov's recollections of his entire imprisonment, Solzhenitsyn limits himself to one day in his hero's life, from the moment he is awakened in the morning to the moment he falls asleep again. There are similarities in the two works which by their nature cannot be attributed to the influence of the earlier writer on the later one, but are due to the situation common to both books. Both heroes share a bunk with a young man. In Dostoevsky's book he is called Alei, and in Solzhenitsyn's, Alesha. The two young men resemble each other not only in name but psychologically and physically. The Daghestani Tatar Alei, whom Goryanchikov teaches to read and write, is described as follows:

His smile was so confiding, so childishly open-hearted, the big black eyes were so mild and affectionate, that looking at him I always felt a particular pleasure, even a relief in my longing and sadness. . . .

He was as chaste as a pure young girl, and a nasty, cynical, dirty, unjust, or violent act on anyone's part in the prison would cause his wonderful eyes to blaze with indignation, which made them even more wonderful.

Solzhenitsyn describes the young Baptist Alesha as follows:

Shukhov stole a look at him. Alesha's eyes glowed like two candles. . . .

. . . and [on the upper bunk] Alesha, Shukhov's clean and tidy neighbor . . . was reading from a notebook in which he'd copied out half the New Testament.

Both characters find intense joy in reading the Gospels. Asked by Goryanchikov what he admires most in Jesus Christ, Alei replies:

"Where he says: Forgive, love, cause no offense and love your enemies. How well he says it!"

Alesha reads out to Shukhov with deep religious conviction:

"If you suffer, it must not be for murder, theft, or sorcery, or for infringing on the rights of others. But if anyone suffers as a Christian, he should feel it no disgrace, but confess that name to the honor of God."

On another occasion:

Alesha heard Shukhov's whispered prayer, and, turning to him: "There you are, Ivan Denisovich, your soul is begging to pray. Why don't you give it its freedom?"

Toward the end of his book, Dostoevsky comments on the Russian lives which have been wasted or destroyed in penal servitude:

And how much youth has been buried for nothing within these walls, what tremendous forces have perished here in vain! After all, the whole story must be told: these people were a remarkable lot. Perhaps they were even the most gifted and the strongest among the whole of our people. But mighty forces died for nothing, died abnormally, illegally, irretrievably. And who is to blame?

Solzhenitsyn, in the words of the squad leader Tyurin, says the same thing. Tyurin is telling about some girls, students from Leningrad, who were traveling in the same railway compartment with him. They knew nothing of concentration camps and, he says, "They were going through life happily. All clear ahead for them." His remarks are supplemented by the critic V. I. Lakshin, writing in *Novy mir* on "Ivan Denisovich: His Friends and Enemies":

When the picture of cruel forced labor fades, as it were, into the picture of free labor, labor done because of an inner driving force, the reader is compelled to realize more profoundly and more clearly the worth of people like our Ivan Denisovich, to realize how criminally absurd it is to keep them far from their homes, under the supervision of automatons, behind barbed wire.

Despite the numerous striking similarities, there are, however, certain essential differences between these two works. Dostoevsky's hero is an aristocrat, an intellectual capable of fathoming the psychology of crime, of criminals and prisoners, whereas Solzhenitsyn's hero is a Russian tiller of the soil, later a private in the Red Army and then an inmate in a prison camp, who sees the hell in which he is living with the eyes of an ordinary uneducated man; all this is conveyed by the language in which the two works are written. Dostoevsky's hero, like the majority of the camp inmates this writer describes, has actually committed a crime, and this enables the author to give us some brilliant insights into human nature. Solzhenitsyn's hero and the majority of his comrades in distress are innocent people who themselves are the victims of crime day and night.

Another difference lies in the fact that Dostoevsky stresses the severity of the regime he describes:

The second category of forced labor, where I was and which consisted of prisoners who were serfs under military supervision, was incomparably more severe than the other two categories. . . .

The "osoblag," i.e., *osoby lager* or "special camp," where Ivan Denisovich is detained is infinitely more bearable than other camps where he has been, both as to food and as to the general mode of life. Ivan Denisovich recalls the camp at Ust-Izhma, where he was "dying of diarrhea":

One good thing about these "special" camps—you were free to let off steam. At Ust-Izhma, you need only whisper that there was a shortage of matches outside, and they'd put you in the guardhouse and add another ten years to your stretch. But here you could bawl anything you liked from the top row of bunks—the squealers didn't pass it on, the security boys had stopped caring.

Despite these important differences, it is interesting to compare the life of prisoners in the nineteenth and twentieth centuries, their psychology and the changes that have taken place in the nature of their imprisonment; for both works in effect describe the attempt to turn human beings into slaves.

The hardest moment in a prisoner's life is when he first wakes. Here there is no difference between the House of the Dead and the "osoblag":

A drum at the guardhouse by the prison gates announced the dawn, and some ten minutes later a noncommissioned officer of the guard began unlocking the barracks. The men began to wake up. In the dim light of a candle bracket containing six tallow candles, the prisoners got up from their bunks, trembling with cold. Many of them were silent and sullen with sleep. They yawned, stretched themselves, and furrowed their branded brows. Some crossed themselves, while others were already beginning to squabble. The stuffiness was dreadful. The fresh winter air rushed in as soon as the door was opened, and spread through the hut in clouds of steam. The prisoners crowded around the buckets of water; in turns, they took hold of the ladle, poured water into their mouths, and with this washed their hands and face. The water was brought the evening before by the man on duty.

Solzhenitsyn's story begins like this:

At five o'clock that morning, reveille was sounded, as usual, by the blows of a hammer on a length of rail hanging near the staff quarters. The intermittent sounds barely penetrated the windowpanes, on which the frost lay two fingers thick, and they ended almost as soon as they'd begun. It was cold outside, and the camp guard was reluctant to go on beating out reveille for long.

The clanging ceased, but everything outside still looked like the middle of the night when Ivan Denisovich Shukhov got up to go to the bucket. It was pitch dark except for the yellow light cast on the window by three lamps—two in the outer zone, one inside the camp itself.

And no one came to unbolt the barracks door; there was no sound of the barrack orderlies pushing a pole into place to lift the barrel of excrement and carry it out.

Shukhov never overslept reveille. He always got up at once, for the next ninety minutes, until they assembled for work, belonged to him, not to the authorities, and any old-timer could always earn a bit—by sewing a pair of mittens for someone out of old sleeve lining; or bringing some rich loafer in the squad his dry *valenki* (knee-length felt boots) right to his bunk so he wouldn't have to stumble barefoot around the pile of boots looking for his own pair; or going the rounds of the warehouses, offering to be of service, sweeping up this or fetching that; or going to the mess hall to collect bowls from the tables and bring them stacked to the dishwashers—you're sure to be given something to eat there, though there were plenty of others at that game, more than plenty—and, what's worse, if you found a bowl with something left in it you could hardly resist licking it out.

Thus we are gradually introduced into the worlds of the respective protagonists. Let us first glance at the external aspect of the lives they lead. There is a difference in the size of the camps and the barrack huts. In each hut in the House of the Dead there were bunks for thirty men; in Shukhov's camp, for four hundred—which is of no small significance in view of Dostoevsky's remark:

Subsequently, I realized that apart from the loss of freedom, the forced labor, there is another form of torture which is almost worse than all the others. This is the enforced living together.

In both cases, the prisoners have their heads shaved. But whereas Dostoevsky's prisoners have chains weighing from eight to twelve pounds fixed to their legs, Ivan Denisovich and his companions merely wear numbers on their caps, on the left knee, on the back, and on the chest, and have to have them renewed from time to time by a prisoner who was formerly a painter. Ivan Denisovich's number is Shch 854, by which he is known to the guards.

In the House of the Dead, the camp is surrounded by a palisade; in Solzhenitsyn's book, this is replaced by barbed wire and searchlights mounted on watchtowers. In the earlier camp, the guards are armed with rifles; in the later, with machine guns. As in all prisons, the prisoners' numbers are changed many times a day; the guards frequently make mistakes, and it is a long time before a prisoner's actual number corresponds to the one assigned him on paper. Dostoevsky writes:

Here [in the prison courtyard] the prisoners parade and the roll is called in the morning, at midday, and in the evening—sometimes several times more a day, depending on the suspiciousness of the guards and their ability to count quickly. . . .

The checkers frequently made mistakes, lost count, went off and came back again. At last the wretched guards managed to reach the desired figure and then locked the huts.

And Solzhenitsyn:

No one dared make a mistake. If you signed for one head too many, you filled the gap with your own. . . .

The escort was worried. There was a discssion over the counting boards. Somebody missing. Again somebody missing. Why the hell can't they learn to count? . . .

What made this recounting so infuriating was that the time wasted on it was the zeks' own, not the authorities'.

In both prison camps, of course, knives and similar objects are strictly forbidden but are nevertheless to be found in some prisoner or other's possession. In both, as in all similar institutions, money has greater value than it does outside. "The most wretched bit of rag," Dostoevsky remarks, "had its price and could be used for something." And Solzhenitsyn:

In forced-labor camps, all prices were local; it was quite different from anywhere else, because you couldn't save money and few had any at all, for it was very hard to come by.

Stealing goes on in both prison camps, with the difference that Dostoevsky's prisoners each have a trunk with a lock, whereas Solzhenitsyn's, whenever they receive a package from home, hand it over for safekeeping to a department where in fact it is not safe at all since it may well be stolen by the keeper. Bribery flourishes in both centuries. Plank beds and refuse pails probably did not change much in the time interval, and in both cases invalids are responsible for keeping the huts clean during the day.

In Dostoevsky's book, only a few wardens accompany the prisoners as they go out in various directions to their place of work after breakfast. The picture Solzhenitsyn gives is a little more modern:

There were guards all over the place. They made a semicircle around the column on its way to the power station, their machine guns sticking out and pointing right at your face. And there were guards with gray dogs. One dog bared its fangs as if laughing at the prisoners.

The degree of isolation in the modern camp is incomparably greater than in the earlier camp. Before the prisoners leave the camp, the commander reads out a formal warning, known to them as "morning prayers":

"Attention, prisoners! Marching orders must be strictly obeyed. Keep to your ranks. No hurrying, keep a steady pace. No talking. Keep your eyes fixed ahead and your hands behind your backs. A step to right or left is considered an attempt to escape and the escort has orders to shoot without warning."

Dostoevsky describes the passage of the column of men through a small Siberian town: the prisoners talk and joke, tease one another, and passers-by stop and give them alms. In Solzhenitsyn's book, there is no question of alms, for in the camps of Stalin's day it was impossible to come anywhere near the inmates. In the few cases where it was possible, ordinary Soviet citizens have been known to help prisoners, like the Russians of the nineteenth century. In an article in *Literaturnaya Gazeta* about a geologist named Kapranov who, while working in the Kolyma region, loses his life after having taken under his protection some of the prisoners from the many camps in this area, Valery Osipov writes:

The camp authorities, of course, realized that Kapranov, to put it plainly, was giving the prisoners extra food at his home, in an attempt to brighten in some way their joyless existence in camp. Such an attitude was widespread in those years among the free population of the Kolyma region. Doctors, engineers, geologists tried insofar as they could to relieve the unjustly convicted of the duty of pushing wheelbarrows and to make use of these men in camp according to their specialties. This helped many to preserve their physical and mental health and in some cases actually saved their lives.

Our reason for comparing the regime in the two camps is that the conditions described indicate the degree of freedom, or rather lack of freedom, of the prisoners. As Solzhenitsyn says:

The thoughts of a prisoner—they're not free either. They keep returning to the same things. A single idea keeps stirring. Would they feel that piece of bread in the mattress? Would he have any luck at the dispensary that evening? Would they put Buinovsky in the cells?

Ivan Denisovich and his companions do not have a minute to themselves. They work all day until dark, with a break for the midday meal, and have supper after they return to camp. This is followed by some renumbering, after which, dead tired, they go to bed. "Apart from sleep, the only time a prisoner lives for himself is ten minutes in the morning at breakfast, five minutes over dinner, and five at supper."

The camp commandant even tries to deprive the prisoners of the opportunity to move about the camp during the brief intervals for dinner and supper:

There was a time when the camp commandant issued still another order: on no account were prisoners to walk about the camp by themselves. A whole squad was to go if at all possible. But when it was not something a whole squad could keep busy on—at the dispensary, say, or at the latrines—then groups of four or five were to be formed and a senior appointed to head them and take them there and back in a body.

The camp commandant took a very firm stand on that order. No one dared contradict him. The guards picked up solitary prisoners, took down their numbers, yanked them off to the cells—yet the order was a flop. It flopped quietly, like many much-touted orders. . . .

With that rule of his, the commandant would have robbed them of their last shred of freedom, but it didn't work, much as he tried, the fat pig.

The prisoners are also deprived of their Sundays and state holidays:

. . . they knew how to keep them jumping even on Sundays. They'd invent something—fixing up the baths, or building a wall somewhere, or cleaning up the yard. There were mattresses to be changed and shaken, bedbugs in the bunk frames to be exterminated. Or they'd have the idea of checking you against your photo. Or of making inventory—turning you with your things into the yard and keeping you there half the day. Nothing seems to make the authorities madder than zeks napping quietly after breakfast.

In *The House of the Dead,* much space is devoted to describing how the prisoners live in their spare time. Compared with twentieth-century conditions, certain scenes from "the worst Siberian prison camp" of the nineteenth century seem idyllic. "At the entrances to the barrack huts," we are told, "the prisoners would sit about with balalaikas."

They did no work on Sundays, celebrated Christmas and Easter for several days on end, and on their name day the prisoners were exempted from work. The Jew Isai Fomich is assured by law of his right not to work on the Sabbath, a right of which he naturally makes good use. Moslems have the same privilege. The prisoners amuse themselves by raising domestic livestock—the billy goat Vaska, and geese. Dostoevsky tells us:

The geese too we started having by chance. I don't know who first kept them or to whom they belonged, but for a while they were a source of much amusement for the prisoners and even became well known in the town. They were even hatched in the prison and were fed in the kitchen. When the brood had grown to a certain size, they fell into the habit of going out in procession with the prisoners to work. . . . They always attached themselves to the largest group and while work was in progress would look for food nearby.

We further learn that the prisoners "organized a theater" on holidays, and occasionally there was even some association with women. "This did, of course, happen, but very seldom and only with the greatest difficulty."

In Solzhenitsyn's camp, women are mentioned only once. Before breakfast, Ivan Denisovich is taken off by the duty officer to the guardhouse for "failing to get up at reveille," but it happens that he only has to scrub the floor in the guardroom:

. . . Barefoot, [he] sloshed the water right under the guards' *valenki*.

"Hey there, you slob, take it easy," one of the guards shouted, putting his feet on a chair. . . .

"How much water are you going to use, idiot? Who on earth washes like that?"

"I'll never get it clean otherwise, citizen chief. It's thick with mud."

"Didn't you ever watch your wife scrub the floor, pig?"

Shukhov drew himself up, the dripping rag in his hand. He smiled ingenuously, revealing the gaps in his teeth, the result of a touch of scurvy at Ust-Izhma in 1943. And what a touch it was—his exhausted stomach wouldn't hold any food, and his bowels could move nothing but a bloody fluid. But now only a lisp remained from that old trouble.

"I was taken from my wife in '41, citizen chief. I've forgotten what she was like."

"That's the way the scum wash. . . . They don't know how to do a fucking thing and don't want to learn. They're not worth the bread we give them. We ought to feed them shit."

Prisoners in the House of the Dead occupy themselves with their own affairs in the evening:

But as soon as the hut had been locked, all [the prisoners] quietly seated themselves, each at his own place, and almost all of them took up some kind of handiwork. The hut was suddenly lit up. Each man held his own candle in a candlestick, mostly made of wood. One started stitching a pair of boots, another making some article of clothing. . . . A small group of idlers squatted in a corner before an outspread rug to play cards.

Such liberalism is alien to the twentieth century. Solzhenitsyn's inmates, after tiresome counts and recounts both outside and inside the hut, lie down and fall asleep immediately. *One Day in the Life of Ivan Denisovich* ends as follows:

Shukhov went to sleep fully content. He'd had many strokes of luck that day: they hadn't put him in the cells; they hadn't sent his squad to the settlement; he'd swiped a bowl of kasha at dinner; the squad leader had fixed the rates well; he'd built a wall and enjoyed doing it; he'd smuggled that bit of hacksaw blade through; he'd earned a favor from Tsezar that evening; he'd bought that tobacco. And he hadn't fallen ill. He'd got over it.

A day without a dark cloud. Almost a happy day.

There were three thousand six hundred and fifty-three days like that in his stretch. From the first clang of the rail to the last clang of the rail.

Three thousand six hundred and fifty-three days.

The three extra days were for leap years.

As for punishments, Dostoevsky describes floggings and the attitude of the Russians toward them. Unforgettable is the character Orlov, who bravely goes to take four thousand strokes in the belief that he will survive to make a break for freedom. The punishment, which itself is for an attempt to escape, is too much for him. In Dostoevsky's day, one sometimes paid for such disciplinary offenses with one's life. What about the Stalin camps? Former Captain (second rank) Buinovsky protests to the guard commander because the commander, when the temperature is twenty-seven degrees below zero, orders the prisoners to undress to see whether they are wearing more than the regulation dress:

"You've no right to strip men in the cold. You don't know Article Nine of the Criminal Code."

But they did have the right. They knew the code. You, friend, are the one who doesn't know it.

"You're not behaving like Soviet people," Buinovsky went on. "You're not behaving like Communists."

Volkovoi had put up with the reference to the criminal code, but this made him wince and, like black lightning, he flashed: "Ten days in the guardhouse."

One would think that ten days in the guardhouse would be definitely better than flogging; but Solzhenitsyn describes the guardhouse:

Brick walls, cement floor, no windows, a stove they lit only to melt the ice on the walls and make pools on the floor. You slept on bare boards, and if you'd any teeth left to eat with after all the chattering they'd be doing, they gave you nine ounces of bread day after day and hot stew only on the third, sixth, and ninth.

Ten days. Ten days "hard" in the cells—if you sat them out to the end, your health would be ruined for the rest of your life. T.B. and nothing but hospital for you till you kicked the bucket.

Imprisonment in the guardhouse is obviously no better than a flogging. After all, it is Siberia, where the normal winter temperature is rarely above twenty degrees centigrade below zero. And what are such punishments meted out for? Solzhenitsyn writes:

Hadn't they been around the barracks and read them that new regulation? You had to take off your hat to a guard five paces before passing him, and replace it two paces after. There were guards who slipped past as if blind, not caring a damn, but for others the new rule was a godsend. How many prisoners had been thrown in the guardhouse because of that hat business?

Despite the guardhouse, however, whipping still survives. Lieutenant Volkovoi is described as follows:

At first, in '49, he'd been in the habit of carrying a whip of plaited leather, as thick as his forearm. He was said to have used it for flogging in the cells. Or when the prisoners would be standing in a group near a barracks at the evening count, he'd slink up from behind and lash out at someone's neck with a "Why aren't you standing in line, slobs?" The men would dash away in a wave. Stung by the blow, his victim would put a hand to his neck and wipe away the blood, but he'd hold his tongue, for fear of the cells.

Now, for some reason, Volkovoi had stopped carrying his whip.

The attitude of the camp authorities toward the prisoners can be seen in a passage in Osipov's article in which Kapranov indignantly exclaims to a member of the camp staff:

"Hurry up, comrade! . . . The men may die."

"What men do you mean?" replied the other with a smirk. "They're enemies of the people."

The major in command of Dostoevsky's camp is no better. It would seem that this type of person has not changed in a hundred years. Only the technique has changed; everything is now on a larger scale. Dostoevsky describes various instances of denunciation, in particular how a certain Ivanov keeps the major informed of everything that goes on in the camp:

As for denunciations in general, they usually flourish. In the prison, the informer is not subjected to the slightest humiliation; indignation is unthinkable. . . . [A certain prisoner] . . . was on friendly terms with the major's batman Fedka and served as his spy, and Fedka repeated to the major everything he heard about the prisoners. We all knew about this, but it never occurred to any of us to punish the rascal or even to reproach him.

Solzhenitsyn describes denunciations on an organized scale. In contrast to Dostoevsky's, his prisoners react to the business of informing:

True enough, something new had started up. Two men, known to be squealers, had been found in their bunks one morning with their throats cut; and, a few days later, the same thing had happened to an innocent zek—someone must have gone to the wrong bunk.

This is almost the only bright feature of twentieth-century prison life.

Flight is risky and almost impossible in both places. Dostoevsky describes how two prisoners escape and hide for three months. Solzhenitsyn observes:

In short, if someone escaped, the guards had had it; they were hounded, without sleep or food. Sometimes they were roused to such fury that the runaway wouldn't get back alive.

The attitude of the prisoners toward those among them who in ordinary life belong to "higher circles" of society is similar in both cases. The inmates of the House of the Dead refer contemptuously to aristocrats as "fly-swatters" ("thumb-twiddlers," idlers) ; those in Solzhenitsyn's camp are no different in their opinion.

If a people has lived too well, it is very difficult to rule it.

TALLEYRAND

Unrelenting hunger is merely one more chain to fetter mankind. A great deal of Solzhenitsyn's story is devoted to food. Shukhov dreams of it continually: all his thoughts revolve around the possibility of getting an extra portion of soup. At the very beginning of the story, we see him hiding half a days' ration of bread (the ration is 550 grams) and sewing it into his mattress to keep it until evening. We follow all his thoughts and actions during breakfast, dinner, and supper. Prison life has developed in Shukhov certain characteristics that are difficult to grasp for people who have not experienced life in one of Hitler's or Stalin's camps. Lakshin writes:

. . . For Ivan Denisovich two things in camp life are of tremendous, sometimes overwhelming, importance—how not to grow weak from hunger and how not to freeze. In conditions reminiscent of the primitive struggle for existence, the value of the simplest "material" elements in life, the things that have always and indisputably been essential to man—food, clothing, footwear, a roof over one's head—is discovered anew. An extra ration of bread becomes a subject of the highest poetry.

How much effort, cunning, and persistence is required to get the best bread ration!

Shukhov's job now was to wedge himself in behind a table, oust two loafers, politely ask another prisoner to move, and clear a little space in front of him—for twelve bowls (to stand close together), with a second row of six, and two more on top. Next he had to take the bowls from Pavlo, repeating the number as he did so and keeping his eyes peeled—lest some outsider should grab a bowl from the table. And he had to see he wasn't bumped by someone's elbow and upset a bowl—right beside him people were leaving the table, stepping over the benches, or squeezing in to eat. Yes, you had to keep your eyes peeled—was that fellow eating out of his own bowl? Or had he wormed his way up to one of the 104th's? . . .

Some of the bowls had been filled before the stuff in the bottom of the kettle had settled after being stirred, and some were duds—nothing but liquid. Shukhov made a mental note of which was which. . . .

He managed, too, to maneuver the tray so that the two bowls with the thickest stew were just opposite the place he was about to sit down at.

Shukhov's great achievement that day is to get a double helping for lunch (by deceiving the cook) and another for supper (his reward for taking Tsezar Markovich's place in line to pick up a package from home). Dinner is not only a physical but a psychological experience:

He dug in. First he only drank the broth, drank and drank. As it went down, filling his whole body with warmth, all his guts began to flutter inside him at their meeting with that stew. Gooood! There it comes, that brief moment for which a zek lives.

And now Shukhov complained about nothing: not about the length of his stretch, not about the length of the day, not about their swiping another Sunday. This was all he thought about now: we'll survive. We'll stick it out, God willing, till it's over. . . .

He began to eat the cabbage with what was left of the soup. A potato had found its way into one of the bowls—Tzesar's. A medium-sized spud, frost-bitten, hard and sweetish. . . .

He ate his supper without bread. A double helping and bread—that was going too far. The bread would do for to-morrow. The belly is a demon. It doesn't remember how well you treated it yesterday; it'll cry out for more tomorrow.

As for the food itself:

The stew was the same every day. Its composition depended on the kind of vegetable there was that winter. Nothing but salted carrots last year, which meant that from September to June the stew was plain carrot. This year it was black cabbage. The most nourishing time of the year was June; then all vegetables came to an end and were replaced by grits (*krupa,* groats). The worst time was July—then they shredded nettles into the pot. . . .

The main thing today was that the oatmeal was good—real oatmeal, the best sort. It wasn't often they had it. . . .

How often had Shukhov in his youth fed oats to horses! Never had it occurred to him that there'd come a time when his whole soul would yearn for a handful of them.

Perhaps the most powerful scenes in Solzhenitsyn's story take place in the dining hall. In a small room, hundreds of prisoners have their lunch and supper. A crowd besieges the entrance, and orderlies maintain order with sticks.

The crowd heaved, pushing away so that no one could breathe. To get its stew. Its lawful stew.

Such constant hunger and on such a scale was unknown in the prisons of the nineteenth century. The description of the dining hall in the House of the Dead seems today truly idyllic:

The prisoners, in their caps and sheepskin coats and girded up, ready to leave immediately for work, seated themselves in all the corners and around the tables. Before some of them, there stood wooden cups containing kvass. They crumbled the bread into the kvass and then sipped it. . . .

Meals are not taken together, but in haphazard fashion, according to who comes first; in any case, the dining hall would not have taken all of them at once. I tried the *shchi* but, being unfamiliar with it, could not eat it and made myself some tea. We took a seat at the end of the table. . . . .

Prisoners came and went. There was, incidentally, plenty of room, for not everyone had come yet. A group of five men seated themselves separately at the large table. The cook poured them out two dishes of soup and set down on the table a whole panful of fried fish. They were celebrating something and eating food of their own.

They brought in the *kalachi* [a kind of fancy bread]. A young prisoner was carrying a whole bunch of them and was selling them around the prison.

Dostoevsky, in the person of Goryanchikov, remarks:

The food, too, struck me as being fairly adequate in quantity. . . . Incidentally, the prisoners, when boasting about the food, referred only to the bread and expressed their appreciation of the fact that the bread was served in bulk, and not doled out by weight. . . . The bread was somehow particularly tasty and was noted for this throughout the town. The explanation usually given was that the prison oven was well designed. The *shchi* was very unattractive to look at. It was cooked in one big boiler, with a little groats added, and—especially on weekdays—was thin and watery.

In the course of a quarrel, one prisoner exclaims: "Look, he's fed himself well on prison bread!" And not only on bread: invalided prisoners could go out into the town, where they bought meat and anything else their fellow prisoners wanted and could afford. Dostoevsky tells us that they brought back tobacco, brick tea, beef, *kalachi,* etc., but no wine. "In the winter," he says, "beef cost us half a kopek [a pound]." On Christmas Eve

. . . the invalids, who had gone to the market on errands for the prisoners, brought back with them toward evening large quantities of all kinds of food: beef, sucking pigs, even geese.

When a prisoner was celebrating his name day, he,

... after rising in the morning, placed a candle before the icon and said his prayers; then he put on his best clothes and ordered dinner for himself. Beef and fish were purchased, Siberian *pelmeni* were prepared; he ate like a horse, almost always alone, rarely inviting his comrades to share his table. Then the wine appeared: the prisoner got as drunk as a cobbler and invariably went from hut to hut, swaying and stumbling in his eagerness to show everyone that he was drunk, that he was "having a good time," and so earn universal respect.

Although alcohol was strictly forbidden, it was brought into the prison by some of the inmates, who ran the risk of being severely punished. "In forced-labor camps, it was sometimes possible to get drunk," Dostoevsky remarks. Elsewhere he points out that getting drunk is an expression of man's freedom: "The word 'prisoner' signifies a man without freedom; but when he spends money he is acting according to *his own will*."

Hunger did not, then, enslave the inmates of the House of the Dead of the nineteenth century. They even kept geese. Their twentieth-century counterparts, on the other hand, compete to see who shall lick clean the dishes left by others. Dostoevsky's prisoners feed Gnedko, the horse which carries the water:

Someone would invariably bring him some bread and salt. Gnedko would eat it and again begin nodding his head, as though he wanted to say: "I know you, yes, I know you! I am a nice horse, and you are a good man."

I also liked to bring Gnedko bread.

Dostoevsky describes the prison dog: "A dog lived there, slept in the yard, and ate the leftovers from the kitchen." Solzhenitsyn relates a conversation between former movie producer Tsezar Markovich and Captain Buinovsky concern-

ing Eisenstein's film *Battleship Potemkin,* in particular about
the scene showing the reaction of the sailors to some worm-
ridden meat. Buinovsky remarks:

"Well, if they'd bring that meat here to camp instead of the fish
they feed us, and dump it straight into the kettle, we'd be only
too . . ."

One more difference. In the House of the Dead, the cooks
are chosen by the prisoners themselves: in Solzhenitsyn's
camp they are privileged persons appointed by the authorities—that is, more or less through bribery.

ii

The desires and dreams of unfree men are determined by the
degree to which they have been deprived of their freedom.
Slaves are always great dreamers, as Dostoevsky noticed in the
House of the Dead. "Here all were dreamers," he remarks.
"This too leapt to the eye." And their dreams revolved
around the subject of freedom: "The goal we all had in mind
was freedom and an end to captivity." Freedom is nevertheless a relative concept. A hungry man dreams of freedom
from starvation. The inmates of Solzhenitsyn's "special
camp" think only of food and sleep:

Shukhov's back was giving him hell. How he longed to be in bed
in the infirmary fast asleep! He wanted nothing else. Under the
heaviest of blankets.

As for getting out of the camp, Shukhov's thoughts run as
follows:

Shukhov gazed at the ceiling in silence. Now he didn't know
either whether he wanted freedom or not. At first he had longed
for it. Every night he'd counted the days of his stretch—how
many had passed, how many were to come. And then he'd grown

bored with counting. And then it became clear that men like him wouldn't ever be allowed to return home, that they'd be exiled. And would his life be any better there than here—who could tell?

Freedom meant one thing to him—home.

But they wouldn't let him go home.

In one very important point, the psychology of twentieth-century prisoners differs from that of their predecessors of the nineteenth century. However much they might dread the beatings and hate their chains, the inmates of the House of the Dead knew that they would be set free after their term was over, so that gaining their freedom did depend for them, to some extent at least, on their conduct. Prisoners in the Stalin camps were simply objects on which nothing depended, not the length of their sentences or their liberation.

Earlier there'd been a spell when people were lucky: everyone to a man got ten years. But from '49 onward the standard sentence was twenty-five, irrespective. A man can survive ten years—but twenty-five, who can get through twenty-five alive? . . .

The law can be stood on its head. When your ten years are up, they can say, "Here's another ten for you."

Later we are told:

He [Shukhov] had been told that this old man had spent years without number in camps and prisons, and that he hadn't benefited from a single amnesty. Whenever one ten-year stretch had run out, they shoved another on him right away.

The inmates of the House of the Dead are serving sentences on various charges. One of them, Baklushin, murdered a German because of a woman; another, named Shishkov, murdered his wife. Three Daghestani Tatars murdered an Armenian merchant; a certain Sirotkin is in prison for murdering a sergeant-major. A young aristocrat killed his father for his inheritance—a charge which later proves to be false;

this provides Dostoevsky with an idea for *The Brothers Karamazov*. Dostoevsky tells us:

Here there were casual murderers and murderers by profession, brigands and brigand leaders. There were ordinary rogues and traveling tradesmen. . . . But each of them had a tale to tell, gloomy and morose like a hangover from yesterday's carousal.

There were a dozen or so "political" prisoners. The sentences were various. Most were in for from eight to twelve years, but some had been sentenced to twenty years followed by exile to Siberia. The "author" of the *Notes*, Goryanchi-kov, is serving a sentence for the murder of his wife.

In Solzhenitsyn's special camp, everyone is in for ten or twenty-five years: *tertium non datur*. The reasons for their imprisonment are as follows: Captain Buinovsky (Shch 331) has found his way into the camp because during the war he was for a time liaison officer on board a British warship under an English admiral, who after the war sent him a present.

"And imagine—after the war the British admiral—only the devil could have put the idea into his head—sent me a gift, a souvenir as 'a token of gratitude,' damn him! I was absolutely horrified. And now here we are, all lumped together . . ."

Alesha, the Baptist, is paying for his religious beliefs. Ivan Denisovich muses about him and his fellow Baptists:

They were an unlucky group, too. What harm did they do anyone by praying to God? Every damn one of them had been given twenty-five years. Nowadays they cut all cloth to the same measure—twenty-five years.

Shukhov tells him:

". . . Jesus Christ wanted you to sit in prison and so you are—sitting there for His sake. But for whose sake am I here? Because we weren't ready for war in '41? For that? Was that *my* fault?"

Like so many others, Ivan Denisovich is in prison because he was captured by the Germans and then escaped and returned to the Red Army lines.

According to his dossier, Ivan Denisovich Shukhov had been sentenced for high treason. He had testified to it himself. Yes, he'd surrendered to the Germans with the intention of betraying his country and he'd returned from captivity to carry out a mission for German intelligence. What sort of mission neither Shukhov nor the interrogator could say. So it had been left at that—a mission.

Shukhov had figured it all out. If he didn't sign, he'd be shot. If he signed, he'd get a chance to live. So he signed.

But what really happened was this. In February 1942 the army was surrounded on the northwest front. No food was parachuted to them; there were no planes. Things got so bad that they were scraping the hooves of dead horses—the horn could be soaked in water and eaten. Their ammunition was gone. So the Germans rounded them up in the forest, a few at a time. Shukhov was in one of these groups, and remained in German captivity for a day or two. Then five of them managed to escape. They stole through the forest and marshes and by a miracle reached their own lines. A machine gunner shot two of them on the spot, a third died of his wounds, but two got through. Had they been wiser, they'd have said they'd been wandering in the forest, and then nothing would have happened. But they told the truth: they said they were escaped POW's. POW's, you fuckers! If all five of them had got through, their statements could have been found to tally and they might have been believed. But with two it was hopeless. You've put your damned heads together and cooked up that escape story, they were told.

Among those imprisoned for similar reasons is Senka Klevskin, hero of a mutiny at Buchenwald, who three times had escaped from German captivity and whose spirit only the Siberian camp has succeeded in breaking:

Senka was a quiet, luckless fellow. One of his eardrums had been smashed in '41. Then he was captured; he escaped, was recaptured, and was sent to Buchenwald. There he evaded death by a miracle and now he was serving his time here quietly. If you show your pride too much, he said, you're lost. . . .

Senka, who had suffered so much, was usually silent: he didn't hear what people said and didn't mix in their conversation. Little was known about him—only that he'd been in Buchenwald, where he'd worked with the underground and smuggled in arms for the mutiny; and how the Germans had punished him by tying his wrists behind his back, hanging him by them, and whipping his wrists.

One Estonian is in prison because his parents, before the Soviets' arrival in Estonia, had taken him to Sweden. He had been a child then, and when he was grown up he had returned of his own free will to Estonia to study—and, of course, to prison.

The squad leader, Tyurin, has been in prison for nineteen years. During the thirties, i.e., during the period of enforced collectivization, he had done his military service in the Red Army. He had been in his twenties. Back home, his parents had been denounced as "kulaks," and Tyurin had broken off all connection with them in order not to suffer himself. But his regimental commander and the commissar one day learned of his "kulak origin" and discharged him without documents or proper clothing, which meant sending him straight to prison. Recalling his former superior officers, Tyurin relates:

"Incidentally, in '38, at the Kotlas deportation point, I met my former squadron commander. He'd been given ten years too. I learned from him that the regimental commander and the commissar were both shot in '37, whether they were of proletarian or kulak stock, whether they had a conscience or not. So I crossed myself and said: 'So, after all, Creator, you do exist up there in heaven. Your patience is long-suffering but you strike hard."

Among the dozen or so characters whose acquaintance we make, only one is a real criminal—a Moldavian, who really is a spy.

On the question of slavery and freedom, Dostoevsky writes:

There are also other [prisoners], men who deliberately committed a crime in order to be sent to a forced-labor camp and so free themselves from an incomparably less bearable life at liberty. There they lived in the utmost humiliation, never ate their fill, and worked for their employers from dawn till dusk, whereas in penal servitude the work was lighter than at home, there was plenty of bread. . . .

Whenever free men and convicts are compared, Dostoevsky writes, there seems to be very little difference between them. The inmates of Soviet prison camps could not boast that they found life in camp easier than life outside; yet they agree with Dostoevsky that there is no essential difference between life in a camp and life outside. As A. Weissberg-Cybulski puts it in his excellent book *Conspiracy of Silence*, they said, referring to those living at liberty: "We are already condemned, while they are still standing trial."

The majority of Soviet critics stress Shukhov's attitude toward work as the most laudable feature of his character. Shukhov works well and with a will, as we see from the way he constructs a building with his squad. On a prisoner's fulfillment of his quota depends his food, his very existence. One of the basic criteria on which a person is assessed in Soviet society is his attitude toward work; *ergo,* prisoners who do not work well are not good people.

None of the critics, however, notices that work—i.e., building—is not the same for Shukhov as for Captain Buinovsky or for any other of the camp inmates. At home, too, Shukhov had done some building, although only with wood; for him, therefore, this work represents in some measure his life outside, work is a function of his freedom. For Buinovsky, on the other hand, who "was fading away under your very eyes," hard work in the camp is not a function of freedom but, on the contrary, one more shackle—and the heaviest one at that. Consequently, a positive attitude toward work cannot in this case be expected from Buinovsky.

Dostoevsky goes deeply into the dialectics of labor in *House of the Dead.* He understands that the same work may constitute slavery or freedom and that the cult of labor is harmful. He writes:

Even the work, for example, seemed to me to be by no means so hard, so much like penal servitude, and it was only quite a long time after that I realized that the burdensomeness and servitude of this work lay not so much in its difficulty or continuity as in the fact that it is forced, obligatory, performed under the lash. The peasant at liberty works, perhaps, incomparably more, sometimes at night, particularly in summer; but he works for himself, he works with a rational aim, and it is incomparably easier for him than it is for the convict engaged in forced labor, which is completely senseless from his point of view. . . . If forced labor is dull and uninteresting for the convict, it is, regarded as work, rational enough: the prisoner makes bricks, digs, plasters, builds; such work has a meaning and purpose. A prisoner may even get carried away by his work and try to do it as skillfully, rapidly, and efficiently as possible. But if he were forced, say, to pour water from one pitcher into another and back again, to grind sand, or to carry a pile of earth back and forth between two points, I imagine he would hang himself after a few days or commit a thousand crimes in order at least to die and so rid himself of such humiliation, shame, and torment. Naturally, such a punishment would become a form of torture, of revenge, and would be pointless, for it would not achieve any rational purpose. But since an element of such torture, pointlessness, humiliation, and shame is inevitable in all forced labor, the convict's work is incomparably more burdensome than any voluntary work, precisely because it is compulsory.

Elsewhere, he says:

All these people [in the convict prison] were working under the lash; consequently they were idle, consequently they became demoralized: if they were not demoralized before, they became demoralized in prison.

With the exception of technical differences such as the organization of squads in the "special camp," Dostoevsky's and Solzhenitsyn's prisoners are engaged in much the same kind of task, as these quotations show. For Solzhenitsyn's prisoners, however, existence itself depends upon the fulfillment of quotas; the inmates of the House of the Dead, who do not always work according to norms, prefer nevertheless to have them.

Then they would be filled with enthusiasm, and although they derived no benefit whatever from it, I myself observed that they exerted every effort to finish as quickly and efficiently as possible; somehow their *amour propre* was involved.

With remarkable lucidity, Dostoevsky distinguishes between creative activity, i.e., voluntary work which liberates the worker, and forced labor, which enslaves and demoralizes him. Convicts who are given a definite task, a norm to fulfill, and then, after its fulfillment, return to their barracks and devote themselves to free, voluntary work, finish their task rapidly and with a will. Dostoevsky remarks that if they had not had jobs of their own to see to—mending boots, sewing, making toys, etc.—the convicts would have gone mad. In Solzhenitsyn's camp there is no possibility of the prisoners' having any time to themselves, and so they long for the chance to stop work and sleep. Only when work is over does one have a chance of indulging in creative activity. Even so, the inmates of the House of the Dead can hardly wait to take up such activity: this we have seen in an earlier quotation. The attitude of Solzhenitsyn's prisoners, not only to forced labor but to any form of movement, comes out clearly in Ivan Denisovich's musings about the doctor who is in charge of the camp infirmary:

. . . a fussy, loud-voiced fellow who gave neither himself nor his patients any peace. He invented jobs in and around the infirmary for all the patients who could stand on their feet— fencing the garden, laying paths, bringing soil to the flowerbeds, and, in wintertime, erecting snow barriers. Work, he said, was a first-rate medicine for any illness.

You can overwork a horse to death. That the doctor ought to understand. If *he*'d been sweating blood laying blocks he'd quiet down, you could be sure of that.

Shukhov calls in the morning at the dispensary and has his temperature taken:

For Shukhov it was a strange experience to sit in that spick-and-span room, in such quiet, to sit under the bright lamps for five long minutes doing nothing.

Marx devoted many pages of his writings to the question of reification and alienation. Unfortunately, the problem of alienated and free work (in our view, the terms "work" and "creative activity" would be better) has still not been dealt with in Marxist literature in its most essential point, i.e., the relation between the individual and work. For it is not a question by any means of the "liberation *of* work" but of "liberation *from* work" for the sake of creative activity, which is essentially different from all work.

Creative activity suffers no compulsion, from outside or from within. Work requires the development of "working habits," but creative activity does not, for man is a creator par excellence, and here nothing has to be consciously developed: all that is required is the chance to pursue such activity. Children never have to be forced to play, and for them play is creative activity; on the other hand, we have to urge them to learn their lessons, to do something useful, etc. Geniuses always have childish qualities, and vice versa: as Tolstoy says, "the majority of people at five years of age are geniuses, and at eighteen mediocrities." Labor requires working habits, discipline, ideology, etc., whereas for creative activity it is essential to do away with all this and to give free rein to spontaneity. According to Marijan Cipra, not until the given world has been destroyed is the possibility created for the world that is given. A classic example of the relation between work and creative activity may be found in Pushkin's little tragedy *Mozart and Salieri:* the childish, frivolous Mozart does no work but achieves success, while Salieri vainly sacrifices himself to work as a composer and, having finally come to the conclusion that there is no justice on earth or in heaven, kills Mozart.

In the Yugoslav Encyclopedia of the Lexicography Institute, "work" (*rad*) is defined as

. . . the expedient and conscious organized activity of human beings, performed in order to achieve some useful result capable of satisfying some particular kind of personal, communal, or production needs. Work is a fundamental requisite for the existence and development of society. . . .

Creative activity, as distinct from work, does not pursue the aim of "achieving some useful result capable of satisfying . . . needs," but is an aim in itself, just as life itself is; as distinct from work, it is a fundamental requisite for the existence and development of the individual. Disaster comes when the two concepts are identified, as in the Bolshaya

Sovetskaya Entsiklopediya (Great Soviet Encyclopedia), which defines creative activity (*tvorchestvo*) as

. . . human activity which creates new material and spiritual values of social import. Creative activity, which is the result of the labor and efforts of the individual. . . .

Certain Soviet critics have stressed as an affirmative characteristic of Communists imprisoned in Soviet camps that they have a positive attitude toward work in the camp, that is, toward their own slavery. These critics come near to the ideologists of the Catholic monastic orders, whose chief motto, designed to guarantee the salvation of the soul, is *Ora et labora*. The Egyptian pharaohs would probably have gladly adopted this motto, too—on behalf of their slaves, of course.

All this suggests that liberation from social exploitation does not immediately imply man's final liberation, but merely opens up possibilities. It is merely one of many stages on this road. Social liberation is not at the same time individual liberation. Marx knew this, and for this reason foresaw that the final liberation of man as an individual would occur only in a Communist society, at an advanced stage in the automation of production. A cult of work and of the proletarian class is therefore quite harmful. Man's liberation is possible only when the proletariat abolishes itself as a class by liberating itself from work. Concentration camps such as the one in which Ivan Denisovich was imprisoned represent the idea of labor materialized *ad absurdum*. All the camp inmates work; they have no choice. And if we take the viewpoint of those critics who maintain that work is the meaning and aim of man's life on earth, labor camps are largely justified. It was not by chance that the inscription *Arbeit macht frei* was placed over the entrance to Hitler's camps.

The inmates of labor camps are a hundred percent social

beings; like ants or bees, if they possess a conscience it is exclusively a "social conscience." The cult of labor inevitably leads to a conflict with all individuality, for all creative activity is essentially individual, however much it may be socially useful: this is a paradox which we have already mentioned. Happily, man is not just a "social being" but a "social being" *inter alia,* and will never reconcile himself to becoming an exclusively "social being," an ant or a labor-camp inmate. Sooner or later this will prove the stumbling block of all totalitarian systems, which are nothing but an attempt to transform a social organism into a social mechanism. The difference between an organism and a mechanism lies in the fact that every constituent part of an organism lives its own life and by virtue of this makes possible the life of the organism as a whole, whereas every constituent part of a mechanism is inanimate and thereby enables the machine to function. This is the explanation of the seeming paradox in the relation between the individual and society: the less man submits to the social mechanism, the greater the extent to which he makes possible the existence of the social organism; the more he submits to the social mechanism and becomes a part of this mechanism without individuality, the more he contributes to the death of society as a living organism. Or, to put it more strongly, extreme uncompromising individuality is of the greatest benefit to society. But a prerequisite for the existence of individuality is creative activity. Forced labor, the lowest degree of human slavery, removes the possibility of creative activity and *ipso facto* of the individual's existence, converting human beings into inanimate though movable parts in a mechanism, thus killing the social organism. Incidentally, the industrial development of the Soviet Union has occurred, not thanks to, but in spite of, Stalinism (Stalinism, not Stalin), which by means of its camp system checked and maimed the tremendous creative forces of the Russian and other Soviet peoples that were awakened by the October Revolution. If Stalinism in the thirties had not taken hold on all spheres of life, the U.S.S.R. today would be an incomparably greater and more powerful industrial and cultural giant. From this point of view, any theory of the so-called "historical necessity" of Stalinism is absurd.

Also in the Yugoslav Encyclopedia of the Lexicography Institute, we read, concerning concentration camps:

Concentration camps [are] places for keeping the civilian population in mass confinement which in their organization and the status of their inmates do not differ essentially from ordinary forced-labor camps. As a rule, imprisonment in these camps occurs without a regular court trial, on the basis of a decision by military or political authorities enjoying in this respect "discretionary powers." Confinement is frequently not individual but extends to whole categories of the population. The introduction of concentration camps signifies an adoption of methods of rule by means of mass intimidation and terror.

Concentration camps came in with the twentieth century and undoubtedly represent one of its chief characteristics, for they are a clear reflection of processes that have occurred during the last fifty years, *viz.*, the attempt to destroy the existence of the individual and transform human beings into working machines. The first concentration camps were established by the British during the Boer War (1899–1902). Later, others appeared in Soviet Russia: in 1919, the Central Executive Committee issued a decree founding forced-labor camps. Until 1929–30, the period of enforced collectivization, these camps were relatively small in number, but from this time on they multiplied in geometrical progression. Later the notorious camps and camp complexes at Solovki, Ust-Izhma, Kolima and Magdan, Vorkuta and Narim came into existence—the last four are mentioned by Alexander Tvardovsky in his excellent satirical poem *Tyorkin in the*

Other World (1963) —and a central camp administration was created under the abbreviated title GULAG.

Concentration camps had a special place in the Hitlerite system in Germany. Before the beginning of World War II, Nazi Germany had six concentration camps; during the war, they reached astronomical figures, the most notorious of them being the so-called death factories at Buchenwald, Dachau, Auschwitz, and Mauthausen. There is little point in saying anything about these camps; they are well known as it is.

On the subject of Stalin's camps, the young Soviet critic V. I. Lakshin has this to say:

The entire system of imprisonment in the camps through which Ivan Denisovich passed was calculated to crush mercilessly, to stifle all feeling of law and justice in the inmates, demonstrating on a large and small scale such tyranny, unmitigated by fear of punishment, that any upsurge of righteous indignation was powerless before it. The camp authorities did not let the inmates forget for a moment that they had no rights and that their sole judge was the dictatorship. They were reminded of this by the whip wielded by Volkovoi, who flogged the men in the cells; they were reminded of it when they were deprived of their rest on Sundays and hustled out to work, whatever time of day it might be.

As for the numbers of people confined in Stalin's camps, not even approximate data are available. All that we know comes from the speeches of Khrushchev at the 20th Soviet Party Congress (1956): that millions of innocent Soviet citizens were subjected to severe reprisals.

We have shown that the penal servitude Dostoevsky went through was like life in a sanatorium, compared with Solzhenitsyn's camp. Even so, Turgenev regarded some of the pages of *The House of the Dead* as a "Dantean hell." Herzen, too, wrote:

Apart from this, it should not be forgotten that this period [the period of social unrest preceding the reforms of the 1860's] has left us a frightening book, a kind of *carmen horrendum*, which will eternally figure over the exit to Nicholas's somber reign, like Dante's famous inscription over the entrance to Hell. This is Dostoevsky's *House of the Dead*, a frightening narrative in which, though probably even the author did not suspect it, in sketching with his manacled hand the figures of his fellow prisoners he was making frescoes *à la* Buonarroti out of life and customs in a Siberian prison.

The emergence of the concentration camp is closely connected with the rise of *étatisme* (in Russian, *gosudarstvennost*) . In *The State and Revolution,* Lenin wrote:

The state is a special organization of force, it is an organization of violence for crushing some class. . . .

Here [in a passage quoted from Marx's *18th Brumaire*] the question is put concretely, and a remarkably clear . . . conclusion drawn: all previous revolutions have perfected the state machine, whereas this machine should be broken, destroyed.

This conclusion is the main, fundamental factor in the teachings of Marxism about the state. . . .

Our ultimate aim is the destruction of the state, i.e., of all organizational and systematic violence, all violence committed on human beings in general. . . .

So long as the state exists, there is no freedom. When there is freedom, there will be no state.

These words make it clear that concentration camps are by no means an immanent feature of a socialist society or of the idea of socialism, and that their existence was a living denial of socialism. In our view, the most positive thing in Soviet society in the past few decades, something that equals the victory over the Fascists in World War II, is the fact that today Stalin's concentration camps are openly discussed and written about in the Soviet Union. On the other hand, the Chinese tendency to minimize the tremendous negative significance of the existence for so many years of the many

Stalinist camps is today unfortunately growing, braking the process of the liberation of the humane element in people's minds and thereby also delaying the necessary and inevitable rehabilitation of the very idea of socialism. Moreover, in the U.S.S.R. itself false notions of Stalinism are still rife and are not being publicly corrected. For example, we read in the latest edition of the Philosophical Dictionary (1963), in the article on the "cult of personality":

Although the personality cult of Stalin was incapable of changing the nature of socialism, nevertheless it was a most serious brake upon the development of Soviet society.

Instead, it should have been stated quite openly that the cult of Stalin had essentially changed the nature of socialism, for if this change is not clear, the essence of the Chinese distortion of socialism is also obscured. Moreover, it then becomes difficult to deal with recrudescences of Nazism in Germany, especially if we recall certain of Hitler's utterances which are so gloomily reminiscent of the Chinese standpoint:

Old Testament or New . . . it's all one and the same Jewish swindle. . . . We want free men who know and feel God to be in them. . . .

Yes! We are barbarians. We *want* to be. It is a honorific title. *We* are the ones who are going to rejuvenate the world. . . .

The era of personal happiness is past. Instead, we shall experience a communal happiness. . . .

Why should we bother about socializing the banks and the factories. We shall socialize human beings. . . .

The Party is an incorruptible judge. . . .

. . . Only deeds and eternal movement give a meaning to human life. . . . All passivity, all inertia, on the other hand, is pointless, an enemy of life. . . .

In lieu of the dogma of the suffering and death of a divine Redeemer on [man's] behalf . . . [I advance the dogma of] the new leader and legislator who lives and acts on behalf of man. . . .

Man is the god of the future. Man must eternally strive to rise above his limitations. As soon as he becomes inert and isolates himself, he degenerates and sinks beneath the level of humanity. He becomes half animal. . . .

Hitler never tires of saying . . . that he is driving the German people and the world into a movement without end, an eternal revolution. This revolution embraces the whole of human existence. . . .

Action is everything.

CONCLUSION

> *But dogs like meekness and submissiveness in their own kind.*
>
> DOSTOEVSKY, The House of the Dead

It is our belief in the possibility of realizing socialism that gives us strength to face up to the terrible marks that the protracted obscurantism of Stalin's "socialism" has left on men's minds. Until the last of the crimes committed during the last half century in the name of humanity has been traced and published, the most terrible consequence of "labor-camp socialism"—fear, which implies being prepared for further slavery—will not have been removed.

Naturally, it is both difficult and painful to look full in the face such facts as the existence of Stalin's camps in the land of the "humane, gentle, great, brotherly Slav nation of Russians," camps which served as a pretext and justification for Himmler's and Kaltenbrunner's camps. But so long as we fail to understand that Fascism is a psychological, not just a social, phenomenon and was not territorially linked only with the Axis countries but appeared everywhere on the globe, under all governments and among all nations whenever men lost their belief in the permanence and absolute value of the most vital reality, *viz.*, the existence of the individual person—so long as we fail to grasp these facts, we risk finding ourselves in the same situation as Senka Klevshin, the hero of the revolt in Buchenwald, whose morale is broken not by the terroristic regime of a Stalinist camp but by the discovery that the evil against which he fought in Germany is also to be found in his homeland. For this reason, the Soviet prison camps seem to him even more dreadful than their German counterparts, though in some respects they were, objectively, less so.

We have attempted to show that the lack of freedom and the pressure designed to convert a human being into an inanimate machine have been incomparably greater in the twentieth century than they were in the nineteenth century. Nevertheless, the very fact that today we can freely discuss this question indicates that man is stronger than this pressure. With respect to the idea of progress, it is perhaps not out of place here to suggest that the most important, the most essential progress is to be found precisely in the strengthening of man's resistance to this pressure. If we consider this point of view for a moment, the entire historical perspective becomes greatly changed and we begin to grasp the meaning of Goethe's remark that "every people has the government that it deserves"—that is, that it is impossible to tyrannize the man who refuses to be tyrannized. Of course, if we take the view that physical death may mean liberation, then an acceptance of slavery always means death.

As long ago as 1921, Ilya Ehrenburg wrote in *Julio Jurenito:*

Humanity is now moving, not toward paradise, but toward the blackest, harshest, sweatiest of purgatories. A complete eclipse of freedom is approaching. Assyria and Egypt will be as nothing compared to the new and unprecedented slavery. But the slave galley will be a preparation, a token of freedom—not of a statue on the marketplace, not of some penpusher's banal invention, but of creative freedom, faultless, perfect harmony. You will ask: what is the purpose of this retrogression, this stepping aside, these aimless crazy months? . . . Freedom that is not fed on blood but is picked up for nothing, received as a gratuity, dies. But remember—this I am telling you now, when thousands of hands are taking up the rod and millions are voluptuously baring their backs in readiness—the day will come when no one will need the rod. A far-off day!

We know that the first part of Ehrenburg's prediction has come true; and we believe that the second part will also be fulfilled.

During the struggle for national liberation [the period of German occupation and partisan warfare, 1941–45] and in the heroic year 1948 [the year of Yugoslavia's expulsion from the Cominform], Yugoslavia herself showed how unlimited pressure gives birth to an unlimited power of resistance and how this power of resistance alone guarantees that freedom shall not be lost, thrown away like a lightly valued gratuity.

Any—even the mildest—form of slavery, whether it be Ivan Denisovich's camp or some other stricter or milder captivity, can be beneficial from only one point of view: if it provokes a resistance which fortifies and hardens the captive's consciousness; for it should be remembered that no one can give another man his freedom or take it away. Man is par excellence a creature of liberty; and whoever does not know that is a slave.

Whether the human race will be transformed into a cog in a machine or after the terrors of this century will become freer than at any time in history we do not know. There are no laws that promise us a future paradise. Everything depends on us—whether we are ready to reconcile ourselves to our fate and be enslaved, or whether the final and dreadful threat of the destruction of life will awaken in man some great power of resistance which will throw back the pressure of death. In any case, the struggle itself, as Dostoevsky through Kirilov prophesies in *The Possessed*, will leave its mark, both literally and figuratively, on man.

[1964]

DOSTOEVSKY TODAY

Dostoevsky is Russia and there is no Russia without Dostoevsky.

ALEXEI REMIZOV

"Tell me the last number, the highest, the greatest."
"But that is nonsense! When the number of numbers is endless, how can there be a last number?"
"So how can there be a last revolution?"

EVGENY ZAMYATIN

The last, the most difficult struggle awaits the human soul.

LEV SHESTOV

*   *   *

IN 1929, People's Commissar Anatoly Lunacharsky in his study "On Polyphony in Dostoevsky" wrote a sentence which is saintly in its simplicity: "Dostoevsky is not dead, either here or in the West, because capitalism is not dead."

More than a quarter of a century has passed since then. The face of the earth has changed several times over. Forced collectivization and the Moscow show trials have thundered by. Hitler climbed to power in Germany, conquered Europe, was bent on exterminating the Jews and the Slavs, and finally shot himself and Eva Braun. Stalin died and is still being laid to rest. Almost half of the world's population has come to live under socialism. The Soviet Union has declared that it built socialism and is going on to build Communism. Several generations of people who know about capitalism only through books have been born and grown old. And still Dostoevsky cannot die.

Quite the contrary, the popularity of his works is increasing from year to year, both in the capitalist world and, especially, in the socialist world. We can honestly say that humanity, in the broadest sense of the term, has only now begun to accept the great Russian classic. Only now is Dostoevsky on the way to becoming our "contemporary."

It is strange that this contemporary of ours stands accused as a reactionary, as an enemy of enlightenment, as a prophet of death and untruth, a bitter enemy of socialism. Why? What exactly are the charges? What is the "progress" against which Dostoevsky so passionately raised his voice?

Is there not a radical misunderstanding, not between us, Dostoevsky's contemporaries, and Dostoevsky himself, but between Dostoevsky and those who have been his accusers for over a century now? We shall attempt to answer this question by analyzing the basic theme of the great writer (and even greater thinker) as well as the charges against him.

The charges are as old as the writer's fame. His early works provoked such public cries of anguish as "A running sore has appeared on the body of Russian literature." And there was worse to come. Dostoevsky's novels followed one upon another: *Poor Folk* (1846), *The Double* (1846), *The Landlady* (1847), *Netochka Nezvanova* (1849). The writer was arrested, condemned to death, and led to a mock execution, after which he did four years of hard labor in the Omsk prison and served five years as an army private in Semipalatinsk. When he returned from Siberia, he continued to write novels and edit journals: *Notes from the House of the Dead* (1862), *The Village of Stepanchikovo* (1859), *Notes from the Underground* (1864). The whole world was moved by *Crime and Punishment* (1866), *The Idiot* (1868), *The*

Possessed (1871), *A Raw Youth* (1875), *The Brothers Karamazov* (1880), *The Diary of a Writer*. Dostoevsky read his famous speech at the unveiling of a monument to Pushkin in Moscow and died a few months later, in 1881. But after his death his fame went on growing, as did the accusations against him. The world split into two hostile ideological camps over him. Indeed, Dostoevsky could justifiably say of himself what that other Great Idealist said twenty centuries ago: "I come to bring not peace but the sword."

His work has inspired a galaxy of philosophers and artists whose names represent the highest points in the development of modern thought. It has also aroused a large group of critics who at the very mention of Dostoevsky's name lose their detachment and adopt a frankly insulting tone.

All of Russian non-Marxist philosophy, from Vladimir Soloviev to Konstantin Leontyev, V. Rozanov, A. L. Volynsky, Nikolai Berdyaev, and Lev Shestov, is rooted in Dostoevsky. The early Russian existentialism and personalism which flowered at the beginning of this century; and Russian modernism, not only in literature but in the other arts as well, epitomized by Alexei Remizov—all that is Dostoevsky.

In the West, too, starting with Georg Brandes's book on Dostoevsky, and with Nietzsche, who wrote: "Dostoevsky is among the most wonderful and happy finds of my life," and right on through André Gide, Stefan Zweig, Hermann Hesse, Adler, and Spengler, to Albert Camus, Jean-Paul Sartre, Remo Cantoni, Reinhard Lauth, J. Van der Eng, and other existentialists and personalists, the word and thought of the author of *The Possessed* and *Notes from the Underground* continue to live, to open ever new horizons, especially in the minds of those who are the makers of modern spiritual history.

On the other side of the ideological barricade, among the

ranks of the revolutionary democrats, from the high-strung, cantankerous exclamations and admonitions of Belinsky, who was provoked by *The Double* and *The Landlady,* and right on through a mass frontal attack by M. A. Antonovich, N. A. Dobrolyubov, D. I. Pisarev, N. K. Mikhailovsky, and later by Gorky and Lenin, antipathy toward Dostoevsky has grown as rapidly as his fame. In his *Notes on the Bourgeois, On Karamazovism,* and in his speech at the First Congress of the Union of Soviet Writers in 1934, Gorky denounced Dostoevsky as "a harmful bourgeois." Lenin, who rarely alluded to his literary preferences, could not conceal his antipathy toward Dostoevsky. In a letter of July 5, 1914, to Inessa Armand, condemning *The Pledge of Our Fathers,* a novel by Vinichenko, he writes: ". . . A superlatively bad imitation of the superlatively bad Dostoevsky." Once in a conversation he exclaimed irritably: "I have no time for that trash."

However, in spite of Lenin's and Gorky's negative attitudes, the first decade after the October Revolution saw the publication of Dostoevsky's *Collected Works* (Moscow, 1926). L. P. Grossman, M. M. Bakhtin, Y. Tynyanov, V. Vinogradov, and numerous other scholars published studies on the life and work of the great writer. Three volumes of letters from Dostoevsky's correspondence were published.

In the thirties the situation changed radically for the worse in all spheres of Russian culture. For almost a quarter of a century, until 1956, Dostoevsky's works were all but banned in Russia. (From time to time there appeared limited editions of *Poor Folk, The Humiliated and the Wronged, Notes from the House of the Dead, White Nights, Crime and Punishment.*) Practically all research on Dostoevsky ceased. Yugoslav students preparing for their examinations in Russian literature of the nineteenth century still use the two-volume *History of Russian Literature* by Pospelov, Zerchaninov, and Brodsky, translated after World War II, in which little more than a page is devoted to Dostoevsky, whereas Saltykov-Shchedrin and Ostrovsky have about fifty pages each.

After the 20th Congress of the CPSU there was a complete change. In 1956, Dostoevsky's *Collected Works* were published in an edition of 300,000 copies (minus just two volumes of *The Diary of a Writer*). A collection of articles, *Dostoevsky in Russian Criticism,* was issued, as well as studies by V. V. Ermilov and D. I. Zaslavsky and a semibiographical novel by Mikhail Nikitin about Dostoevsky's years in Semipalatinsk. In the following years the number of essays and books on Dostoevsky increased steadily, and in the past decade a considerable literature on Dostoevsky, his life, and creative work has accumulated. Numerous monographs and comparative studies have appeared. The Academy of Sciences has brought out a large collection of critical articles written by the most prominent Soviet literary historians. An edition of Dostoevsky's letters is being revised and its fourth volume is now out.

The majority of Soviet literary historians and critics (including A. A. Belkin, U. A. Guralnik, I. Oksman, A. V. Chicherin, V. S. Nechayeva, D. O. Zaslavsky, I. M. Strochkev, V. V. Ermilov, I. L. Motyleva, G. L. Abramovich, B. A. Byalik, V. I. Kirpotin, F. I. Evnin, G. M. Fridlender, M. Gus, and B. S. Ryurikov) staunchly defend the correctness of a kind of vulgar sociologizing, the foundations for which were laid by the revolutionary democrats of the last century. With varying degrees of passion they reiterate the accusations against Dostoevsky as a reactionary. In general, they feel that, although the writer cannot be ignored, only part of his work is acceptable and total war must be waged against all those who glorify "bad" Dostoevsky. B. S. Ryurikov brashly writes: "Reactionary criticism has defended Dostoevsky in the past and continues to do so. Idealists and enemies of enlightenment have written whole volumes praising him for his mysticism, his pessimism, his nationalist tendencies. . . . The same tenor prevails today in the works of his reactionary 'interpreters.' They emphasize the pessimistic, the anti-humane ideas in his writing and use them for their own unclean purposes."

Two voices can be heard above this uniform chorus: those of Viktor Shklovsky, the founder of the formalist school of literary criticism and one of the most important modern Russian literary critics, and I. A. Golosovker, who, in his short book *Dostoevsky and Kant,* opened totally new horizons in Dostoevskian criticism. Drawing a parallel between *The Brothers Karamazov* and Kant's *Critique of Pure Reason,* he shows how Kant and Dostoevsky, though in different languages, speak about identical things. This comes close to the existentialist thinker, Lev Shestov, who said some decades earlier that *Notes from the Underground* was a more consistent and powerful critique of pure reason than Kant's work. This is how matters stand in the Soviet Union today.

During the years of silence on Dostoevsky in the U.S.S.R., numerous works devoted to him appeared in the West. On the whole, these are much more scholarly and serious than the majority of their Soviet counterparts, most of which suffer from schematism and oversimplification. At the same time, the Western literature is free from a certain lack of understanding of Dostoevsky's spirit and spirituality which has always been the main objection to studies published by authors of non-Russian origin. In Prague, the Free Russian University published a three-volume collection of articles on Dostoevsky, edited by A. L. Beme, with contributions from the most eminent scholars among the Russian émigrés: D. Chizhevsky, N. E. Osipov, V. V. Zenkovsky, R. V. Pletnev, P. M. Biccili, and others. In addition to Shestov and Berdyaev, a number of scholars published detailed monographs on Dostoevsky: Mochulsky in Paris (1946), P. M. Biccili in Sofia (1925), Alexander Pogodin in Belgrade, Marc Slonim in New York, Nina Gourfinkel in Paris, etc.

The ideological struggle surrounding Dostoevsky, far from abating, rages on with growing intensity. This is due first of all to a certain degree of liberalization in the spiritual life of the U.S.S.R. and also to increasing opportunities for contact between the Soviet and non-Soviet worlds. The polemic concerning Dostoevsky has taken on international proportions, and one may assume that an already vast literature on Dostoevsky will continue to grow. In Russian alone, there are already several hundred books on Dostoevsky.

Here in Yugoslavia the attitude of the literary critics toward Dostoevsky has never been clearly defined. On the one hand, Dostoevsky has been considered ideologically suspect. On the other, certain critics have shown strong emotional affinity with the Russian writer, one of them being August Cesarec, a revolutionary and a Marxist, who wrote one of the most profound studies on the Grand Inquisitor in his essay *Dostoevsky and Lenin: The two poles of Russian imperialism* (1922). It must be admitted that Yugoslav criticism has so far not produced a single attack on Dostoevsky of the Zhdanov-Ermilov variety, in spite of a wide range of opinion among critics, both those who wrote about his Pan-Slavism (Dragutin Prohaska, Josip Badalić, and Iso Velikanović) and others (such as Radovan Kazimirović, Momčilo Natasijević, Branko Lazarević, Juraj Lončarević, Petar Mitropan, Milivoje Jovanović, Petar Džadzić, Aleksandar Flaker, Branko Kreft, Dragan M. Jeremić, Radovan Lalić, Nikola Milošević, Milisav Babović, Ervin Šinko, and Josip Vidmar).

In spite of a certain duality in the attitude of our Marxist critics, exemplified most recently by Vinko Cecić's study

"Dostoevsky in Relation to Religion and the Church," Yugoslav literature on Dostoevsky remains within the limits of scholarly good taste.

If it is no surprise to find such Soviet statements as Ermilov's "We must confess before the conscience of all mankind that Dostoevsky's moral crime is great" (the "moral crime" being *Notes from the Underground*), it is fairly surprising to read in a Yugoslav journal that Dostoevsky "has become a prophet of death and untruth"; that the theme of *The Brothers Karamazov* is "repugnant and incomprehensible"; and "how far Dostoevsky went in his foul dealings with darkness and misery."

To set the record straight we must point out that this attitude of denigration is not the exclusive monopoly of the Soviet critics and our own Cecić. In 1925 in Germany a pamphlet appeared entitled *Idiotführer durch die russische Literatur* and signed "Sir Galahad." It is a worthy rival to Ermilov's book, and its opinion of Dostoevsky differs little from Upton Sinclair's.

To wage war on Dostoevsky, however, is remarkably difficult. Almost all his attackers believe that art is a reflection of an objective social reality, that the greater the art, the more objective the reflection, which in turn should inspire readers with confidence in precisely those ideals which the attacking critics hold dear: science, social revolution, progress, atheism, etc.

Since Dostoevsky's works destroy faith in these ideals, he distorts the image of objective reality, say these critics, and compromises his art. In his first period (in his early works up to but not including *Notes from the Underground*), Dostoevsky more or less meets the requirements of "progressive" criticism which labels his later period "reactionary."

If art really is a reflection of an objective reality, then it follows logically that Dostoevsky's later works are artistically less valuable. The difficulty lies in the fact that the artistic value of his later works is incomparably higher than that of his earlier works. It would seem that the more "reactionary" Dostoevsky becomes, the greater an artist he is.

One way to get around this difficulty would be, of course, to proclaim his second period (the period of *Crime and Punishment, The Idiot, The Possessed, A Raw Youth, The Brothers Karamazov*) as decadent, and this is, in fact, what the more naïve critics do. M. A. Antonovich, one of the first to attack *The Brothers Karamazov,* wrote in 1881: "We shall not analyze the novel from the aesthetic point of view. We consider that the novel contains very little which could be called artistic."

Wiser and more serious opponents of Dostoevsky do not deny the artistic value of his "reactionary" works. They maintain that because he is a great artist he reflects reality despite his reactionary ideas. His characters lead the independent lives created for them by the artist and, in living these lives, prove their creator wrong. Unfortunately, this is not true. If it were, no war would be waged over Dostoevsky's ideas. We must conclude, therefore, either that art is not a reflection of objective reality or that the "enlightened" ideas which Dostoevsky opposed do not spring from and are not confirmed by objective reality.

Dostoevsky called himself a realist, but a "more profound and more real realist than all other realists." We agree with this. We also agree that art is a reflection of objective reality (and, in Dostoevsky's case, an anticipation of things to come as well). We grant too that Dostoevsky did not give satisfactory answers to all the questions posed by his rebellious characters. But he was not supposed to give them, according to George Lukács: "For raising questions and formulating problems in the shape of new men and new human destinies is the real task of poetry. . . . The concrete answers which poetry, of course, always gives are frequently of an incidental nature."

We shall prove that the century-old hostility to Dostoevsky stems neither from his inability to provide answers nor from his providing wrong answers while rejecting possible "progressive" answers, but from the fact that Belinsky and Mikhailovsky, Gorky and Lenin themselves failed to provide answers to Dostoevsky's questions. This failure is also the cause of a neurotic aversion to Dostoevsky which, in the case of the more emotional critics, is translated into open denigration.

The charges against Dostoevsky include: (1) that he was a reactionary because he actively opposed the revolution and socialism, because he ridiculed revolutionaries (among them Chernyshevsky), and because he foresaw that the Russian Revolution would end in unparalleled tyranny; (2) that he was an enemy of the very idea of progress and therefore an enemy of reason and science; (3) that he preached belief in God and in the immortality of the soul and glorified suffering and resignation as the only possible expiation for sin; (4) that he was a mystic.

We do not intend to follow in the footsteps of the more naïve defenders of Dostoevsky, who wish to demonstrate that he was progressive, that he *did* believe in revolution, in socialism, in human reason, and that it is ridiculous to label him reactionary. Thus, for example, the Soviet critic Kirpotin, trying to prove that Dostoevsky remained under Belinsky's influence all his life, wrote: "And as Jacob could not conquer the Lord, so Dostoevsky could not conquer Belinsky." A. S. Dolinin's "defense" of Dostoevsky is not very different.

No, a progressive Dostoevsky was not. He was not progressive in the sense in which revolutionary democrats were progressive, and we do not consider it necessary to "defend" him by trying to prove the contrary. We agree with his opponents that the charges against Dostoevsky are correct on every count and that they not only apply to all his works but are the *spiritus rector* of his creativity.

However, we wish also to show that there exists a patent misunderstanding between Dostoevsky and his accusers on more than one of the charges leveled against him. Let us analyze these charges, one by one.

DOSTOEVSKY AND THE REVOLUTION

> *Counterrevolution is not a revolution in reverse, but the reverse of a revolution.*
>
> JOSEPH DE MAISTRE

> *The spirit of the revolution does not recognize the revolution of the spirit.*
>
> NIKOLAI BERDYAEV

Every revolution is parricide. Revolution destroys the social structure which engenders it. Dostoevsky wrote about revolution not only in *The Possessed* but also in *The Brothers Karamazov, A Raw Youth, The Idiot, Crime and Punishment,* and, of course, *Notes from the Underground.* Thus, all the works of his second, and most important, period treat revolution implicitly or explicitly.

In his early period, Dostoevsky merely observed life and wrote about what troubled him most: human suffering, humiliation, etc. In his later works he tried to find a solution to man's problems in the destinies of his characters, each of which represents a living idea, and delved into the possibilities and consequences of certain courses of action. Yes, we accept the verdict of his accusers: Dostoevsky did not find an answer to the question what is to be done. Had he found it, he would not have written his novels, which may be considered in fact experiments.

The answer to the questions raised by Dostoevsky's characters, however, was not provided either by any socio-revolutionary ideology (Marxist ideology included). It was not provided by the October Revolution and it will not be provided by Communist society, which has already been realized. This explains both Dostoevsky's rejection of social revolution and the hostility toward him on the part of advocates of socio-historical progress.

"The Possessed is a virulent attack against revolution and socialism, and has been, and always will be, used as such by all reactionaries in their struggle against revolution and socialism," writes the Soviet critic M. Gus. Further on he says: "Dostoevsky did not understand that the real history of mankind has an inner logic and is governed by objective laws . . ." The critic Belkin, in his study *On Dostoevsky's Realism,* writes: "Dostoevsky failed to grasp the great concept of Karl Marx, the basic tenets of which were to be found in the French materialists of the eighteenth century: if human nature is conditioned by its environment, then we must make this environment more humane."

Dostoevsky believed in something altogether different. This is what he wrote in his *Diary of a Writer:* "It is patently clear that evil lies hidden deeper in man than the physician-socialists suppose, that a social system free from evil is impossible, that the human soul will always be, that immorality and sin come from the human soul, that the laws governing the human soul are still to such an extent unknown and alien to science and to such an extent undefined and shrouded in mystery that there are no physicians, or even judges, nor can there be any, except one who says 'Mine is the vengeance which I shall give.' "

The critic Ermilov, in his book on Dostoevsky, writes:

"Dostoevsky has expressed in his writings the immeasurable suffering of insulted, wronged humanity in a society based on exploitation, and has pointed out the limitless pain caused by this suffering. Yet, at the same time, he fought rabidly against any attempt to find realistic ways to struggle for the liberation of humanity from the insults and the wrongs." In short, Dostoevsky saw more clearly than anyone man's misery and suffering but refused to follow a path that would lead to their elimination, that is, the path of revolution. What misery and suffering are we talking about? In the answer to this question lies the crux of the misunderstanding between Dostoevsky and the socialists.

Referring to *Crime and Punishment,* Ermilov says in his book on Dostoevsky: "This is a book full of compassion for humanity, one of the most powerful works in Russian literature; it exposes the inhumanity of capitalist society. The objective content of the book is the utter impossibility of finding any solution within the framework of that society. In a terrible portrayal of human misery, humiliation, solitude, and life's unbearable pressures, the suffering of humanity stares one in the face. To live in such a society is impossible. That is the basic conclusion of the novel . . ."

G. M. Fridlender in his study of *The Idiot* has this to say about the tragedy of the dying youth, Ippolit: "Dostoevsky wanted to show that Ippolit's sufferings would disappear with his arrogance. In fact, he realistically showed that Ippolit's very "arrogance," his neurotic egocentricity, the anarchic individualistic rebellion from which he suffers and by which he is tortured, are but a reflection of his loneliness and the inhumanity of his social environment and are caused by his alienation from people, from other human beings, an alienation which turns his thoughts into delirium."

V. I. Kirpotin in his analysis of *Notes from the House of the Dead* explicitly states: "A bad environment makes men bad. If you wish to change man, you must first of all change his environment." Similarly, Lukács says: "Dostoevsky's characters fearlessly follow the socially necessary path of self-revelation. They follow it to the bitter end, and this self-destruction, this self-annihilation is the most passionate protest against the existing social order ever heard."

Our own Cecić repeats: "The artistic force with which Dostoevsky reveals the profound truth about bourgeois society has invested his works with eternal artistic value. But that is all. This is not to say that his truth *indicts bourgeois society exclusively*" (Cecić's italics).

He means that the causes of Dostoevsky's characters' tragedies are to be found only in the capitalist social system. The solution, therefore, lies in changing the system. This is precisely what the critic Kirpotin says: "The story of Raskolnikov proves to us that the masses, rather than one individual, should have risen and that they should have risen for the sake of universal liberation and not for the sake of improving anyone's personal lot."

Dostoevsky's reasons for not taking this as a solution remain unclear. B. S. Ryurikov offers the following explanation: "Dostoevsky sees evil in the world but fears active struggle against evil. He is afraid of the force with which the people in European countries will rise against the rich, the force with which the Russian peasantry rose against the Russian landlords." Why is he afraid? The usual answer is that his spirit was broken by years of hard labor in Siberia. Recently an interesting variant of this answer has appeared: "The collapse of the 1848 revolution in Europe and his own painful personal drama together broke the spirit of the writer."

Were we to ask Dostoevsky's characters themselves, we would see that they do not accept this simplistic explanation that the solution of all problems lies in the struggle for socialism. The hungry student Raskolnikov, the dying young Ippolit, Ivan Karamazov, and the underground man, standing on the brink of death, be it a physical death as for Ippolit or a spiritual and intellectual death as in the case of Ivan Karamazov or a moral and social death, which the underground man and Raskolnikov face, would all laugh at any offer of consolation in the form of an idealized realm of liberty or any practical solution in terms of socio-revolutionary action. Let them speak for themselves.

Raskolnikov: "Why did that fool Razumikhin rant against the socialists so? Worthy people, and industrious—in pursuit of 'universal happiness . . .' No, this life was given me only once, it will never come again! I don't want to wait for 'universal happiness.' I want to live myself, otherwise it is better not to live at all. So what? Only I refuse to pass by a hungry mother, awaiting 'universal happiness,' tightly clasping my ruble in my pocket. Here am I, carrying my little brick for 'universal happiness' and because of it I feel peace in my heart. Ha, ha, ha! I live only once, and I also want . . . Something needs to be done now, don't you understand? With what will you keep them, you future millionaire? In ten years' time? In ten years . . ."

Ivan Karamazov: "I need revenge or I shall destroy myself. And I need it now, not in eternity, somewhere, sometime . . . but here, on this earth, so that I can see it."

In answer to Myshkin's advice to accept his fate with resignation: "Pass, and forgive them their happiness," Ippolit, the young man who is dying of tuberculosis while his friends rejoice in life, laughs wickedly.

What is most interesting is that the opinions of Dostoevsky's characters are shared by Vissarion Belinsky. "What good is it to me to know that reason will triumph, that the future will be fair, when I'm destined to witness the triumph of contingency, absurdity, and brutal force? What good does it do me to know that my children and your children will be all right, if I suffer, and suffer undeservedly?" (Letter to Botkin, March 1, 1841).

Dostoevsky's characters and Belinsky, in the letter just quoted, demand something which historical social progress cannot provide, an answer to all their questions, the elimination of injustice, suffering, and humiliation *now*, in their lifetime—as Ivan Karamazov puts it: "So that I can see it."

And very often the suffering is not of a social nature. The suffering of Ippolit, dying in the prime of youth, dying in accordance with those objective laws which Dostoevsky refuses to recognize, can hardly be explained by "alienation from people." And even if, in spite of Raskolnikov's views, we could accept the thesis that revolutionary action can solve everything, what action is Ippolit to take, revolutionary or otherwise? Can he be satisfied with the words of Myshkin, the fool in Christ: "Pass and forgive them their happiness"?

That would be resignation indeed, and capitulation before death and destiny. It can be said that Dostoevsky's rebellious characters are egoists and individualists who put their own happiness before the happiness of mankind (mankind in the future). Just before his repentance, Raskolnikov admits to Sonya Marmeladova: ". . . Sonya, I wanted to kill, without casuistry, to kill for myself, only for myself! I did not want to lie about it even to myself. I did not kill to help my mother— what nonsense. I did not kill in order to become the benefactor of mankind that becomes rich. What nonsense. I have simply killed. I have killed for myself. You know, Sonya," he suddenly spoke as if inspired, "you know what I'm going to tell you now? Had I cut her throat simply because I was hungry," he continued mysteriously and stressing every word but looking at her candidly, "I would . . . now . . . be happy. Do you know that?"

The underground man answers his own question: "If I were to choose between the end of the world or drinking my tea—I would drink my tea." Belinsky's egoism goes further. It embraces all the victims of social conditions, of Phillip II's inquisition, etc., and thereby becomes a kind of altruism. Like Ivan Karamazov, he rejects "future harmony" out of love for his blood brothers.

We can see that the problem is far more complex than Dostoevsky's critics suppose. Even the question of egoism is not simple. Who can guarantee that Pavel Korchagin, the main character of Nikolai Ostrovsky's *The Making of a Hero,* is not an egoist, that his motives for fighting in the October Revolution for the "future happiness of the world" were not personal egoism? (In Biblical language, he was striving to "save his soul" through his revolutionary struggle.)

In 1884, Engels wrote to Marx: "Before we can do anything for an idea, we must make sure that that idea is personal, egotistic. Our own egoism consists in being Communists, in wanting to be human beings, not just individuals. As for individualism, we must remember that in the beginning even Marx was an extreme ideological individualist who destroyed the collective conscience of his time and that Lenin, with his collectivism, was also an extreme individualist since he preached collectivism at a time when social individualism reigned supreme in human consciousness."

Ermilov juxtaposes the egoism of the underground man to that of the protagonist of Chernyshevsky's novel *What Is to Be Done?* "Yes," says Chernyshevsky's protagonist, "I will always do what I want. I will never sacrifice anything, not even a whim, for the sake of something I do not desire. What I want, with all my heart, is to make people happy. In this lies my happiness. Mine! Can you hear that, you, in your underground hole?"

The difficulty lies in the fact that even if a man were able to satisfy his every urge, be it to drink tea or to make people happy, he cannot determine these urges himself. As Schopenhauer says: "Man can do or not do, but he cannot will what he wills." Pavel Korchagin and Yuri Zhivago both live truly personal lives, "egoistic" lives, and Zhivago dies spiritually only because he did not fight hard enough for his personal happiness, because he betrayed it for one moment. Pavel Korchagin would have died the same death had he betrayed the revolution.

The critic Ryurikov wrote: "Ivan Karamazov, in his rejection of the existing world, argues so passionately, so forcefully that the characters representing Dostoevsky's ideas cannot refute his anguished doubts." It is interesting that no one has noticed that Ivan's arguments refute not only Dostoevsky's religious ideas but also the socio-progressive ideas of Ryurikov himself. Belinsky demands an accounting for "all the victims in history." Ivan Karamazov demands punishment for torturers and rejects, as does Belinsky, "future harmony" if "children's tears" are not avenged. Can progress satisfy the demands of Belinsky and Ivan Karamazov? No, it cannot. For Ivan Karamazov, or Belinsky, or the underground man, or any individual, "future paradise on earth" is no different from "heavenly paradise" inasmuch as they both require *credo quia absurdum est,* a creed which neither Karamazov nor Raskolnikov nor the underground lover of paradoxes can have, as they are ruled wholly by reason.

Dostoevsky answers all this rebellion with religion. And the profound belief that the world moves according to the plan and will of a sentient and all-knowing superior being, moreover a merciful and all-forgiving being, who sooner or later will reward the suffering and the just and punish the wicked, would pacify the rebellion of Ivan Karamazov and other Dostoevskyan heroes and reconcile them to this life because their rebellion is a revolt of externals against the essence.

The difficulty lies in the fact that in order to believe it is not enough to want to believe. The essence of belief was best expressed by Tertullian, who said: "I believe because it is impossible." If a man possesses reason, or is possessed by reason, which is hostile to Tertullian's formula or to any belief, then his capacity for belief is in inverse proportion to his dependence on reason. Faith does not and cannot offer any arguments on its own behalf. In this lies the essence of all faith. Christ, for Dostoevsky, is the symbol of faith—not of historical Christianity, which is, in turn, symbolized by the Grand Inquisitor.

However, Raskolnikov, Karamazov, and Belinsky (in the letter quoted above) not only reject faith in God; they also refuse to believe everything which Dostoevsky's critics accept. The point is not whether Dostoevsky's characters believe in the possibility of building an earthly paradise. The point is that reason tells them: "What good is it to us? Will the future avenge the suffering of innocent children, the victims of the Inquisition? We shall no longer be there, and the innocent children and the victims of the Inquisition have forever lost their case against life."

That reason is on their side, and not on the side of the advocates of a "paradise on earth," is irrefutable. At the heart of every ideology we find an unconscious social mysticism. There is nothing more tragic or more laughable than to see the advocates of progressive ideas hold up reason as their standard—reason, which is the greatest enemy of faith in a better future for mankind, not because this future is not realizable but because it is meaningless for those living now. (I can suggest an experiment for those who consider this strange: try to console a mother who has just lost her child by telling her that a day will come when medicine will be so advanced that such tragedies will no longer occur.)

It follows, therefore, that if the building of a paradise on earth is not going to provide all the answers and solve all the problems, the very idea of a "better future" for man (which will come after death), and his struggle for this future, is meaningless and an obstacle to man's finding another solution to the problems that have beset him from the beginning of time. Nor is this all. Dostoevsky sees that the peculiar "negative religiosity" of the advocates of an "earthly paradise" which cannot solve man's existential problems leads inevitably, as does every institutionalized religion, to the loss of human freedom, to the Grand Inquisitor.

It is curious to note that in his study of Dostoevsky, August Cesarec, in the spirit of so-called "reactionary criticism," identifies Lenin with the Grand Inquisitor. For this he would have been anathematized by Lunacharsky then or by Ermilov today. "We are not with you, but with Him," says the Inquisitor to Christ. "Him" means the devil, reason. It is clear that if there were no higher being to judge, at the end of history, those guilty of sins against life, then love for mankind itself dictates the building of an earthly paradise, of a "crystal palace of Communism." However, this "crystal palace" cannot solve man's problems. It can only offer an opportunity for more humane relations among men and protect men from certain natural inconveniences, such as sickness, etc.

You believe in a crystal edifice that can never be destroyed; that is, an edifice one would not be able to stick out one's tongue at or thumb one's nose at on the sly. And perhaps I am afraid of this edifice just because it is crystal and can never be destroyed and one cannot even put out one's tongue at it, even secretly.

You see, if it were not a palace but a chicken coop, and it started to rain, I might creep into the chicken coop to avoid getting wet, and yet I would not call the chicken coop a palace out of gratitude to it for sheltering me from the rain. You laugh, you even say that in such circumstances a chicken coop is as good as a mansion. Yes, I say, if one lived just to avoid getting wet.

But what is to be done if I have taken it into my head that this is not the sole object in life . . .

It is precisely against proclaiming a chicken coop a palace that Dostoevsky was protesting. Of course, for those Marxists who consider Marxism a science for healing the social organism and preserving it in good health, rather than a religion offering all solutions, Dostoevsky is not an enemy. He is an enemy of those for whom Marxism has become a "religion without a God."

It was while analyzing the origins of the Russian revolutionary "negative religiosity" that Dostoevsky wrote *The Possessed*, which is, in spite of all attacks, one of his most powerful, most significant works. As the Russian critic Pereverzev clearly showed, Dostoevsky depicted Russian revolutionaries with psychological accuracy and fidelity.

Both Peter Verkhovensky and Shigalev, as well as the Grand Inquisitor, envisage an earthly paradise achieved through violence. For how else can this paradise be created if not all men believe in its meaningfulness or its validity? The genius and forcefulness with which Dostoevsky anticipated Russian history find their confirmation in Stalinism and the "personality cult." This is Shigalev's plan for the future "paradise on earth": "All members of society must watch each other and are obliged to denounce each other. Each belongs to all and all to each. All are slaves and equal in their slavery. In extreme cases there is slander and murder. But the main thing is equality. First of all we must lower standards in education, in science, in talent. High standards in science and talent are of advantage to the most capable only. The most capable have always taken power into their own hands and become despots. The most capable cannot help becoming despots and they have always done more harm than good. They must be exiled and executed. Cicero's tongue is cut out. Copernicus' eyes are gouged out. Shakespeare is stoned. That's Shigalevism for you. Slaves must be equal. There has never been freedom or equality without tyranny, but within a herd we must have equality. That's Shigalevism for you," says Peter Verkhovensky to Stavrogin. Later, in his famous novel *We* (1922), Evgeny Zamyatin depicted in even greater detail the totalitarian society that Dostoevsky the visionary feared and foresaw. Vladimir Dudintsev, in his novel *Not by Bread Alone* (1956), describes the conflict between a talented and independent inventor and a Soviet administrator. The representative of authority tells the worker: "And you, genius, independent worker, are not needed with your grandiose ideas on glass legs. There is no capitalist who would buy your idea, and the people cannot use these elemental passions which only rock the economic boat. We shall solve this problem gradually, without panic, on the appointed day, even on the appointed hour." The inventor, Lopakhin, meditates: "That I should have lived to see this. That a Russian should sit across from me and threaten me. You genius, it is not allowed. A river is not allowed to exist. Only a little drop can exist. And who should think so? A son of a fatherland which can boast scores, masses of great talents." Dostoevsky would have rejoiced in Dudintsev's book, which shows to what extent he was right. In the same vein is Alexander Tvardovsky's portrayal of Soviet society during the "personality cult," his excellent satirical poem *Tyorkin in the Other World* (1963).

For man to attain paradise on earth, there must be violence; that is, those who refuse to recognize the chicken coop as a crystal palace must be destroyed or rendered ineffective. "But what is significant in history is not the aims but the acts of the participants." This is what V. I. Talin, an eminent Russian publicist, wrote in 1928. We find a similar thought in Marx and Engels' *German Ideology:* "Whereas in everyday life every shopkeeper can distinguish perfectly well between what something actually is and what it is considered to be, our historiography is not yet capable of this distinction. It takes the word of each era for what that era has to say and what it imagines about itself."

The genius of Dostoevsky is demonstrated in his ability to see the roots of totalitarianism in the parricide which precedes it, a parricide which is every revolution. "I have come to an amazing conclusion," says Shigalev. "Extreme freedom leads to extreme slavery." Penetrating the subconscious, Dostoevsky perceived the dialectic of future social consciousness. (Incidentally, any philosophical theory which holds that the human psyche mirrors external reality might well be put in doubt by Dostoevsky, who foresaw the future development of society. So with Alexei Remizov and Franz Kafka, who depicted identical realistic subconscious visions and identical situations in which the forces of the subconscious are essentially the real social forces of the future.) The individual subconscious is the social consciousness of the future. The future is already in us, and an introverted artist was able to perceive it there.

The advocates of social progress do not realize that they base their ideas on a naïve religious foundation, namely that man will be happy if he is good and that therefore he must be given an opportunity to be good with an impunity that will guarantee the resolution of all problems. Belinsky, at the point in his development that earned him claim to fame as a writer and a revolutionary democrat, wrote: "Man is born not for evil but for good, not for crimes but for the reasonable enjoyment of the riches of this life. His urges are just, his instincts noble. Evil lurks not in man but in society." Chernyshevsky in his novel *What Is to Be Done?* confirms this: "Then the wicked will see that they must no longer be wicked, and those among them who are human will become good. After all, they are wicked only because it is harmful for them to be good . . ." Leaving aside our national proverb "It is easy to be good when things go well; heroes are proved by suffering"; leaving aside the question whether the good or heroes are more necessary in life, let us consider another question: Who says that the good are at the same time happy ("rewarded," in Christian language)? Death and suffering strike good and bad alike. The belief that the good will be happy presupposes a belief in the existence of a God, or of certain natural laws according to which, in spite of the contingencies of this life, the good will be rewarded in this life. However, we do not believe in God and we know of no such natural laws. Empirically we are convinced of the opposite. As for the theory that the environment determines whether man will be good or bad, the advocates of progress refute it themselves, since they are constantly pointing out that the negative characters in Dostoevsky's novels (Versilov, F. P. Karamazov) generally belong to the upper, to the wealthy social classes and could therefore do good with impunity, instead of the opposite.

Moreover, there is another strong argument against the enforced organization of life on a "reasonable and scientific" basis. The argument is offered by the underground man:

Advantage! What is advantage? And will you take it upon yourself to define with perfect accuracy exactly what man's advantage consists of? And what if it happens that a man's advantage not only may, but even must, *sometimes* consist exactly in his desiring under certain conditions what is harmful to himself and not what is advantageous? And if so, if there can be such a condition, then the whole principle becomes worthless. . . . Oh, tell me, who first declared, who first proclaimed, that man does nasty things only because he does not know his own interests; and that if he were enlightened, if his eyes were opened to his real interests, man would at once cease to do nasty things, would immediately become good and noble, because, being enlightened and understanding his real advantage, he would see his own advantage in the good and nothing else, and we all know that no man can knowingly act to his own disadvantage. Consequently, he would begin doing good, so to speak, out of necessity. Oh, the babe! Oh, the pure, innocent child.

The most important thing in man's life is freedom, says Dostoevsky, and every planned, organized life is inevitably not free. Hence the appearance of the man with the "reactionary physiognomy" in the *Notes*.

And yet, today, to take a stand against the revolution and the ideals of socialism would be to negate oneself. Revolution is, first of all, nonconformism to the point of parricide. To take a stand against the revolution in a society in which the revolution has been raised to the level of an a priori truth would mean being a nonconformist and negating oneself. We might say that this happened to Pasternak, who wrote in *Doctor Zhivago:* "Reorganize life! This is the approach of those who have perhaps lived through a lot, but have never once understood life or felt its spirit, its soul, its reason. For them, existence is a chunk of rough material which their touch has not yet made noble and which remains to be processed. Yet life is never material, never an object . . . It is, if you must know, the first cause, continuously self-regenerating, constantly self-modifying, it remodels and reorganizes itself eternally. It stands incomparably higher than all our obtuse theories." In saying this, Pasternak has talked himself into an untenable position. The very fact that he writes this means he is trying to reorganize life. Were he to leave everything to life itself, he would be silent.

Revolution is a means to attain progress. Dostoevsky was an enemy of revolution because he was an enemy of progress in the sense in which the revolutionary democrats understood progress and in which it is still understood today.

DOSTOEVSKY AND PROGRESS

Of course, a lecturer or a professor whom the state pays a good salary would say with unpleasant ease that man exists in order to build a future culture and future universal happiness. But for an ordinary man all this is nebulous and even repulsive. Only then do other strange questions arise. Why does a ladybird exist, and why a jackdaw? They obviously are of no use to anyone, certainly not to any future culture. And why is a man's life more important than that of a jackdaw?

MIKHAIL ZOSHEHENKO

What will become of an ax in space? Quelle idée! *If it found itself at some distance from the earth, then, I think, it would start orbiting the earth in the guise of a satellite, not knowing itself why. Astronomers will calculate the rising and the setting of the ax: Gatzuk will make entries of it in the calendars. That's all.*

The devil to Ivan Karamazov

In the January 1876 issue of *The Diary of a Writer* Dostoevsky included this short discussion:

What would be the result, for instance, should the devils all at once reveal their might and overwhelm man with discoveries? If, let us say, all of a sudden they were to "invent" electrical telegraphy (that is, if it had not already been invented), or to divulge various secrets to man: "Dig over there and you will find a treasure, or deposits of coal" (by the way, firewood is so expensive!) —well, all this is but a trifle! Of course, you understand, science is still in its infancy—actually, it is only just beginning its work; if it has achieved anything solid, it is only that, for now, it stands firmly on its feet. And, unexpectedly, a series of discoveries would come showering down, such as the fact that the sun remains motionless while the earth revolves around it (because surely there are many discoveries of the same magnitude which have not yet been made and which our sages have not even dreamed of). All of a sudden, all-important and altogether gratis, as a gift! I ask you: what, in that event, would happen to men? —Oh, it goes without saying that at first they would be enraptured. People would ecstatically embrace one another; they would rush to study the discoveries (and this would take time); they would feel, so to speak, overwhelmed with happiness, buried in material blessings; they might be walking or flying on air; they would fly over immense distances ten times more quickly than they now travel on railroads; they would extract fabulous harvests from the earth; perhaps they would create organisms chemically, and there would be three pounds of meat for every person, as our Russian socialists are wont to dream. In short: eat, drink, and be merry. "Well," the philanthropists would exclaim in unison, "now that man is provided for, only now will he become what he really is! No material privations any more; no degrading "milieu" that used to be the cause of all vices; now man is going to be beautiful and righteous! No longer is there need of incessant work to earn one's subsistence; now all men will occupy themselves with lofty and profound thoughts—and with universal phenomena. Sublime life has now begun!" And what clever and good people perhaps would shout this in unison, and possibly in the beginning they would sway all others, and they would all vociferate one common hymn: "Who is equal to this beast? Praise to him who has brought us fire from heaven!"

But it is doubtful if these raptures would suffice even for one generation! People would suddenly realize that life is no more for them; that there is no freedom of spirit, no will, no personality; that everything has been stolen from them; that the human image has vanished and the bestial image of a slave, the cattle image, has come into being, with the difference, however, that cattle do not know they are cattle, whereas men would discover that they had become cattle. And mankind would begin rotting; people would be covered with sores and ulcers; they would bite their tongues in pain, seeing that their lives had been taken from them in exchange for bread, for "stones turned to bread." Men would realize that there is no happiness in inaction; that idle thought dies; that one cannot love one's neighbor by sacrificing one's labor to him; that it is a nasty thing to live gratuitously; that happiness is not in happiness but in its pursuit. Tedium and anguish would ensue: everything has been accomplished—there is nothing more to accomplish; everything is known—there is nothing more to know. There would be crowds of felos-de-se, and not as now—merely in miserable tenement houses; people would gather in multitudes, seizing each other by the hand and spontaneously annihilating themselves by the thousands by means of some new device revealed to them along with other inventions. And then perhaps the ones who were left would cry out to God: "Thou art right, O Lord: Man shall not live by bread alone!" Then they would rise against the devils and would forsake witchery . . . Oh, never would the Lord inflict such torture upon mankind! And the devils' kingdom will be destroyed! No, the devils will not commit a political error as momentous as this. They are shrewd politicians, and they pursue their goal by the most subtle, the sanest means (that is, if devils in fact exist).

In this short piece Dostoevsky gives us a critical analysis of the concept of progress, carrying it to the absurd, that is, to its realization.

Let us consider what progress actually is. We read in the Encyclopedia of the Lexicography Institute: *"Progress.* Advance, forward movement in the sense of a change which is in the course of time directed toward a higher level of development, toward what is better, more humane, more perfect, more worthy." As for social progress, the Great Soviet Encyclopedia gives: "Gradual development, forward movement of a society, change for the better; more advanced, more perfect transition from the lower to the higher, from the simple to the more complex."

First of all, the idea of progress is not clear in itself and is profoundly alien to all cultures except our Judaeo-Christian culture. This is often overlooked. The idea of progress contains in itself a belief that in the continuum of time and space life develops *for the better,* whether it is the question of the coming of the Messiah or of the building of the Kingdom of Freedom. So the idea of progress has two aspects: religious, the end of history and the coming of the heavenly kingdom; and secular—meaning the end of prehistory, of the *kingdom of exigency,* and the beginning of real history, the *kingdom of freedom.* However, there is an essential difference between these religious aspects and the secular socio-historical aspects of progress. The religious belief is based on the dogma of the immortality of every soul. Therefore, everyone who has done his duty to God (to existence, to life) will attain the kingdom of heaven at the end of history, and *the life eternal,* and will be free in God and be immeasurably happy. Socio-historical progress is not concerned with individual souls, either past or present. It promises a happy and free life (not eternal, to be sure) for future generations. For one who unconsciously identifies his life with the life of all humanity, the secular idea of progress represents the old Judaeo-Christian faith translated into the dimensions of socio-historical reality. The *kingdom of freedom* will exist when we shall no longer exist, so what good is it to us? This is what reason tells us. But if struggle for freedom alone gives us freedom, freedom is possible now and all ideas of a future "crystal palace" are superfluous. The only thing that is necessary is the struggle itself. This is the basic paradox of all revolutionary ideologies marching under the standard of reason, the natural enemy of any struggle at all, and therefore the enemy of life itself. Revolution always means *rather the grave than a slave,*[1] which is an irrational formula. The position of reason

1 This is the slogan with which the Serbian segment of Yugoslavia's population answered the pro-German policy of the Yugoslav government before March 26, 1941. That government fell on March 27, 1941. [Trans.]

is always that *it is better to be a living ass than a dead lion.* It was no accident that, remembering an eruption of Vesuvius, Pliny the Younger, an excellent dialectician and a very reasonable man, at the time of the fall of the Roman Empire said: "At that moment my only consolation was the thought that all of humanity was dying with me."

Dostoevsky was one of the first men after the Renaissance to realize that reason, for whose victory all Russian revolutionaries from Belinsky to Lenin fought with such passion, is the greatest enemy of struggle. Hence the contradiction: on the one hand, the rejection of any ideology based on social progress, since its acceptance presupposes *credo quia impossibile est,* which reason rendered impossible for Dostoevsky; and, on the other hand, struggle against this same reason in the name of life, which also means in the name of revolution.

I repeat: due to the unconscious irrationality of all the ideologists of progress, all the problems which Dostoevsky had formulated from the position of reason are false problems. From this it follows that all stands taken against Dostoevsky by critics of this kind are doomed to failure.

Even if we could forget that we are mortal and that we shall never live to see the "kingdom of freedom," so that, from the point of view of reason, it is irrelevant for us—even then, as in the case too of those who will live in it, that kingdom of freedom is no more than a shelter from rain, no more than the chicken coop, as the man from the underground says. Neither the justice of a just social system nor liberation from enslaved labor nor even the highest level of science and technology can ever resolve the existential questions which beleaguer man, nor can any of these solve that most important question, without which no other questions would exist, the question of death. This brings up the question of the meaning of human existence. A just social system, all the material advantages, highly developed technology, in a word, the crystal palace, are meaningful only as a means, never as an end in themselves. And that end we cannot see. Man cannot accept the idea that he lives merely to live well . . . And yet the advocates of social progress do not even try to offer an answer to that question. *But what if I've got it firmly in my head that men do not live just to keep dry in the rain?* This is what the underground man, the "I" in every one of us, as Shkolvsky so lucidly points out, says so justifiably.

Another question arises, a question connected with progress, which Nikolai Berdyaev criticized so irrefutably. A future earthly paradise is immoral with respect to all those generations that lived before its realization. There is still another question, that of the existence of this earth and our universe. The devil says to Ivan Karamazov: "You keep on thinking about our earth. But this earth may have renewed its existence a million times already. It may have died, frozen over, exploded, shattered, disintegrated into its component parts, land may have changed to water, water may have become a comet, the comet a sun, the sun this earth again. This evolution may have been repeated countless times already . . . the same way to the least little detail. It is so boring, so indecently boring. . . ."

Of course, in relation to the span of a man's life, this question does not arise. It does not arise even in relation to humanity as a whole. *But what is unfortunate is that a thinker cannot not think,* as Dudintsev says in *Not by Bread Alone.* If one is expected to fight and make sacrifices in the name of something, then that something had better be a *crystal palace* and not a *chicken coop,* which would sooner or later be destroyed. Everyone who asks such radical questions is, like Dostoevsky, labeled a pessimist, which is absurd. Real pessimism is to pretend that the question does not exist because we cannot answer it. And to ask such extreme questions, to put them as sharply and uncompromisingly as Dostoevsky did, means to believe that they can and must be answered, which is real optimism.

It is interesting that criticism of the idea of progress as a socio-historic-scientific advance has recently begun in Dostoevsky's own country. Thus, in Dudintsev's book, Drozdov, the representative of the older generation, and one of the main characters, says to his young wife: "You told me once that I go to extremes. But extremes cannot exist for a man who is building a strong material base. Because this base is what comes first. The more I build it, the stronger our country becomes. This is not Turgenev, my dear." His wife replies: "You are mixing up your categories. Bases are human relations; they are relative to matter, not matter itself . . ."

As for the use of the adjectives *progressive* and *reactionary,* one must realize that *progressive* and *reactionary* are dialectic relationships and *not qualities* in themselves. An idea which was very progressive yesterday can be reactionary today, and vice versa. The same is true of ideals. There is no reason why life on this earth should be just, why it should be free from slavery and exploitation. This is purely irrational. It is because man wishes it to be so without any proof or reason. There are no objective laws according to which the kingdom of freedom will come to pass. Lucien Goldmann, the Marxist critic, in his essay on Pascal writes: "Let us add finally that in the great work of tragic philosophy whose author, George Lukács, has become one of the greatest Marxist thinkers of today, we find the idea expressed that to be a man means to wager unreservedly one's whole existence on the eternally unproven affirmation of a possible relation between sensory data and perception, between God and the empirical reality behind which God hides, a relation, let us repeat, which can never be proved, on which, nevertheless, we must wager all our existence . . . I have already said that the idea of the

Pascalian wager is central to Marxist thought as a wager on the historical future which is never a simple and complete certitude. It is absolutely certain and absolutely uncertain because it is a future which we must realize by our own action."

It is paradoxical that those very critics of Dostoevsky who believe that man is naturally good but needs to be assured that he can be good with impunity are the ones who accept violence, shaping a new man, etc., just as if they believed that man is naturally bad and must, therefore, be changed. On the other hand, Dostoevsky, who considered that man's nature was sinful, rejected violence as a means of changing man for the better because he knew that all violence is evil, that violence corrupts man and reduces him to slavery, even when it is carried out from the noblest motives.

DOSTOEVSKY AND REASON

> *Man is stupid, phenomenally stupid.*
> The underground philosopher

> *To understand this world means to make it unknown.*
> HEINRICH RICKERT

The question of the meaning of life, which means the question of human reason, arises only when that meaning no longer exists. When everything is clear in itself, even the possibility of such a question cannot exist—which means that the question, that is, the rationale, arises only when man becomes alienated from life. Dialectics are over, life has begun, says Dostoevsky about Raskolnikov's resurrection. Paradoxical though it may seem, the very fact that man thinks tells us that he is not free while he thinks. To understand nature through intellect is the same as the parricide of the Karamazovs. Reason gives us power over nature, and the will to power appears only when nature and life become objects, when living contact with life is lost. Nature is the primary, the main enemy of modern man, who forgets that not only misery (sickness, death, etc.) but also the greatest blessings (such as love) are gifts of nature.

The point is not that man cannot understand everything but that he gains nothing by understanding nature. To be more precise, what man gains—power over nature—is not equal to his loss, which is his love of nature, of life itself. (Similarly, power over a loved woman makes love impossible, since love is always free.) The relationship man–nature is analogous to the relationship man–woman. For several centuries now, our civilization has tried to violate nature. The point is not that this is impossible but that the greatest misfortune would lie precisely in the success of this venture. This would finally break all ties with life for good and would destroy all possibility of love.

To understand life means to enslave it. "Bow before me and I will give you power over all earthly kingdoms" is Satan's way of tempting Christ. This means the elimination of everything that is miraculous, and renders all things natural. To render a phenomenon understandable and *natural* means to create in the mind the counterpart of the phenomenon, a concept, an idea, a thought, a system, which then separates man from life. But as life changes constantly, and with it the so-called natural laws, and the system remains the same, the deeper man's knowledge of life, the wider the rift between him and life. At the moment when the system falls apart, which is what happens at breaking points in history, in periods of the so-called death of old cultures and birth of new cultures, man awakens from his peaceful slumber and suddenly sees that life is mysterious, extraordinary, inexplicable, *mystical*. Dialectics cease and man begins to live, that is, to love.

This is why all glorification of human reason leads directly to alienation and solipsism in man. To free man from this solipsism by reason is as impossible as freeing a slave by violence, since violence itself makes him a slave. (Stalin and Robespierre are excellent examples of this. Robespierre sent to the guillotine all those who were against absolute freedom of expression.)

"Life is a mode of existence of the albumen," wrote Engels. Then, to the question *what is a mode of existence?* there is an answer which in turn is followed by a question and another and another, and so on ad infinitum. Science is nothing more than $X=Y$, $Y=Z$, $Z=$ ... etc.

Lev Shestov, who all his life crusaded against rationalism, was the first to notice that it was not Kant who gave the strongest critique of pure reason, but Dostoevsky in what is in our view his most important work: *Notes from the Underground*. In 1963, following in Shestov's footsteps, the Soviet critic Golosovker reiterated the same views: "It was not Mitia, not Ivan, not Smerdiakov who was guilty of the murder (of F. M. Karamazov), but the devil, reason, the dialectic hero of Kant's antinomies. That was the murderer. And conscience, the knight of fear and remorse armed with one argument only, *credo quià absurdum est,* conquered the hero, driving him to insanity . . . The murderer of all suicides and of all the victims of murder is a formula: 'Everything is allowed,' which, as its author intended, must kill itself in the person of these suicides; it must kill its own idea . . . Not twenty human corpses, but one single corpse of the 'suicide-idea,' bathed in blood—that is what Dostoevsky wished to place in triumph before his readers. It is a corpse of antithesis." And what is most interesting, Golosovker comes to the conclusion that Dostoevsky's hell is not a social hell but an intellectual hell. "Together with the moral hell of Dante's *Divine Comedy* and with the social hell of Balzac's

Human Comedy, stands Dostoevsky's many-volumed Devil's Comedy, intellectual hell."

Dostoevsky's work is a ceaseless struggle against reason and for life. In that struggle he has no reasoned arguments at his disposal, nor can he have them. All arguments are on the side of the Grand Inquisitor. Dostoevsky has only one argument: I will or I will not, with no reasons given. Free will, whim, which is more valuable than all other blessings of this world, because it is free, which means alive—that is his argument. All Dostoevsky's heroes are alive when they act irrationally. The motivation of their acts is expressed in the formula: *absence of reason as the greatest of reasons.* When Raskolnikov acts rationally, when he kills the parasitical old woman in order to save himself, he is punished by spiritual death, a death which is alleviated by hard labor since hard labor diminishes the distance between spiritual death and actual physical being, and, in so doing, diminishes the cleavage between the conscious and the subconscious, which, in Marxist terminology, is alienation. This is also the experience of Sonya Marmeladova, who sacrifices herself to save her family —which is reasonable. But man's life, not only the life of another but also one's own, is not man's property (the idea of possession is tied to the idea of slavery, and man, free at the outset, is a slave only when he is ignorant of this fact) —and so Sonya is punished, just as Raskolnikov is. To allow violence to be done to oneself and to do violence to another are one and the same sin. That Dostoevsky's critics should have taken Sonya for his ideal is incomprehensible. His ideal might rather be the underground man, in whom Shestov was the first to see a true medieval martyr and saint who refuses to bow before precisely those objective natural laws which Dostoevsky's critics glorified. And yet it is in the underground man that these critics might have found proof of their belief that man is born good and that it is circumstances which make him bad. "They won't let me be good," says the underground man. One more step and he would have become the founder of a new religion. But he was not to take that step. He is not convinced that he is right. He still suspects that others may be right. His belief in his rebellion is not strong enough. Yet it is only extreme individualism, it is only the underground man who can, at a given moment, unexpectedly attain the ultimate collectivism (Berdyaev would have called it *sobornost*[2]), a collectivism that stands far higher than the collectivism of the revolutionary democrats, organic collectivism, the collectivism that destroys all social systems and prepares the way for the living social organism. The difference between the organistic and the mechanistic lies in the fact that in an organism every component part (the "I" of each one of us) by its very life guarantees the life of the organism, whereas in the mechanism it is the nonlife of every part, its obedience to the system (to any social system), which ensures the seeming life, the functioning of the mechanism, of the machinery. Absolute freedom is necessary if the individual, the smallest part of the organism, is to live. It is this freedom which the Grand Inquisitors of all churches are forever trying to take away, arguing that man is not free, that he must bow before the *objective laws of life,* of social progress, of history, etc., so that one day, when he will no longer exist, he may be free. But these "laws" exist only insofar as man believes in them, just as in chess the castle can move down or across the chessboard, never diagonally—but only as long as man agrees to play the game this way. Belief in these laws allows man to understand them in order to possess life, the possession of which gives him nothing but spiritual death.

2 There is no accepted translation of this word. Dostoevsky scholars use the Russian, which means, spiritual community held together by oneness of mind; more literally, worshippers in one cathedral *(sobor)*. [Trans.]

"I think that, first of all, everybody must love life," says Alyosha Karamazov to his brother Ivan. "To love life more than the meaning of life?" asks Ivan. "That is the only way. To put love before logic is the only way to understand meaning," repeats Alyosha. "Cognition of life is superior to life . . . knowledge of the laws of happiness is superior to happiness. This is what must be fought, and I will fight it," says the protagonist of *The Dream of a Strange Man,* published in *The Diary of a Writer* for April 1877. And Dmitri Karamazov quite irrationally exclaims: "I shall conquer all, all suffering, if only I can tell myself at every moment that I exist. I'm paralyzed but I exist. I can see the sun, and even if I cannot see it I know that it exists. And to know that the sun exists, that is already a whole life." There is no rational answer to the question why it exists. Reason does not justify life.

In the Bible, man's most profound book, or, as Pasternak calls it, the *notebook of mankind,* men at the very beginning of history noted something which had suddenly been revealed to them, that the *tree of knowledge* kills life.

DOSTOEVSKY AND RELIGION

There is one thing I cannot understand: why must Dostoevsky bring Christ into his detective stories?

IVAN BUNIN

As we have said, Dostoevsky's writing is a battle against reason. "I am a child of this century, a child of unbelief and doubt to this very hour. I know this and I shall so remain, even to the grave. What terrible tortures have been the price for my thirst for faith, a thirst which grew stronger in my soul with every counterargument I found in myself. And yet, from time to time, God sends me moments of complete peace. In these moments I worked out a Credo for myself, a Credo in which everything is clear and luminous for me." Thus wrote Dostoevsky to N. D. Fonvizina. He also wrote: "Even Europe has never known such force of atheistic expression" (*The Diary of a Writer*, 1876). To his very death he could not conquer reason in himself, and, like Shatov in *The Possessed,* he could only say: "I shall believe in God."

This explains why Dostoevsky failed to create a positive hero, a hero who would finally believe, rather than heroes who merely promise that they will believe. Dostoevsky has often been reproached for this failure. Father Zosima is a contrived, two-dimensional figure. On this, both Lev Shestov and the censorious Soviet critics agree. Dostoevsky kept promising to create such a hero, but he never succeeded. He describes in a few words Raskolnikov's spiritual regeneration and his conversion, and says that a new book is needed for the new, regenerated Raskolnikov. We feel that the problem of the positive hero, the true believer, as conceived by Dostoevsky, has not been correctly formulated.

It is often stated that an artist can create only the image of what he carries within himself. Had Dostoevsky carried within him a true believer, he would have created his image. The problem is a little more complex, however.

All Dostoevsky's works are products of a struggle against doubt and reason. A true believer does not doubt and does not struggle. Had Dostoevsky been a believer, he would not have needed to struggle against reason and by the same token he would have had no reason or cause to write. This is what Raskolnikov's conversion is like: *"Now he could no longer decide anything consciously, he simply felt. Instead of dialectics, life had begun."* In those moments when for Dostoevsky *life came to replace dialectics,* he could not write, or, for the same reason, create the image of the man he was. When he could write, or more precisely when he was compelled to write, he did not live and did not carry within himself the image of a true believer—which is why he had to create types like Zosima from memory and why they are two-dimensional.

In the October 1876 issue of *The Diary*, Dostoevsky published what purported to be the reflections of an atheist on the verge of suicide. These reflections are so significant that I must quote them here in full:

The Verdict

Incidentally, here are the deliberations of a man committing suicide *out of tedium*—a materialist of course.

". . . Indeed, what right did nature have to bring me into this world in accordance with some eternal laws of hers? I am created with consciousness and I *conceived* nature: what right had she, therefore, to beget me without my will, without my will as a conscious creature? Conscious implies suffering, but I do not wish to suffer. Why should I consent to suffer? Nature, through the medium of my consciousness, proclaims to me some sort of harmony of the whole. Human consciousness has produced religions out of this message. Nature tells me—even though I know well that I neither can nor ever shall participate in this 'harmony of the whole,' and besides, that I shall never even comprehend what it means—that nevertheless I must submit to this message, abase myself, accept suffering because of the harmony of the whole, and consent to live. However, if I were to make a conscious choice, of course I would rather wish to be happy at that moment when *I* exist. I have no interest whatever in the whole and its harmony after *I* perish, and it does not concern me in the least whether this whole with its harmony remains in the world after me or perishes with me. Why should I bother about its preservation after I no longer exist? That's the question. It would be better to be created like all animals—i.e., living but not conceiving myself rationally. But my consciousness is not harmony, but, on the contrary, disharmony, because with it I am unhappy. Look: who is happy in this world and what kind of people *consent* to live? Those who are akin to animals and come nearest to their species by reason of their limited development and consciousness. They readily consent to live but on the specific condition that they live as animals, i.e., eat, drink, sleep, build their nests, and bring up children. To eat, drink, and sleep, in the human tongue, means to grow rich and to plunder; and to build one's nest preeminently signifies—to plunder. I may be told perhaps that one may arrange one's life and build one's nest rationally, on scientifically sound social principles, and not by plunder, as heretofore. All right, but I ask what for. What is the purpose of arranging one's existence and of exerting so much effort to organize life in society soundly, rationally, and right-eously in a moral sense? Certainly no one will ever be able to answer this question. All that could be said in reply would be: 'To derive delight.' Yes, were I a flower or a cow, I should derive delight. But, incessantly putting questions to myself, as now, I cannot be happy even in the face of the most lofty and *immediate* happiness of love of neighbor and of mankind, since I know that tomorrow all this will perish: I and all the happiness, and all the love, and all mankind will be naught, will fall into its former chaos. And on such a condition, I can under no circum-stances accept any happiness—and I do not refuse to accept it because I am stubbornly adhering to some principle, but for the simple reason that I will not and cannot be happy threatened with tomorrow's zero. This is a feeling—a direct and immediate feeling—and I cannot overcome it. All right: if I were to die but mankind, instead of me, were to exist forever, then perhaps I might be consoled. But our planet is not eternal, and mankind's duration is just as brief as mine. And no matter how rationally, happily, righteously, and holily mankind might organize its life on earth—tomorrow all this will be zero. And even if all this might be necessary according to some almighty, eternal, and fixed law of nature, yet, believe me, in this there is some kind of profound·disrespect for mankind which to me is deeply insulting, and all the more unbearable as no one is guilty.

"And, finally, even if one presumed the possibility of some

truth in that tale about man's ultimate attainment of a rational and scientific organization of life on earth—were one to believe in this tale and in the future happiness of man, the thought that, because of some inert laws, nature found it necessary to torture man thousands and thousands of years before granting him that happiness—this thought itself is unbearably repugnant. And if you add to this that that very nature which finally had admitted man to happiness will, for some reason, tomorrow find it necessary to turn all this to zero despite the suffering with which mankind has paid for happiness and—what is most important—without even bothering to conceal this from my consciousness, as it did conceal it from the cow—willy-nilly there arises a most amusing but unbearably sad thought: 'What if man has been placed on earth for some impudent experiment—solely to ascertain whether this creature is going to survive on earth?' The chief sadness of this thought is the fact that here again no one is guilty; no one has conducted the experiment; there is no one to damn, since everything came to pass as a result of the inert laws of nature, which I do not understand at all, and with which my consciousness is altogether unable to reconcile itself. *Ergo:*

"Inasmuch as to my questions on happiness I am receiving from nature, through my own consciousness, only the answer that I can be happy not otherwise than within the harmony of the whole, which I do not comprehend, and which, it is obvious to me, I shall never be able to understand——

"Inasmuch as nature not only does not admit my right to demand an account from her, but even gives me no answer whatsoever—and not because she does not want to answer, but because she is unable to——

"Inasmuch as I have convinced myself that nature, to answer my queries, designates (unconsciously) *my own self* and answers them with my own consciousness (since it is I who say all this to myself) ——

"Finally, since under these circumstances I am assuming both the role of plaintiff and of defendant, both of accused and of judge; and inasmuch as I consider this comedy on the part of nature altogether stupid, and my enduring this comedy humiliating——

"Now, therefore, in my unmistakable role of plaintiff and of defendant, of judge and of accused, I sentence nature, which has so unceremoniously and impudently brought me into existence for suffering, to annihilation, together with myself. . . . And because I am unable to destroy nature, I am destroying only myself, weary of enduring a tyranny in which there is no guilty one.

N. N."

A contemporary replied to Dostoevsky in the journal *Razvlechenie* (Moscow, 1876) under the pseudonym N.P.:

I have received the last issue of *The Diary of a Writer*. I read it and began to think. There are many good articles in this issue, but there are also many strange ones. We will express our confusion as concisely as possible. Why was it necessary, for example, to publish the "reflections" of a suicide committed "out of tedium." I really fail to see why this is necessary. The reflections, if the delirium of a near madman is worthy of that name, represent nothing new to anyone who should know about such things. This is why their appearance today in *The Diary* of such a writer as Dostoevsky is both ridiculous and pitifully anachronistic. This is an era of cast-iron ideas, this is a century of positive knowledge, an era whose slogan is "live at all costs." Of course, there are exceptions to everything. Suicides are committed with and without reflections. But today no one any longer pays attention to such commonplace heroism: such heroism is too stupid. There was a time when suicide, especially with reflections, was upheld as the highest degree of "consciousness" (consciousness of what, one would like to know!) and heroism, although what this heroism consisted of was also not known. However, that decadent time is gone, gone never to return, thank God, and is not to be regretted. No suicide who dies with reflections, like the suicide of Mr. Dostoevsky's *Diary*, is worthy of pity. He is a vulgar egoist, an ambitious and extremely harmful member of society.

Dostoevsky's reply appeared in the December issue of *The Diary:*

Having read this, I was seized with despondency. Good Lord, is it possible that I have many such readers, and can it be that Mr. N. P., in asserting that my suicide does not deserve sympathy, seriously maintains that I depicted him for the purpose of arousing his, Mr. N. P.'s, "compassion"? Of course, Mr. N. P.'s isolated opinion would be of little importance. But the point is that in this case undoubtedly he represents a certain type, a whole collection of fellows of his own pattern, an impudent type with those very "cast-iron conceptions" to which Mr. N. P. himself refers in the lines I have quoted from his article. This is a suspicion concerning a whole group of people. Honest to goodness—I am scared. . . .

My article—*The Verdict*—refers to the basic and loftiest idea of human existence: the necessity and inevitability of belief in the immortality of the soul. The underlying idea of this confession of a man perishing as a result of "logical suicide" is the necessity of realizing immediately that without faith in the soul and its immortality, man's existence is unnatural, unthinkable, impossible. It seemed to me that I had clearly expressed the formula of a logical suicide, that I "discovered" it. In him there is no faith in immortality; this he explains in the beginning. Little by little, the thought of his aimlessness and his hatred of the muteness of the surrounding inertia lead him to the inevitable conviction of the utter absurdity of man's existence on earth. It becomes clear as daylight to him that only those men can consent to live who resemble the lower animals and who come nearest to them by reason of the limited development of their minds and their purely carnal wants. They agree to live specifically as animals, i.e., in order "to eat, drink, sleep, build their nests, and raise children." Indeed, eating, sleeping, polluting and sitting on soft cushions will long attract men to earth, but not the higher types. . . .

My *felo-de-se* is precisely a passionate exponent of his idea—i.e., the necessity of suicide—and not an indifferent, cast-iron man. He really suffers and is tormented, and it seemed to me that I had expressed this clearly. To him, it is quite obvious that he cannot live; and he knows only too well that he is right and that it is impossible to refute him. Irresistibly, there stand before him the loftiest, the most pressing questions: What is the use of living if he has already conceived the idea that for man to live like an animal is disgusting, abnormal, and insufficient? And what, in this case, can hold him on earth? He cannot solve these questions and he knows it. Even though he realizes that there is what he calls a "harmony of the whole," still he says: "I do not understand it, I shall never be able to understand it, and of necessity I am not going to partake of it; this comes of its own accord." Now, it is this lucidity that finished him. Well, where is the trouble? In what was he mistaken? The trouble is solely the loss of faith in immortality.

However, he himself ardently seeks (that is, he was seeking while he was living, seeking in suffering) conciliation; he meant to find it in "love for mankind." "Not I but perhaps mankind will be happy and some day may attain harmony. This thought could hold me on earth"—he drops the word. And, of course, this is a magnanimous thought and one full of suffering. But the irresistible conviction that the life of mankind—just as his own—is, substantially, a fleeting moment, and that on the morrow of the realization of "harmony" (if one is to believe that this dream can be realized) mankind will be reduced to the same zero as he, by force of the inert laws of nature, and that after so much suffering endured for the attainment of that dream—this thought moves his spirit; it sets him in revolt precisely because of his love of mankind; it insults him on behalf of mankind, by law of the contagion of ideas; it even kills in him the love of mankind. Similarly it has been observed many a time that in a family dying from starvation, father and mother—when at length the suffering of their children grows intolerable—begin to hate them, those hitherto beloved ones, precisely because of the *intolerableness* of their suffering. Moreover, I assert that the realization of one's utter impotence to help, to render some service, to bring alleviation to suffering mankind—while at the same time there is a firm conviction of the existence of that suffering—*may convert love for mankind in one's heart into a hatred of it.* Gentlemen of cast-iron ideas, of course, will not believe this and will be utterly unable to understand it: to them, love of mankind and its happiness are such cheap things; everything is so conveniently fixed; everything has been set and described so long ago that these things are not worth a thought. But I intend to make them really laugh: I assert (again, as yet, without producing any proof) that love of mankind is unthinkable, unintelligible, and *altogether impossible without the accompanying faith in the immortality of man's soul.* Those who, having deprived man of the faith in his immortality, are seeking to substitute for it—as life's loftiest aim—"love of mankind"; those, I maintain, are lifting their arm against themselves, since in lieu of love of mankind they are planting in the heart of him who has lost his faith seeds of hatred of mankind. Let pundits of cast-iron ideas shrug their shoulders at this assertion. But this thought is wiser than their wisdom, and unhesitatingly I believe that some day humankind will embrace it as an axiom—though, once more, I am setting forth this idea without any supporting proof.

I would even assert that love of mankind *in general, as an idea,* is one of the most incomprehensible ideas for the human mind. Precisely as an idea. Sentiment alone can vindicate it. However, sentiment is possible only if there is a conviction of the immortality of man's soul. (Another arbitrary assertion.)

It is clear, then, that suicide—when the idea of immortality has been lost—becomes an utter and inevitable necessity for any man who, by his mental development, has even slightly lifted himself above the level of cattle. Immortality, on the other hand—promising eternal life—ties man all the more strongly to earth. Here there is a seeming contradiction: if there is so much life—that is, if in addition to an earthly existence there is an immortal one—why should man treasure his earthly life so highly? And yet, the contrary is true: only if he has faith in his immortality does man comprehend the full meaning of his rational destination on earth. Without faith in his immortality, man's ties with earth are severed, they grow thinner and more putrescent, and the loss of the sublime meaning of life (felt at least in the form of unconscious anguish) inevitably leads to suicide.

Hence, the reverse moral of my October article: "If faith in immortality is essential to man's existence, it is, therefore, a normal condition of the human race, and, this being so, the immortality of the human soul exists undeniably." In a word, the idea of immortality is life itself—"live life," its ultimate formula, the mainspring of truth and just consciousness for humankind. This was the substance of my article, and I supposed that everyone who read it would so comprehend it.

To refute Dostoevsky with rational arguments is impossible. Reason is on the side of the suicide. Could anyone lead a normal life or carry on his everyday work knowing with certainty that execution awaits him tomorrow? Leonid Andreyev, in his superb story *The Seven Who Were Hanged,* showed that this was impossible. Knowledge of certain death has always meant horrible, unbearable suffering for man. Man is not conscious of death until he finds himself face to face with it, as in the case of Ivan Ilyich in Tolstoy's famous tale. Yet the difference between dying tomorrow and dying in fifty or a hundred years is not great. But man is unaware of this.

In his early book *The Soul and the Forms* George Lukács says:

God's gaze robs events of their temporal and spatial character. Before his eyes all difference between appearance and essence, phenomenon and idea, event and destiny, disappears . . . Tragic life is the life which is most exclusively of this earth. This is why its boundaries are always intertwined with the boundaries of death. Real life never reaches these boundaries and knows death only as something frightening, deprived of all meaning, which brings it to an abrupt end. The mystic goes beyond this boundary and in so doing robs death of all reality. The opposite is true of tragedy; there death, itself the boundary, always represents imminent reality . . .

All his life Dostoevsky carried in himself a tragic consciousness, and he never did become a real mystic, in spite of his passionate desire. To the end of his life, he struggled against doubt. To the end he suffered and rejected this life.

DOSTOEVSKY TODAY—CONCLUSION

Tragic consciousness is pregnant with striving for faith. As we indicated, socialism does not provide answers to the questions that engender tragic consciousness in man, and this is why Dostoevsky tried to "deceive himself," as Marx would say, with the illusion of the existence of God. Dostoevsky opposed revolutionaries because he knew that the "crystal palace" does not make this world much better than it is and does not solve either the problems of man today or the problems of the generations to come until the "kingdom of freedom" arrives. If we turn back to prehistory and for a moment imagine our far-off, primitive ancestors, for whom the world and existence were an endless round of struggle and suffering and chaos, we will see that the emergence of the idea of God (that is, the idea that in all this chaos there is sense and order) is one of the greatest spiritual revolutions, the one that marks the border between man and animal. When Spinoza concluded that man lives in a world governed by "objective laws of nature," a world comprehensible by reason and not governed by a personal being, God (whose will, according to Spinoza, is related to human will and destiny in the same way as "a dog, an animal that barks, is related to the Dog constellation"), man suddenly found himself once again in senseless chaos, though this time in the chaos of the "laws of nature." For primitive man the world was incomprehensible; death was a horrible phenomenon. The man of the new age understands the world through science and regards death as quite "natural."

The laws of nature provide for the eternal existence of matter and energy, but they ignore human beings. Reason and science claim that man must obey. At the most he can count on prolonging his life by a few years through medical progress. But compared to eternity, fifty or even a thousand years is nothing. (Let us remember the verdict of the rational suicidal man.) What is to be done if death is a natural phenomenon with inherent laws? All we can do is accept the fact and resign ourselves to it.

There are people who do not agree with this. According to Lev Shestov: "As a matter of fact, the most puzzling thing in life is the regularity of natural phenomena." Even in this present-day era of "iron concepts," there are still people who regard the human soul as immortal, and they are not primitive in the intellectual sense or in any other, because a belief that the human soul is mortal is not based on empiricism.

If the Middle Ages used to burn the body to save the soul, the New Age does the opposite: it destroys the soul to save the body. The results are identical. In both cases, man dies.

Religiosity, however, is a phenomenon that, unfortunately, because of such concepts as Lenin's "the idea of God was always the idea of slavery," is still rejected a priori. The sense of one's own immortality—belief in God is how religious people express this, whereas moderns would point to the certainty of laws establishing the fact that the human soul is, like matter and energy, immortal—is a fact. The sense of their immortality strengthened the first Christians, the heretics of the Reformation, and (unconsciously) the Russian revolutionaries, as well as all who accept pain and suffering (which they could have avoided) in the name of the struggle for freedom, i.e., their life. "Here with us, it is just the same as with you," says the devil to Ivan Karamazov. And Euripides wrote: "Who knows, maybe to live means to die and to die means to live."

Now we come to one of the greatest of paradoxes (or to the answer to our problem) : that only faith in the immortality of the soul gives rational justification to life. Hence, faith in the immortality of the soul does not exclude the struggle for the "kingdom of liberty." On the contrary, faith justifies the struggle, and it is reason, which does not believe in immortality, that negates struggle.

Dostoevsky, however much he might have been aware of the necessity of belief in the immortality of the soul, also knew that in order to attain faith it is not enough to wish for it, to be conscious of the need for it. Searching for the path to faith, he discovered that it leads through suffering. Only the most extreme, most profound suffering destroys the "glass test tube of reason" and saves man from isolation and, through love, binds him to the life eternal. For his belief in suffering as a remedy, Dostoevsky has been assailed by all his revolutionary critics. Lev Shestov, a faithful follower of Dostoevsky, said: "There are no unhappy men. All unhappy men are pigs." On the surface this is a contradiction. But, as a rule, something has been overlooked. The suffering of Judas Iscariot, which brings him to suicide, and the suffering of Christ, who ascends Golgotha to "conquer the world by death," are not identical. Not resigning oneself to the world as it exists requires suffering. Resignation is the easiest course. It is evident, then, that there is a misunderstanding here too between Dostoevsky and his critics.

What man means by eternity is not clear either. In *The Possessed*, Stavrogin has the following conversation with Kirilov:

"Have you come to believe in a future, eternal life, then?"

"No, not in a future, eternal life, but in this present, eternal life. There are moments—you can reach moments—when time suddenly stops and becomes eternal."

"In the Apocalypse, the angel promises that there will be no more time."

"I know. There's a lot of truth in it. It is clear and precise. When man attains happiness, there will be no more time because there will be no more need for it. It's a very true thought."

"Where will they hide time?"

"Nowhere. Time is not a thing, it's an idea. It will vanish from the mind."

At the moment when man completely frees himself from the rational, from regarding himself as an object, time will vanish and eternity will take its place. Time exists only for the "alienated man." And it exists to the highest degree, to use Beckett's phrase, when it stands at "the zero point."

[1964]

NOTES ON DOSTOEVSKY

It is impossible to insult Dostoevsky without at the same time offending all of humanity in its myriad directions and intentions . . .

VIKTOR SHKLOVSKY

Judging from the vehemence with which you deny my existence, I am convinced you believe in me.

The Devil to Ivan Karamazov

*   *   *

CECIĆ AND DOSTOEVSKY

It is almost impossible to debate in any meaningful way with Vinko Cecić, whose essay "Dostoevsky in Relation to Religion and the Church" contains opinions almost diametrically opposed to my own. If what seems black to me is white to Cecić, I can only refer to an aphorism of Lev Shestov's to explain the anomaly:

One part of man sprang from fallen Adam, whose sin courses in the bloodstream, stirring longing and striving for Paradise Lost. The other part, originating in the ape, has a clear conscience; it never suffers or dreams about the unattainable.

However, I would like to point out certain historical inaccuracies which Cecić appears to have picked up from such oversimplifiers as Zhdanov and Ermilov and upon which he builds his central idea, namely, that Dostoevsky's religiosity and mystic "obscurantism" are directly related to his epilepsy and to his having limited his reading to the Bible during his years of exile. Dostoevsky's abandonment of his earlier views on the church and religion and his conversion to belief are not linked to his Siberian exile, Cecić's opinion notwithstanding. In his *Diary of a Writer,* a work with which Cecić is evidently not acquainted, Dostoevsky not infrequently delves into the subject which had been the cause of a debate between him and the Russian critic Belinsky: the significance of Christ and Christianity. Belinsky's ironical attitude toward Dostoevsky's deep faith was the basic reason for the rapid deterioration of their friendship, a process which began before his exile and which, after the publication of *Poor Folk,* led to increasing animosity. So it is not at all a question, as Cecić would have it, of "dissent from his previous positions on the church and religion."

Cecić's whole discussion, as it relates to the church, is an oversimplification, for Dostoevsky was never pro-clerical (we need only recall his mocking of the orthodox monks in *The Brothers Karamazov*). Rather, he advanced the idea (through Father Zosima) of a "Church Universal," which meant a uniting of man not in a worldly institution such as the Catholic Church, but in God. If he is more sympathetic to the Orthodox than to the Catholic Church, it is because the former is less institutionalized, less a church, than the latter.

Cecić also errs in maintaining that Dostoevsky was "broken" by his confinement. He only parrots what official Soviet criticism has been proclaiming for decades. Leonid Grossman, one of the ablest commentators on the life and work of the great writer, in his book *Dostoevsky's Road* (Leningrad, 1924), makes the following statement on the basis of concrete historical data:

He did not return from exile broken, shattered, disappointed or morally mutilated. He amazed all about him with his exuberant vitality and boiling energy.

Cecić writes further:

Under Chernyshevsky's attack, old Russian philosophy and aesthetics were dying, disappearing forever. The birth of a new materialistic aesthetics, based on philosophical materialism, was at hand.

It is difficult not to become agitated by an untruth of this kind. For, far from dying and disappearing, it was only *after* Chernyshevsky that "old Russian philosophy and aesthetics" really blossomed forth in the genius of Vladimir Soloviev (1853–1900) and Konstantin Leontyev (1831–91). This flowering of original Russian philosophic thought continued during a most fruitful span of years between 1900 and 1917 (the period of the "second ideological offensive," precursor of today's existentialism and personalism in Western Europe) in the works of Berdyaev, Shestov, Lossky, Gershenzon, Bulgakov, Struve, Tikhomirov, Rozanov, Ern, and others.

Cecić writes that Dostoevsky lived "physically in Russian reality without comprehending its essentials . . ." Of course, from the "progressive" viewpoint, it is possible to label Dostoevsky a conservative, but this allegation is patently untrue, given the fact that Dostoevsky, more than any other writer, was close to and intimately familiar with everyday social and journalistic-political reality, as Cecić himself inadvertently proves by directly linking *The Possessed* with the Nechaev affair, not to mention the whole range of Dostoevsky's own extraordinarily important political and journalistic activity. In his study of him, George Lukács says:

The real genius of Dostoevsky is revealed in the fact that he could discern the future shape of social, moral, and psychological processes in the germs of something only beginning to appear. We may also add that Dostoevsky by no means limited himself to description and analysis . . . but also delved into genesis, dialectics, perspectives . . .

The best proof that Dostoevsky saw and understood the essentials of Russian reality is provided by the passionate accusations which have been directed at him for a century.

This has nothing to do with whether he upheld the idea of "progress" or not. No one pays any attention to people who fail to notice and understand essentials.

I do not like statistics because the only thing that is really important and essential, that is, freedom and happiness, cannot be statistically measured. Cecić likes to cite statistical data on the production of grain in Russia. But I too can provide statistics which support Dostoevsky as much as they refute Cecić. In the Great Soviet Encyclopedia, under the entry *forced labor,* we find that the number of prisoners working at forced labor in Tsarist Russia ranged from 5,000–10,000 in the nineteenth century to a peak of 31,000 in 1912. But in his speech to the 20th Party Congress, Khrushchev referred to millions of concentration-camp inmates. Thus, while the population grew less than 50 percent, the number of prisoners rose 10,000 percent, an eloquent statistic in itself.

It is somewhat futile to attack Cecić for many of his opinions since they are so obviously conditioned by an emotional, irrational antipathy toward Dostoevskyan Christianity, a kind of "negative religiosity" in Cecić himself which cannot be rationally examined. We may cite a few "pearls" in his essay by way of illustration:

Thus Dostoevsky's brilliant beginning as an artist in *Crime and Punishment* is brought to its futile demise. Sadder still is the fact that the downfall of the genuine artist, heralded in that novel, is made even more explicit in the works which followed. *The Idiot* puts this conclusion beyond all doubt.

The artist who became a preacher of death and lies.

The idea underlying this novel [*The Brothers Karamazov*] **is** disgusting and inconceivable.

Does Cecić consider everything he cannot understand disgusting? He goes on:

Freedom from self, which allegedly only the Christian religion can bestow—this is what Dostoevsky proposes in his works. What spiritual poverty! Especially in the way this "philosophy" is revealed in *The Brothers Karamazov*.

We feel that the sole worth of Cecić's essay is that its radical, oversimplified approach is developed to its logical conclusion and, thus, fully reveals the indefensible theoretical positions taken by enemies of Dostoevsky.

In this connection it is worth quoting Lucien Goldmann, one of France's leading Marxists:

We completely agree with the idea . . . that modern socialist thought has been able to thrive only within the intellectual world which Christian thought and culture created.

Attitudes toward Christianity like those of Cecić are undoubtedly the root cause of the great struggle presently being waged by the Soviet government against mystic and religious sects which are growing by leaps and bounds in the U.S.S.R. Some thirty years ago, during a visit to the Soviet Union, André Gide noted the danger of "negative religiosity" in Soviet atheism and wrote prophetically:

I doubt that the U.S.S.R. was very clever in instigating an anti-religious war. The Marxists could have easily stuck to history, denied Christ's divine origin, even, if you will, his existence, rejected the dogmas of the Church and discredited Revelation— observed in a very human and critical way the idea which still brought the world hope and a most unusual revolutionary fermentation which was possible at the time. They could have easily said that the Church's principles have failed, and shown how the liberalizing doctrines of Gospel could, unfortunately with the consent of Church, lead to the worst abuse of power. All of this would have been better than simple silence and denial, the existence of which cannot be denied, and the ignorance in which it consequently keeps people in the U.S.S.R., leaving them without a critical defense and unvaccinated against an epidemic of mysticism, which is always to be feared. There is something even worse than that . . . ignorance and denial of the Gospel and of everything which originated from it can only impoverish mankind and culture to a miserable degree.

DOSTOEVSKY AND MYSTICISM

> *The most beautiful excitement which we can experience is mystical. This is the progenitor of all real art and science. The man to whom this excitement is foreign is no longer able to experience wonder, or to stand bewildered and in fearful admiration, just as if he were dead.*
>
> ALBERT EINSTEIN

Dostoevsky has been frequently attacked for his mysticism, a belief that the world is mysterious, unknown, guided by strange powers either conscious (ghosts, Satan) or unconscious, gloomy or bright.

Mysticism flourished during the Renaissance and the Reformation, transitional epochs when one cultural, religious, and social organism was disappearing and another was emerging. Although Dostoevsky was interested in all the mystical literature he could get his hands on (his library included all the Russian translations of Swedenborg, Alexander Aksakov's classic work on spiritualism, studies of animal magnetism and other psychopathological phenomena, etc.), he did not consider himself a mystic. He saw himself as a realist in literature and an orthodox Christian in belief—at least, he tried to become one.

However, his achievement centers on his struggle with rationality, which he waged by leading reason to its ultimate conclusion in his heroes' actions and thus destroying it, and by investigating the relationship of the mind to other aspects of being and thus provoking an ideological clash among them.

What is the relationship between reason and mysticism (in its extreme form, belief in ghosts and phantoms)? Can reason confirm or deny the existence or nonexistence of ghosts? This seems a ridiculous question in the twentieth century, when men are convinced that reason has brought light to darkness and dispelled superstition and prejudice and that obscurantism can be overcome by science.

The mark of genius is its ability to perceive a problem in something which others hold unproblematic. Dostoevsky caused reason to clash with mediocre, vulgar spirits and discovered that reason—and consequently science and logic as well—is helpless when confronted by vulgar superstition. Thus, he demonstrates that an inner feeling that spirits, that is, mystical good or evil powers, do not exist is based not on reason or reasoning, but on belief without proof.

In *Crime and Punishment* Svidrigailov, when he first visits Raskolnikov, tells how he has been visited by ghosts of his dead wife and servant, who talk with him. The passage continues their conversation. Svidrigailov says:

"I asked you: Do you believe in ghosts?"

"No, I shall never believe in them!" exclaimed Raskolnikov with a kind of rage.

"Now what do they usually say?" muttered Svidrigailov, as though to himself, looking away and inclining his head somewhat. "They say: You are sick, therefore what you imagine is just a nonexistent hallucination. But this isn't strictly logical. I agree that ghosts appear only to sick people; but then all this proves is that ghosts appear only to sick people, not that they don't exist in their own right."

"Of course they don't!" insisted Raskolnikov irritably.

"They don't? You think so?" went on Svidrigailov, after casting a brief glance at him. "Well, but what if we argue in the following way (you can help me here): Ghosts are, in a manner of speaking, scraps and fragments of other worlds, their beginning. The healthy man, naturally, has no reason to see them, because the healthy man is the most earthbound, and must therefore live a life solely of the here and now, for the sake of fullness and order. But the moment he falls ill, the moment the normal earthly order of his organism is breached, the possibility of another world begins to make itself felt, and the more ill he becomes, the greater are his contacts with the other world, so that when a man dies completely he passes straight into the other world."

Svidrigailov's logic is irrefutable. Like solipsism, mysticism cannot be refuted by logic. No science can exclude the possibility of the existence in our time and space continuum of x more worlds, with which man, with his normal, healthy philosophical constitution, cannot have contact, just as he cannot see electromagnetic waves or hear ultrasonic waves.

Dostoevsky is not trying to prove the existence of ghosts. He is showing how impotent reason is. The rational in its ultimate consequences destroys faith and, in so doing, not only does not exclude, but on the contrary admits the possibility of, the existence of all kinds of superstitions. Dmitri Merezhkovsky said:

The sun of human reason did not illuminate the gloomy sides of life. On the contrary, they became darker like shadows become more intense as light increases.

With respect to Father Zosima's tract "Of Hell and Hellfire: a Mystic Reflection," it is worth remembering that the greatest misunderstandings and hostilities are often created by different terminology and that there is no essential difference between confession in church and psychoanalytic therapy. Zosima says:

Fathers and teachers, I ponder "What is hell?" I maintain that it is the suffering of being no longer able to love. . . . They talk of hell-fire in the material sense. I don't go into that mystery and I dread it. But I think if there were fire in the material sense, they would be glad of it, for I imagine that in material agony their still greater spiritual agony would be forgotten for a moment. Moreover, that spiritual agony cannot be taken from them, for that suffering is not external but within them.

If we compare this to recent research in "depth psychology"; the results of the Institute for Parapsychological Research of the U.S.S.R. Academy of Medical Science; the novels and long stories by the modern Soviet mystic Alexander Grin; and Antonioni's films—we will reach the conclusion that they have a lot in common. It is the same thing with the other mystical passages in the works of Dostoevsky. *Mystikos* means mystical, unknown. For a mystic the world is full of secrets. If someone tells us that we know this world very well, it is very simple to refute him by saying: "Open your eyes and look at the world."

When, after the catastrophe in Skoplje, newspapers said that the animals in the zoo had been uneasy the whole night before the earthquake, a Viennese zoologist declared that this could not be since animals have no organs for foretelling an earthquake. But the Japanese have for centuries kept in their houses aquariums with little fish which forewarn them of earthquakes, although the fish also have no organs for forecasting earthquakes. That Rose Kuleshov, as the Soviet press reports, "sees with her hands" seems impossible, though it is so. As Hamlet said: "There are more things in heaven and earth . . . than are dreamt of in your philosophy."

CONCLUSION: GOD EXISTS, BUT HE WAS ON LENIN'S SIDE

> *Matter and energy are indestructible and Socrates and Giordano Bruno are destructible. So proclaims reason. And everyone accedes to this without protest. Nobody dares*

*even to raise the question why reason proclaimed this;
why it so paternally spared matter and energy and forgot
about Socrates and Bruno.*

*But there is no doubt. Only he who does not know
where he is going can arrive at the Promised Land.*

LEV SHESTOV

How can those who rebel be happy?

ALEXEI REMIZOV

*No Marxist ever saw in Marxist theory any general, com-
pulsory philosophical, historic schemes or anything more
than an explanation of a certain socioeconomic formation.*
All that is done in the name of love will be forgiven.

LENIN

Even if, theoretically, we completely agreed with the critics
of Dostoevsky, it would still not mean that he is a reactionary.
For history has borne out many of his predictions. Of course,
if something worthwhile emerges from the horror of the first
half of the twentieth century, from cults of personality, secret
police, concentration camps, totalitarianism of every color,
etc., as Ehrenburg predicted in his *Julio Jurenito,* and as we
ourselves believe, then and only then we may say that
Dostoevsky was reactionary. But that would happen only if
we ignore all existential questions in his heroes and refer
solely to socio-historical progress.

Dostoevsky is the most existential and consequently the
most social writer in world literature. Leonid Grossman was
right when he wrote:

Eternal protest against the idea that live souls are only material
for building future cultures, eternal struggle against the legaliza-
tion of individual suffering in the name of general welfare,
passionate defense of the sacred inviolability of the human

personality against all attempts of world historic progress to tyrannize over it—this is the theme implied in Dostoevsky's strange, tortured first novel and in all his early stories. This same theme is central to the humane sermon in *Notes from the House of the Dead*. It stands as an insolent challenge to self-willed tyranny in his *Notes from the Underground* and issues as a satanical demand for supêr-human morality in *Crime and Punishment*. Finally, symbolic unity of many motifs, all of which support humanistic individualism and titanic personal volition, is reached in *The Brothers Karamazov*.

In his defense of the inviolability of the individual personality against the "tyranny of the world historical process," in defending individuals from forced socialization (Adolf Hitler: "We will socialize men . . . The time of individual happiness is over. We will feel general happiness instead. The Old and New Testaments are one and the same Jewish swindle") , Dostoevsky was defending the life of society itself because society in which the integral parts, individuals, are dead (that is, without freedom) is dead also.

Like Dante, Dostoevsky stood at the crossroads of two eras, and their views of the universe have much in common, down to the smallest details. "The real hero in Dostoevsky, just as in Dante, is the reader," wrote P. M. Bicilli. Between Dante and Dostoevsky came a period in our European culture which will never return. The misunderstandings, presently growing harsher, between the advocates of socio-historical progress and Dostoevsky must be reconciled in the near future because the problems which tortured Dostoevsky are our own. The questions which he had to answer face us squarely and we cannot avoid them.

All modern philosophy and literature is under the shadow of Dostoevsky, and nothing can be solved by proclaiming him a "reactionary who will die with capitalism." It is in socialist society that Dostoevskyan problems become the problems of all mankind.

In a similar juncture of history, a great ideological dispute arose between the theoretician and precursor of the Reformation, Erasmus, and the leader of the Reformation, Martin Luther. Erasmus wrote a debate, *On the Freedom of the Will (De Liber Arbitrio)*, in which he claimed that since man is free, his own salvation and destiny depend on himself. Luther countered Erasmus in *On the Bondage of the Will (De Servio Arbitrio)*, in which, following St. Augustine, he refuted the assertions of Erasmus and supported the thesis that whether a man is to be saved or not is predetermined by God. Luther himself, however, in a revolutionary way and by his own free will, declared himself against Catholic spiritual hegemony. Something similar also happened during the Russian Revolution. Lenin, who, like Luther, was breaking regular evolutionary progress and was creating a revolution (revolution being precisely an expression of free will[1]), held that world historical progress is based on social laws (every law is essentially predicated on lack of freedom, no matter if it was perceived or not). Ideologically, Lenin has the same relation to Dostoevsky as Luther had to Erasmus, the same relation that conscience has to life. Viktor Shklovsky in his book on Dostoevsky wrote: "Man escaped either to the revolution or to the underground." Had Dostoevsky succeeded in becoming a true believer in either progress or Christianity, he would not have written novels but would have been an active revolutionary or a "holy hermit" like Father Zosima. Dostoevsky is really the conscience of the Russian Revolution. Precisely for that reason, he recognized all the detours and traps and foresaw that an Ivan Karamazov unconsciously incites the action of a Smerdyakov, just as Lenin unconsciously opened the way for Stalin. Dostoevsky provided no solution either for himself or for any other man. He knew what was wrong but he did not know what was to be done.

[1] Berdayev: "Man has to fulfill God's will and God's will is that man should be free." [M.M.]

Defending the individual, he defended society; fighting the rational, he defended the revolution; struggling for religion and belief in immortality, he rebelled against any church. Dostoevsky did not preach resignation. He knew that resignation, as such, is the greatest sin. Luther knew this, too: "Blasphemy is sometimes dearer to God than prayer." Dostoevsky wanted to demonstrate that parricide is wrong. It is not by chance that Smerdyakov says to Ivan Karamazov: "You have most of your father's devil." But Dostoevsky never pointed out the right way. Both he and Marx answer the sick man's question: "How do I get well?" by saying: "By being healthy." It is for us to find the way.

Even more basic is the fact that no insuperable contradictions exist between Marxism as a science of the life of society and Dostoevsky. If Marxism does not provide answers to the questions posed by Raskolnikov, Ippolit, or Ivan Karamazov, it is as unjust to blame Marxism for this as to blame medical science for not being able to bring the dead back to life. The problem appears only when Marxism becomes "negative religiosity," as in Cecić. Medical science is of benefit to man, but if we maintain that the only goal and purpose of human existence is physical health, we would render medicine a disservice. Similarly, "negative religiosity" renders a disservice to Marxism. By negative religiosity we mean not only the belief that Communism and classless society will solve all problems but also the belief that science will discover everything about life and that the meaning of all human existence is cognition of life. We have demonstrated that the idea of the immortality of the human soul does not contradict the struggle for a better life here and now (no matter what kind of struggle and no matter whether the path taken by the Russian Revolution was right or not). Only the idea of immortality justifies the crystal palace of a Communist society.

Recently, especially following the publication of the complete works of that Christian and personalistic philosopher, "the heretical Jesuit," Teilhard du Chardin (whose ideas are more and more at the center of ideological disputes in the West, and about whom comment has even begun to appear in the Soviet press), it has become easier to predict a future ideological synthesis of Marxism and Christianity, Dostoevsky and Lenin. This looks especially probable with the growing popularity of a so-called "third power," the father of modern personalism, Emmanuel Mounier. Naturally, by Christianity we do not mean any church organization but only faith in the immortality of the human soul and the superiority of love for life over the striving to know life. Let's remind ourselves that the Christ of the Gospels did not resign himself: "I come to bring not peace but the sword." However, nonresignation has nothing to do with oppression.

The question whether the social environment conditions man or vice versa is relevant only for the "alienated" man. "It is about time to stop blaming the environment for everything," wrote Dostoevsky in his *Notes from the House of the Dead:* Only the "alienated," that is, unliberated man, can hold the environment responsible for everything. Awakened by his liberation and a true meeting with life, when he has broken the restrictions of the rational, man ceases to blame external circumstances. "The very moment you start believing that you yourself are responsible for everything, you will understand that it is so," wrote Dostoevsky. And perhaps the greatest result of "saving the world" (Marx says "change" the world; a more adequate expression would be "attempt to change") is that, in the attempting to change the world, man changes himself, and all "external" achievements (like science and technology, etc.) are only by-products of lesser value. The death of the idea of progress as socio-historic and sociologic advancement will come only when this "progress" materializes. Perhaps this progress consists only in the growth of resistance to that sort of "natural law" which fails to avenge Socrates, Giordano Bruno, or the victims of the Inquisition and the Gestapo. This is why we can accept Ehrenburg's thesis about a new, "unheard-of slavery" brought by the revolution as a "schoolroom" for genuine creative freedom. In that case, the first half of the twentieth century has been only profitable in the negative sense. Only the greatest dangers in life—the loss of freedom and the transformation of a living individual into a part of a mechanism—incite the resistance that develops into immense strength, a strength which guarantees that freedom won't be lost. We also emphasize that pressure on the individual in the twentieth century is occurring everywhere, that it is now spreading beyond Europe, whatever the color of the flag of the ruling ideology (hence the essential and substantial similarity between Stalinism and Hitlerism).

Just as slavery in the "name of liberty" is the "schoolroom" for creative freedom, rationalism in the name of irrational values (the future paradise on earth) may lay the basis for a genuine (not "future") irrationalism that is the "life eternal"—life free from the test tube of reason and dialectics—and a time when men will not know, to use the expression of Emmanuel Mounier, whether they think their life or live their thoughts. Zhdanov[2] did incomparably more for the development of future Russian modernism in literature and art than any influence from the West.

It is an interesting fact that all Dostoevsky's critics hold against him his self-confessed doubt, when this is the very argument in his favor. "Scoundrels were teasing me with bad education and reactionary faith in God. Those stupid idiots did not even dream of so forceful a denial of God as can be found in the Inquisitor and in the preceding chapter. The

[2] Andrei Zhdanov, Soviet cultural commissioner under Stalin. [Trans.]

whole novel serves as an answer to that chapter. I do not believe in God like a fanatic. They wanted to teach me and laughed at my stubbornness. Their stupid nature did not even suspect the strength of denial that I passed through, and they wanted to teach me!" wrote Dostoevsky in his notebook.

To the question what is God for Dostoevsky, we can answer: immortality. The idea of immortality brings freedom, not slavery. Dostoevsky's thought that "if there is no immortality, everything is permitted" elucidates this much better than any undefined God. If all disappears with physical death, if the criminals who escape punishment in society really will never be punished or the martyrs revenged, then "everything is permitted." Although rationalism suggests that this is, in fact, the case, an instinct much deeper than reason suggests the contrary. One need only read *The Death of Ivan Ilyich,* one of Tolstoy's most significant works, in which the great writer brings out the "natural agony" of his hero and his terrible mental sufferings—a genuine medieval last judgment over a human soul, an eternity of torments experienced by Ivan Ilyich in a relatively short time (short especially for his milieu) —to comprehend that our notions about time and eternity are largely undefined. Einstein created a revolution in physics by proving that the stream of time is different in different inertial systems. A similar notion seems to apply to living human beings. Dostoevsky described in *The Idiot* how a human being experiences a whole eternity before death. The same thing was noted by Leonid Andreyev in his celebrated story *The Seven Who Were Hanged,* where the girl revolutionary, Musya, moments before death, suddenly feels

seized with an unspeakable joy. There is no more doubt; she has been taken into the pale. She has a right to figure among the heroes who from all countries go to heaven through flames and executions. What serene peace, what infinite happiness! And—this is death! What sort of death is that? . . . And if from all the corners of the worlds would gather in her cell scientists, philosophers, and hangmen, lay before her books, scalpels, axes, ropes, and start proving to her that death does exist, that man does kill himself and dies, that immortality does not exist—they would only surprise her. How come that there is no immortality when she is now already immortal. . . . The important thing is that we should ourselves be ready to die. What do those people think? That there is nothing more terrible than death? They have invented it themselves, they constantly fear only it, and frighten us with it.

Man also experiences eternity in real love and, generally speaking and using existentialist terminology, in all "crucial situations," that is, in the moments when the test tube of reason is destroyed by happiness or suffering and when man becomes a part of life itself. Thomas Mann devoted the first third of *The Magic Mountain* to the first week of his hero Hans Castorp's stay in the sanatorium, the second third to the next several weeks, and the last third to years. In the works of Beckett, time ceases to move; it rests on zero point because there is no longer any contact with life. In "crucial situations," on the contrary, time is replaced with eternity.

Only in a "crucial situation" does man come to accept faith, and in order voluntarily to accept a crucial situation (man is always escaping into the test tube), he must pass through doubt, that is, reason. Fear of death, crucial situations, freedom ("Escape from Freedom," as the American Marxist Erich Fromm called it) is the same as fear of real love because it is connected with an illusory loss of personal individuality. (Christ said: "He who will save himself will lose himself, and he who loses himself will save himself.") And Lev Shestov said: "Fear is not an attribute of freedom but an expression of its loss." The road to faith leads through doubt, but to seek faith means, in a great measure, to have found it, just as the struggle for freedom is, in a certain sense, freedom itself. St. Augustine best expressed this in the phrase: "You were looking for me because you had found me."

Nikolai Berdyaev wrote:

Human nature is bi-polar, antinomian, irrational. The urge for the irrational, for senseless freedom, for suffering, cannot be uprooted in man. Usefulness is not of prime importance to man. He doesn't accept a rational system of life. Freedom is more highly esteemed than welfare. . . . The truth makes man free but he has to accept it freely. He cannot be led to it by oppressive, compulsory means. Imposed good is not good any more; it becomes evil.

This is only a comment on Dostoevsky. But the fact that human nature is irrational (that is, alive) does not mean that it is also evil. Here we agree with Dostoevsky's critics. But from this fact it does not follow that evil lurks outside man either, and here is where we do not agree with the critics. If Alyosha Karamazov is not reconciled with his father, neither does he kill him. Dostoevsky did not write "love" or "family" or "social" novels. All that he wrote was relevant to existence as a whole. The Russian critic, V. Kirpotin, wrote:

Unlike the decadent psychologism of Proust and Joyce which marked the fall and decline of bourgeois literature, the psychologism of Dostoevsky in his positive works is not subjective, but realistic. His psychologism is a special artistic method, the penetration into the objective essence of paradoxical human society; into the very core of social relations which were upsetting him, and the transformation of this method into words. Dostoevsky, with the whole strength of his agitated, impatient temperament experienced all the ideological gropings of his contemporaries and re-created them in psychologically colored characters.

Dostoevsky thought in psychologically elaborated characters but he thought socially.

The critic is right only to the point that society, as a part of the universe, is made up of individuals. The ultimate goal of Dostoevsky's study was the individual, because he himself was isolated from the unity of life by the same rationalism that his critics argued for. As Viktor Shklovsky puts it: "The notion of crime in Dostoevsky is linked not to the question 'against what?' but to the question 'who?' " However, Kirpotin is wrong when he states "that men have long since passed judgment on Dostoevsky. The mystery of man which tortured Dostoevsky all his life has been explained. The causes of the suffering that he proclaimed to the world have been defined. Dostoevsky is not a prophet or a teacher of life, or an interpreter of the 'Russian soul' as has often been alleged."

Dostoevsky is linked to capitalist society in that the eternal problems of existence (eternal as much as man is eternal) are the problems crystallized in a capitalist society. In a non-capitalist society, the same tragedies will occur, though in different form (the issues of life and death are not only historico-social but also existential and universal).

The problems that obsessed Dostoevsky are of an existential nature, which is why all modern artists and thinkers keep going back to him. He is related to modernists, however, as Molière was to his contemporary misanthropes. Dostoevsky discovered us, that is, twentieth-century men. And he did it in the middle of the past century. By describing us, by defining our problems, he carried out a revolution of immense importance.

Dostoevsky, like Columbus, did not know himself what he had discovered: he was sailing for India and found the New World. Dostoevsky was constantly preparing himself for a creative victory without realizing he had already won this victory, that his achievement had already radically changed "the face of the world," that he had become the engine of a huge cultural revolution.

These words were written by the critic Chulkov in a book on Dostoevsky, the only almost completely non-Zhdanovist work to appear in the gloomiest quarter century of modern Russian history.

Dostoevsky no longer belongs to the era that began with the Renaissance. Nor does he belong to the future, because he had to write novels. This may seem paradoxical, but a man alive, not an "alienated" man, would not read or write, at least not artistic literature. He who loves and is loved does not need to read love novels. No one at the front reads war novels. One either lives life or perceives it, that is, reads and writes about it.

Just before his death, Dostoevsky wrote in his notebook, under the rubric "I": "I am, of course, of the people (because my path originated in the depths of the people's Christian spirit). Although I am not known to the Russian people of today, I will be known to the future." If we take a look at the number of works on Dostoevsky that are now appearing in the U.S.S.R.—the surest sign of his growing popularity in his own country, particularly among the young—our conclusion must be that Dostoevsky's prediction is coming true. In the U.S.S.R. in 1952 it was possible to publish a textbook on Russian literature containing not a single reference to Dostoevsky; today this is no longer possible. Dostoevsky has become socialism's conscience.

In this discussion we have touched upon a few basic problems relating to the misunderstanding between Dostoevsky and his critics. An end to this misunderstanding would bring about the beginning of a new spiritual era.

We love and defend Dostoevsky because he is completely ours, because he experienced what we experience and suffered the agonies which have tormented us men of the twentieth century and which continue to torment us. We agree with Vladimir Solovyev's words:

More than anything else, he loved the living human soul in everything and everywhere . . . he believed in the limitless strength of the human soul which triumphs over every outward oppression and every inner fall.

[1964]

HOW RUSSIA WAS CRUCIFIED:
SEEDS OF TOMORROW,
BY MIKHAIL SHOLOKHOV

*　　*　　*

RUSSIAN FASCISM has produced no better, more talented writer than Mikhail Sholokhov. His Nobel Prize is helping to make his books known the world over, and this is only to be welcomed. Despite his personal convictions, despite his many years of Communist Party membership, the power of his talent has outweighed official falsehoods and the author has left future generations a truthful description of the horrors his great people suffered during long years of totalitarian enslavement.

This great literary artist has recorded the two most important episodes in recent Russian history: the revolution and the civil war in *And Quiet Flows the Don* and the collectivization in *Seeds of Tomorrow*. Although *Seeds of Tomorrow* has less literary merit than *And Quiet Flows the Don* it is unsurpassed as a document of that terrible operation performed on the living body of the Russian people as a result of which Russia agonizes on her sick bed to this day.

The first half of *Seeds of Tomorrow* came out in 1932, when the author's impressions of the events described were still fresh. The second half *(Harvest on the Don)*, which appeared nearly thirty years later, in 1960, revealed a loss of spontaneity in the depiction of Russian village life. From the opening to the closing lines the novel presents a historically truthful account of the destruction of a Russian village and of its "socialization" at the hands of totalitarian dictatorship.

The roots of the deplorable fact that a country once enormously rich in agricultural produce is now constrained to import grain lie deep in the historical events of the 1930's described in this book. In order to understand what happened in 1929–30, however, one must first glance at the Russian peasantry of the nineteenth century.

The 1861 reform which liberated the Russian man on the land from serfdom unfortunately retained the traditional village commune, which prevented the development of individual initiative and innovation in farming. The size of per capita land allotments diminished quickly, owing to the growth of village populations. It was only in 1906 that Stolypin, one of Russia's greatest statesmen, opened the way to development of individual farming by new agrarian reforms. The Bolsheviks refer to his policies as "the Stolypin reaction." Within a decade, 38 percent of peasant farms were privately owned.

The February Revolution set Russia on the road to completion of the agrarian reforms begun by Stolypin and provided economic support for villages. Cooperation among peasants was already developing freely. This was a European road and it promised Russian villages the same kind of evolution that took place in France, Germany, and the Scandinavian countries. The seizure of power by the Bolsheviks and Socialist Revolutionaries in the October coup (it was a coup, not a revolution!), and the Decree on Land which was issued forthwith, set the Russian village back half a century by reestablishing communal farming. This destroyed the individual productive farmers (called kulaks in Leninist terminology), who had just come into their own. The Soviet government came to be represented in the villages by "Committees of Poor Peasants." Of course, Lenin was aware of the negative effect the decree would have on Russian villages, but Party dictatorship meant more to him than strengthening agriculture. Stalin, similarly motivated, forced the peasants into collective farms en masse and, in that sense, was "a true follower of Lenin." Economically independent farmers were intolerable to a dictatorship.

The New Economic Policy (NEP), a breathing spell during the process of "socialization," granted because of the catastrophic condition into which industry and agriculture had fallen, offered the Russian peasantry some possibilities, however limited, for progress and a better life. The hardest working and most capable farmers, who were getting on their feet rapidly and becoming increasingly independent, represented a constant threat to the government and an impediment to socialism. The short NEP breathing spell moved the country swiftly toward economic recovery. The Party realized, however, that this was only a respite and that if NEP were to continue, Party dictatorship would soon end. It was at this time that Trotsky came up with the slogan "Total collectivization." In connection with intra-party friction among "leaders" and factions, Stalin upheld a contrary point of view, and it was only after Trotsky's fall that Stalin snatched up his idea of collectivization.

Collectivization began in the winter of 1929–30. By that time, of a total of 25 million peasant families, 2 million were considered "kulak elements"; 18 million, "middle peasants"; and 5 million, "poor peasants." Middle peasants were constantly being reclassified into "kulaks." Naturally, the kulaks and the greater number of middle peasants had no desire to join a kolkhoz and give up private farming, which was becoming more and more progressive and modern. The poor households had nothing to lose by joining kolkhozy, and it was upon this one fifth of the rural population that the authorities were counting to accomplish collectivization. All kulaks, as well as any other farmers who refused to join collectives, saw their goods confiscated or were arrested and sent into exile.

By March 1930, 58 percent of all peasant households had

been forced into the kolkhozy. But the peasants frantically resisted collectivization, and in some parts of the country there were armed uprisings. Stalin, realizing the danger of the situation, on March 2, 1930, published an article in *Pravda* carrying the headline "Dizzy With Their Success" in which he laid the blame for forced collectivization and for the extreme measures being used to implement it upon local government representatives.

For a while forcible collectivization ceased and many kolkhozy were disbanded. Peasant protests ceased as well. Stalin's maneuver had succeeded. However, the pressure was soon renewed, and by 1934–35 collectivization was an accomplished fact.

Through starvation, police terror, reprisals, deportations, and deception, the Party succeeded in liquidating all free farmers. The peasants became hired laborers for the kolkhozy, whose directors were henchmen of the government. Economically speaking, agriculture was dealt a blow from which it has not yet recovered. The power of the Party, on the other hand, was preserved and strengthened. Farmers were allowed to own tiny personal plots and a few head of cattle, but this was the only concession.

Approximately 10 million peasants were victims of calculated starvation during the years of forced collectivization. It is unknown how many perished in concentration camps. But the main goal, the consolidation of Party rule, was achieved.

It was this process of liquidating a Russian village that Mikhail Sholokhov powerfully and truthfully described in *Seeds of Tomorrow*. No other Soviet novel contains an account as candid as Sholokhov's. Paradoxical as it may seem, the explanation lies in the fact that Sholokhov had been dedicated to the Party heart and soul all his life and was a true believer in Communism, just like the people who crucified Russia, and he could therefore allow himself to depict reality much more truthfully than those who did not share his belief. He described reality honestly because he believed that in spite of all sacrifices the imposed collectivization would benefit Russia in the long run. And we ought to be grateful to him for his candor. For any reader who does *not believe* in Communism, this novel will always provide a key to understanding the evil which dictatorships, be they Communist or Fascist, bring to the world—a total, final evil: death of the soul and then of the body.

The first part of the novel, *Seeds of Tomorrow,* starts with the arrival of a future chairman of a future collective farm at the village of Gremyachy Log. His aim is to put into effect the Party decree on 100 percent collectivization. The Party had sent 25,000 factory workers (the so-called Twenty-five Thousand) to carry out the dispossession of kulaks and organize collective farms.

The secretary of the Party District Committee exhorts the new chairman, Davidov:

"And then you'll make a drive for a hundred percent collectivization. We shall judge your work by the percentage you achieve. We'll create a gigantic collective farm out of our eighteen village Soviets. How's that?"

When Davidov, himself one of the Twenty-five Thousand, arrives at the village assigned to him, he in turn explains to the Party nucleus:

"Davidov sat down at the table, told them of the tasks which the Party had set in connection with the two months' advance towards complete collectivization and proposed that a meeting of the poor Cossacks and active workers be called for the very next day."

At that meeting, thirty-two "poor Cossacks and active workers," empowered by the government to make decisions concerning the life and death of the remaining villagers (the *majority*), are addressed by the chairman-to-be, Davidov:

"So what's to be done?" Davidov went on, ignoring the reply. "The Party proposes complete collectivization, so as to hitch you on to the tractor and lift you out of your want! What did Comrade Lenin say just before his death? 'Only on the collective farm can the peasant find salvation from his poverty. Otherwise he is doomed. The vampire kulak will suck him as flat as a board.' And you must walk quite firmly along the road he pointed out. In alliance with the workers the collective farmers will sweep away all the kulaks and enemies. I'm speaking the truth. . . .

"Why must you join a collective farm? Because it is impossible to go on living as we are! The difficulties we're having with the grain have arisen because the kulak lets it rot in the ground. We have got to get the grain from him by force! You would be glad to give your grain, only you haven't got much. You can't feed the Soviet Union on the grain of poor and middling peasants. We've got to sow more. But how are you going to sow more with only a wooden or a single-share plough? Only the tractor can get us out of that difficulty. Fact! I don't know how much you can plough here in the Don with one plough during the autumn."

This evokes an immediate response. A certain Lyubishkin says:

"You're crazy, aren't you, agitating among us on behalf of the Soviet Government? It was us who set it on its feet during the war, it was us who supported it with our shoulders, so that it didn't break down. We know what a collective farm is, and we're all for it. Give us machines!" He stretched out a fist the size of a turnip. "A tractor's fine, we know, but you workers have only made a few of them, and that's what we swear at you for. We haven't got anything to lay hold of, that's the trouble. And we can plough with oxen, one hand driving, the other wiping away our tears, without joining a collective farm. I myself was think-

ing of sending Kalinin a letter before the collective farm movement began, to ask them to help the grain-growers to begin a new
life. For the first few years were just like the old regime—pay
your taxes, live as best you can, and what was the Russian
Communist Party for? Well, we won the civil war and then what?
Again the old style: follow the plough, those who had anything
to harness to a plough. And those who hadn't—were they to
stretch out their hands and beg at the church door? Or to wait
with a wooden club under a bridge and frighten Soviet mer-
chants and co-operative managers? They allowed the rich to rent
land, they allowed them to hire labourers. Was that what the
Revolution dictated in 1918? You've closed the eyes of the
Revolution!"

And again:

"It seems I fought the Cadets for the rich to live better than me.
For them to have the sweets while I get bread and onion."

And, at last, comes the main demand:

"What are you talking to me about the collective farm for? Cut
the veins of the kulaks, and then we'll join. Give us their
machines, their oxen, give us their strength, then we shall have
our equality! But now it's all talk and talk about 'destroy the
kulak' while he grows from year to year like a burdock and keeps
the sun off us."

So there it is: "Cut the veins of the kulak!" "Lead us to
smash up the kulaks!" Naturally the mobilized worker,
Davidov, upholds the "voice" of the people:

"That is the policy of our Party," he declared. "What are you
knocking at an open door for? Destroy the kulak as a class, hand
over his property to the collective farms! Fact! And you, comrade
partisan, you threw your cap under the table for nothing; you'll
still need it for your head. The renting of land and hiring of
labourers can't go on any longer. We put up with the kulaks
because of our need, *they supplied more bread than the collec-*

tive farms did. But now it's the other way round. Comrade Stalin has reckoned it all up to the last figure and said: 'free the kulak of his life! Hand his property over to the collective farms . . .' You've all been crying out for machines . . . Five hundred million whole roubles are going to be given to the collective farms to get them on their feet. What d'you think of that? Have you heard about that? Then what are you shouting about? First you've got to start your collective farm and then worry about machinery. But you want to buy the collar first, and when you've got it, you'll buy a horse! What are you laughing at? That's true!"[1]

Thus, thirty-two dissatisfied people come to a decision to liquidate all the kulaks in the village, simply throw the "wealthy" out of their houses and exile them to Siberia. Yet who are these "vampires," "surviving landowners," "idle rich?" These labels do not appear to fit them well at all:

"You see," Nagulnov began irresolutely. "This Borodin—we call him Titok—voluntarily joined the Red Guards together with us in 1918. *He was the son of a poor Cossack,* and fought bravely. He was wounded and was given a distinction, a silver watch, for his revolutionary conduct. So you see, comrade worker, how he has touched our hearts. When he came home he got his teeth into his farm like a hound into carrion. And *he began to get rich, although we warned him again and again. He worked day and night,* grew a shaggy beard all over him, went about in a single pair of canvas trousers winter and summer. He got himself three yoke of oxen, and ruptured himself through lifting heavy weights, and still it wasn't enough for him! He began to hire workers, two or three at a time. He got a windmill, and then he bought a five-horsepower steam engine, set up an oilmill, and began to trade in cattle. He doesn't eat much himself, and he starves his labourers, although they work twenty hours a day and have to get up five times a night to see to the horses and cattle.

1 Italics here and in following passages quoted from Sholokhov are Mihajlov's. [Trans.]

We've had him before the nucleus and at the Soviet more than once, we've tried to make him feel ashamed of himself, we've told him: 'Stop it, Tit, don't stand in the way of our own Soviet government! You've suffered for it yourself, fighting the Whites at the fronts . . .' " Nagulnov sighed and spread out his hands. "What can you do when the devil gets hold of a man? We could see he would be eaten up with his property. We called him before us again, reminded him of the civil war and our common sufferings, argued with him, threatened we would trample him into the earth if he stood in our way, became a bourgeois, and didn't want to wait for the world revolution . . ."

"Don't be so long-winded," Davidov impatiently demanded.

Nagulnov's voice trembled as he went on more quietly:

"I can't cut it any shorter. It hurts till the blood comes . . . But he always replies: 'I'm carrying out the orders of the Soviet government, I am increasing my sowings. And I'm allowed by law to have labourers, my wife is ill with women's sickness. I was nothing and I've become all; I have got everything, and that's what I fought for. And it isn't the likes of you who keep the Soviet government going. With my hands I give it something to chew. And you're only paper-spoilers. I see you for what you are."

And finally:

"And we took away his vote. He tried to ride the high horse, wrote letters to the district and to Moscow. But as I understand it, there are old revolutionaries sitting in the chief positions in the central institutions, and they realize that once a man's become a traitor he's an enemy and there's no mercy for him. . . . And they didn't give him back his vote, but he's gone on just the same, only he's got rid of his labourers . . ."

At this, Davidov

pressed his lips together and his face darkened: "What are you telling us these pitiful stories for? He was a Partisan, and all honour to him for that! But now he's become a kulak, become an enemy, crush him! What is there to talk about?"

Here is the story of Gaev, who was dispossessed as a kulak and exiled:

"The middling peasant Gayev was treated as a kulak and exiled although he was not in the least to be regarded as a kulak as far as possession of property was concerned. But on Nagulnov's demand he was treated as one because he employed someone in 1928. But what sort of labourer did he employ? Comrades, Gayev hired a girl from Gremyachy Log for a month during the harvesting period, and he hired her only because his son had been called up to the Red Army in the autumn of 1927, and with his many children Gayev could not manage the work by himself. Such exploitation of hired labour was not prohibited by Soviet law. Gayev hired this girl on the basis of a contract with the Labourers' Committee and paid her wages in full. That fact I have checked."

The main enemy of collectivization in the village, Yakov Lukich Ostrovnov, who, because he joined the collective at once, was not dispossessed, is also no country gentleman or capitalist:

"What is there to talk about, Alexander Anisimovich?" he said. "There's no joy or pleasure in life these days. The Cossacks had begun to build up their farms again and to get rich. In 1926, and even in 1927, the taxes were, well, comparatively bearable. But now they've turned the clock back again. How are things in your district? Is there any talk of collectivization there?"

"There's talk," his guest briefly replied, licking a cigarette paper and staring attentively from under his brows at Lukich.

"*So everywhere tears are falling because of that cheerful song, are they?*" Lukich said. "I'll tell you my story. I returned from the retreat in 1920. I left a pair of horses and all my goods down by the Black Sea. *I came back to a bare hut. Ever since then I've worked day and night.* The first time the comrades troubled me with their grain requisitions, they raked up every bit of my grain. I've lost count of the wrongs I've suffered since then. I could reckon them up though; they do you a wrong and then write you out a receipt so that you won't forget." He rose, slipped his hand behind the mirror, and, smiling into his clipped moustache, drew out a sheaf of papers. "Here they are; here are the receipts for what they took in 1921, and I gave up grain, and meat, and butter, and skins, and wool, and fowls, and I took whole oxen into the collection office. And here are the receipts for the single agricultural tax, for self-taxation, and these are for insurance. I've even paid for the smoke that came out of the chimney and for the cattle standing alive in the yard. I'll have a sackful of such papers soon. In a word, Alexander Anisimovich, I've lived, and fed myself from the earth, and fed others around me too. They've skinned me again and again, but I've grown a new skin every time. I got a yoke of young oxen to begin with, and they grew up. I sold one at a good price for meat, but I bought another with my wife's sowing machine. After a time, in 1925, I got another yoke of oxen from my own cows. So I had two yoke of oxen and two cows. They didn't take my vote from me, but for the future they wrote me down among the middling to rich peasants."

What are the farming methods of this peasant? This is how he works:

"I began to listen to the agricultural inspectors, started a proper rotation of crops, and looked after my land as though it was a sick wife. My corn is the finest in the village, and I get the best harvest of all. I treated my grain chemically and took steps to keep the snow on my fields. I sowed the spring seed grain immediately after plowing, without any spring tilling, and my sown fallow was always the first. In a word, I became a scientific farmer, and I've had a letter of praise from the District Agricultural Department. . . . During the first years after my return I sowed twelve acres; then, as I got on, I bent my back to it even more. I sowed thirty, then fifty, and even seventy-five acres, think of that! I worked, and my son and his wife. I only hired a labourer a couple of times at the busiest season. What was the Soviet government's order in those years? Sow as much as you can! And I sowed until my back well-nigh broke, by the true Christ! And now . . . I'm afraid! I'm afraid that because of my seventy-five acres they'll drag me through the needle's eye and call me a kulak."

Here is what others say of him:

"They ought to have had Yakov Ostrovnov for chairman. He's got a good head! He had some wheat of a new, finer sort sent him from Krasnodar, which lives through the worst of drought; he always keeps the snow on his autumn-ploughed land, and his harvest is always among the best in the village. He's raised first class cattle, too. He groans a bit when we press him for his taxes, but he's a good farmer and has a letter of praise from the Agricultural Department."

While the "vampire" himself thinks:

"If they didn't hunt the rich Cossacks, I might now, with my efforts, be the first man in the village. In a free life I might be driving my own car."

And it is peasants of this sort, the most advanced and capable farmers, the "kulaks and middle peasants," who are to be "dispossessed by decision of the village poor," headed by an "active element."

And dispossessed they were, like the "kulak" Frol Damaskov, for instance:

"Come in and sit down, my dear government officials!" he invited them.

"We haven't got time to sit down," Andrei Razmiotnov replied, pulling a paper out of his brief-case. "The meeting of the poor peasants has decided *to evict you from your house, Frol Damaskov, and to confiscate all your property and your stock.* So finish your meal and then get yourselves out of the hut. We shall make an inventory of the property at once."

"What's all this for?" Throwing down his spoon, Frol rose to his feet.

"We intend to destroy you as a kulak class," Diemka Ushakov enlightened him.

His solid, leather-soled felt boots creaking, Frol went into the sitting-room and brought back a document.

"Here's the statement; you signed it yourself, Razmiotnov."

"What statement?"

"The statement that I handed over my grain tax."

"The grain tax has got nothing to do with this."

"Then what am I being driven out of my home and my property confiscated for?"

"That's what the poor peasants have decided, as I've already told you."

"There's no law which allows it!" Timofei sharply exclaimed. "You're organizing robbery. Father, I'll ride to the District Executive Committee at once. Where's a saddle?"

"You'll go to the committee on foot if you want to. I shan't let you have a horse." Andrei sat down at the edge of the table and took out a pencil and paper. Frol's torn nose was flooded with blue, and his head began to shake. He suddenly crumpled to the floor where he stood, and muttered, with difficulty moving his swollen, blackened tongue:

"Sons of bitches! Sons of bitches! Rob on! Cut us down!"

"Father, get up, for the love of Christ!" The girl burst into tears and tried to lift her father with her hands under his armpits.

Frol recovered, got up and lay down on the bench, listening impassively as Diemka Ushakov and the tall, sheepish Mikhail Ignationok dictated to Razmiotnov:

"An iron bedstead with white balls, a feather bed, three pillows and two wooden bedsteads. . . . A cupboard full of crockery. Am I to go all through the crockery? Damn the whole lot! Twelve chairs, one long armchair with a back. A three-tiered accordion."

"I'm not going to let you have my accordion," Timofei shouted, snatching it out of Diemka's hands. "Hands off, squint-eye, or I'll smash your nose in!"

"I'll smash you so that your mother won't be able to wash you clean," Diemka retorted. "Hand over the keys to the chests, old woman!"

"Don't give them to him, mother. Let them break the chests open, if they've got the right."

. . . . .

Andrei could not get all the items written down. From the best room and from the hall Diemka Ushakov, Arkashka and Aunty Vasilisa, the only women in Andrei's party, outvied one another with their shouts:

"A woman's fur coat."

"A sheepskin."

"Three pairs of new shoes and galoshes."

"Four lengths of cloth."

"Andrei! Razmetnov! You'll never get all these goods on one sledge, old man. There's calico and black satin and all sorts of other stuff . . ."

As he went towards the best room, Andrei heard a girl's lamentations, the housewife's voice and Ignationok's persuasive tones coming from the porch. He threw open the door.

"What's up here?" he demanded.

Her face swollen with tears, the snub-nosed daughter was leaning against the front door, bellowing like a calf. Her mother was bustling and cackling around her, while Ignationok, his face crimson and wearing an embarrassed smile, was pulling at the girl by the edge of her skirt.

"What the—? Damn you!" Not realizing what was the trouble, Andrei began to choke with rage and gave Ignationok a violent push. His long legs engulfed in his ragged felt boots, Ignationok fell on his back. "Fine politics that!" roared Andrei. "We're attacking the enemy, and you're pawing girls in corners? But you'll answer to a court for your—"

"Here, hold on, wait a bit!" Ignationok jumped up from the floor in alarm. "As if she could turn my head! Pawing her! Look at her: she was just drawing on the ninth skirt around her. I was trying to stop her, and you flare up like that!"

Only then did Andrei notice that the girl, who under cover of the general confusion had dragged a bundle of clothes out of the best room, had already managed to wrap a heap of woolen dresses around her. Hampered in her movements by the abundance of her clothes, looking strangely awkward and dock-tailed as she huddled in the corner, she was adjusting the hem of the top skirt. Andrei felt pity and aversion for her with her wet eyes, which were pink like a rabbit's. He slammed the door and said to Ignationok:

"You can't undress her. *What she's managed to put on she can keep, but take the bundle away from her.*"

The inventory of the goods in the house was finished at last.

"The keys of the granary," Andrei demanded.

Frol, as black as charred wood, waved his hand. "We haven't got them," he declared.

"Go and break the door open," Andrei ordered Diemid, who went to the barn, pulling a swivel-bolt out of a cart as he went. The five-pound padlock was broken off with difficulty by resort to an ax.

"Don't smash the door post! It's our barn now, so take care with it. Gently, gently!" Diemka counseled the sweating Diemid.

They began to measure out the grain. "Perhaps we'd better sift it at once. There's a sieve lying in the bin," Ignationok, *drunk with joy,* proposed.

And the last scene:

In the best room Andrei found Diemid squatting on his heels. On his feet were Frol's new leather-soled felt boots. As Andrei entered unnoticed, Diemid scooped up a tablespoonful of honey from a large iron bucket and ate it, screwing up his eyes with delight, smacking his lips, and letting the sticky, yellow drops run down his beard.

And here is how they evicted old Lapshinov from his house:

The women ceased their hubbub and sighed. Razmiotnov finished his writing, then said harshly:

"Well, Daddy Lapshinov, clear out of here. Your tears aren't so pitiable as all that. You've done wrong to many in your time, and now we're going to settle with you ourselves, without God's help. Out with you!"

Lapshinov put his three-cornered cap on his head, took his stuttering, half-witted son by the hand, and left the hut. The crowd rushed after him. In the yard the old man spread the edge of his fur jacket out over the snow, and fell to his knees. He signed the cross before his furrowed forehead and bowed down to the ground in all four directions.

"Get on! Get on!" Razmiotnov ordered. But the crowd began quietly to boo, and shouts were heard:

"Let him say good-bye to his own farm at any rate!"

"Don't be a fool, Andrei! A man with one foot in the grave, and you—"

"After the life he's lived he ought to crawl in with both feet," Kondrat shouted. He was answered by old Gladilin, the church-warden:

"Currying favour with the government? Men like you ought to be whipped."

"You old fox, I'll give you such a blow that you'll forget your way home," Kondrat replied.

Lapshinov bowed, crossed himself, and, appealing to the easily affected women's hearts, said stentoriously, so that all could hear:

"Good-bye, true believers! Good-bye, dear kindred! May God give you health—to enjoy my property. I lived, I worked honestly, I—"

"Bought stolen goods," Diemka prompted him from the porch.

"In the sweat of my brow I earned my bread—"

"Ruined other men, took interest, and even stole! Go on, confess! You old lecher, you ought to be taken by the throat and your head knocked against the ground."

"My daily bread, I say, and now in my old age . . ."

The women began to snivel and drew the ends of their kerchiefs up to their eyes. Razmiotnov was about to raise Lapshinov and push him out of the yard and had got as far as: "Don't you try to work up an agitation here, you—" when there was a sudden tumult on the porch, where Diemka had been leaning against the balustrade. Lapshinov's wife came running out of the kitchen; in one hand she had a basket containing a

nest of goose eggs, in the other was a goose lying quiet and
blinded by the snow and sun. Diemka had no difficulty in taking
the basket from her, but the old woman clung to the goose with
both hands.

"Let go, you wretch! Let go!" she shouted.

"The goose belongs to the collective farm now," Diemka
roared, seizing the bird by its outstretched neck.

The woman hung on to its legs. They each pulled in the
opposite direction and furiously dragged each other about the
porch.

"Give it back, squint-eye!" she screamed.

"I won't."

"Let go, I say!"

"It's a collective farm goose," Diemka pantingly shouted.
"It'll give us goslings in the spring. Get away, old woman, or I'll
kick you in the ribs. You've eaten your fill of goose. . . ."

Dribbling with spittle, her feet firmly planted against the step,
the dishevelled woman pulled the bird towards her. The goose
had at first given voice to a stupid cry, but now it was silent, and
evidently Diemka was choking it. But it flapped its wings madly,
and white down and feathers whirled like snowflakes about the
porch. It seemed that in another minute Diemka must be victorious and tear the half-dead goose out of the woman's knotted
hands. But at that moment the bird's feeble neck quietly cracked
at the joints and came apart from the body. The woman's skirt
flew over her head, and she tumbled thunderously down from the
porch, her body bumping heavily on each step. Groaning with
surprise, Diemka, holding only the goose's head in his hands, fell
into the basket on the floor just behind him and crushed the half-
hatched eggs. A tremendous outburst of laughter shook the icicles
from the roof. Lapshinov rose from his knees, pulled on his cap,
furiously tugged his dribbling, impassive idiot son by the arm,
and dragged him out of the yard almost at a gallop. Black with
anger and pain, his wife scrambled to her feet. After dusting her
skirt she stretched out her hand to pick up the beheaded goose,
which was still writhing by the steps. But a tawny Borzoi hound
hanging around the porch steps saw the blood spurting out of the
goose's neck and, its hair on end, made one sudden spring, seized

the bird from under the woman's nose, and dragged it around the yard to the whistling and hallooing of the lads.

It all ended in a carefree, jolly manner:

Throwing the goose's head, with its eternally astonished orange eyes still staring out on the world, after the woman, Diemka went into the hut. And for a long time the sound of voices, of laughter, and excitement hung about the yard and the street corner, frightening the sparrows out of the dry brushwood.

Great fun, isn't it? And Sholokhov himself is amused.

The kulaks were then deported to labor camps far in the northern regions. Some even survived and were still alive by the 20th Party Congress. It did happen sometimes.

The Germans deported Jews to camps in the same way. That was fun, too. There were even a few survivors. For the Germans it was race; for the Communists it was class. In the words of Davidov, who had been sent by the Party: "I was sent to you by our own Communist Party and by the working-class to help you organize a kolkhoz and crush the kulak as the bloodsucker who preys on us all."

And so they crushed the "bloodsuckers." They crushed them so thoroughly that even one of the active Communists, Andrei Razmiotnov, began to object:

"I'm not going on."

"What d'you mean? 'Not going on'?" Nagulnov pushed the abacus to one side.

"I'm not going to do any more of this breaking up the kulaks. Well, what are you staring at? Do you want to send yourself into a fit?"

"Are you drunk?" Davidov asked, looking anxiously and attentively at Andrei's face, which was expressive of angry determination. "What's the matter with you? What d'you mean by you're 'not going on'?"

His calm tenor voice infuriated Andrei, and, stuttering with his agitation, he shouted:

"I've not been trained! I've not been trained to fight against children! At the front it was another matter. There you could cut down who you liked with your sword or what you liked. . . . And you can all go to the devil! I'm not going on!" His voice rose higher and higher, like the note of a tautened violin string, and seemed about to snap. But, taking a hoarse breath, he unexpectedly lowered his tone to a whisper:

"Do you call it right? What am I? An executioner? Or is my heart made of stone? I had enough in the war. . . ." And he again began to shout: "Gayev's got eleven children. How they howled when we arrived! You'd have clutched your head. It made my hair stand on end. We began to drive them out of the kitchen. . . . I screwed up my eyes, stopped my ears, and ran into the yard. The women were all in a dead fright and pouring water over the daughter-in-law. . . . The children—Oh, by God, you—"

"Cry! It'll ease you!" Nagulnov counselled him, pressing the twitching muscle in his cheek until it swelled, his inflamed eyes staring fixedly at Andrei.

"And I shall cry! My own little lad maybe—" Andrei broke off, bared his teeth, and abruptly turned his back on the table.

There was a silence.

Davidov slowly rose from the table. And just as slowly was his unbound cheek flooded with a deathly blue, and his ear went white. He went up to Andrei, took him by the shoulder, and gently turned him round. Breathing heavily, not removing his eyes from Andrei's face, he began to speak:

"You're sorry for them. . . . You feel pity for them. And have they had pity on us? Have our enemies ever wept over the tears of our children? Did they ever weep over the orphans of those they killed? Well? After a strike at his factory my father was discharged and sent to Siberia. My mother was left with four children. I was the oldest, and I was nine. We had nothing to eat, and so my mother went—you look at me!—she went on the streets so we shouldn't die of starvation. She brought her guests into our little room—we were living in a cellar. We had only one bed left. And we children slept on the floor behind a curtain. . . . And I was nine years old. . . . Drunken men came home with her. And I had to put my hands over my little sisters' mouths to prevent them from crying. . . . Who wiped away our tears? Do you hear? In the morning I would take the accursed rouble—" Davidov raised his leathery palm to the level of Andrei's face and tormentedly ground his teeth—"the rouble my mother had earned, and go to get bread. . . ." Suddenly he swept his leaden-hued fist down on the table and shouted: "How can you pity them?"

And again there was a silence. Nagulnov dug his nails into the table-top and clung to it like a kite to its prey. Andrei said nothing. Panting violently, Davidov paced up and down the room for a minute, then embraced Andrei around the shoulders and sat down with him on a bench. In a breaking voice he said:

"You've lost your senses! You come and start bellowing: 'I won't work . . . children . . . pity. . . .' Well, that slanderous attack of yours just now, do you take it back? Let's talk it over. You think it's a pity we're clearing out the kulak families? Think again! We're clearing them out *so they shan't prevent our organizing a life without any of those* . . . so it shan't happen again in the future. You're the Soviet government in Gremyachy, and yet I've got to make propaganda for you!" He smiled forcedly. "We'll send the kulaks to the devil, *we'll send them to Solovky in the White Sea. They won't die, will they? If they work we'll feed them.* And when we've built the new life, their children will no longer be kulak children. The working class will re-educate them." He pulled a pack of cigarettes out of his pocket, but for a long time his trembling fingers could not grip one.

While Davidov was speaking, Nagulnov's face had broken into a deathly sweat. Andrei sat watching him, not taking his eyes off him for a moment. Now, to Davidov's surprise, he swiftly rose to his feet, and at the same moment Nagulnov jumped up as though tossed into the air by a springboard.

"Snake!" he gasped in a penetrating whisper, clenching his fists. "How are you serving the revolution? Having pity on them? Yes. . . . You could line up thousands of old men, women, and children and tell me they'd got to be crushed into the dust for the sake of the revolution, and I'd shoot them all down with a machine-gun." Suddenly he screamed savagely, a frenzy glittered in his great, dilated pupils, and foam seethed at the corners of his lips.

After the dispossession of the kulaks, the villagers gathered and voted: "Out of the two hundred and seventeen heads of households present, only sixty-seven raised their hands "in favor of joining the kolkhoz. And that after the peasants had seen what would happen to them if the Poor Peasants' Committee declared them to be an "anti-Soviet element." The worker-agitator, Davidov, "could not understand the stubborn reluctance of the majority of middle peasants to join the collective farm despite the tremendous advantages of collective agriculture." But the other active Communist, Razmiotnov, had said: "We'll show them! They'll all come into the farm!"

And they were shown. During the village meeting, Nikolai Lushnia, a Cossack just this side of poverty, asks to be allowed to speak:

"But no arguments! The question's quite clear," Nagulnov warned him.

"How'd you make that out? Maybe I do want to object! Or am I not allowed to speak against your opinion? I say this: the collective farm's a voluntary matter. If you want to you join, and if you want to you watch it from outside. And we want to look on from outside."

"Who are 'we'?" Davidov asked.

"Those who grow the grain, I mean."

"You speak for yourself, Daddy. Each has got a free tongue and will speak for himself."

"And I can for myself. It's for myself I'm speaking. I want to see what sort of life there'll be in the collective farm. If it's good, I'll sign up; and if not, why should I join it. It's a stupid fish that swims into the net . . ."

"That's true!"

Nothing seems more natural than such a wish. But to allow freedom of choice in the matter of joining a kolkhoz would mean saying goodbye to collectivization and, in the long run, to totalitarian government. Therefore, to all their arguments the peasants receive one answer: "You're speaking like an enemy!" "Counter-revolutionary!"

Then the inexplicable occurs: "I'll tell you how it is; now almost the whole village has joined the collective farm. They keep coming in." As for any who refuse to come in, the government has a new weapon. A decree is issued stipulating that all grain must be placed in communal granaries, presumably to safeguard it. This is supposed to be voluntary, so it naturally calls for propaganda. Finally, everyone brings in his grain. Consider this interesting conversation:

"Sit down, Gregor Matveich!"

"Thanks for the invitation." Bannik sat down, planting his legs wide apart.

"Why haven't you brought in your seed grain, Gregor Matveich?"

"What have I got to bring it in for?"

"That was the decision of the general meeting. Both collective and individual farmers have got to bring in seed grain. Have you got any?"

"Of course I have."

Nagulnov glanced at the list; against Bannik's name, in the column "proposed area for spring 1930 sowing," was the figure fifteen.

"So you intended to sow fifteen acres with wheat this spring?" he asked.

"That's right."

"That means you've got forty-two poods of seed grain?"

"I've got it in full, sifted and cleaned grain as good as gold."

"Well, you're a hero!" Nagulnov praised him, sighing with relief. "Bring it to the communal granary tomorrow. You can leave it in your own sacks. We'll accept it from individual farmers in their own sacks if they don't want the grain mixed. Bring it in and have it weighed by the foreman. He'll seal up your sacks, hand you a receipt, and in the spring you'll get back the whole of your grain. But there are lots who complain that they haven't kept their grain, they've eaten it. It'll be kept safer in the granary."

"You can give up that idea, Comrade Nagulnov!" Bannik smiled jauntily and stroked his fair whiskers. "That game doesn't come off. I won't give you my grain."

"Why not, if I may ask?"

"Because it will be safer with me. If I give it to you, in the spring I shan't even get back the empty sacks. We've grown wiser now, you don't get round us that way."

Nagulnov raised his eyebrows and his face paled a little. "How dare you distrust the Soviet government!" he demanded. "So you don't believe what I say?"

"That's right. I don't believe it. We've heard that sort of yarn before."

"Who's told you yarns? And what about?" Nagulnov turned more noticeably pale, and slowly rose to his feet.

But as though he had not noticed anything, Bannik continued to smile quietly, revealing his few, firm teeth. Only his voice quivered with a note of grievance and burning anger as he said:

"You'll collect the grain, and then you'll load it into trains and send it abroad. You'll buy automobiles, so that Party men can ride around with their bobbed-haired women. We know what you want our grain for. We've lived to see equality, all right!"

"Have you gone mad, you devil? What are you babbling?"

"You'll go mad all right if they take you by the throat! A hundred and sixty poods I brought in for the grain collection.

And now you want our last seed grain . . . so that my children
. . . may starve . . ."

"Hold your tongue! You're lying, you reptile!" Nagulnov
thundered his fists on the table.

. . . . .

"What's that? . . . Whose words are these? What are you
saying to me, you counter-revolutionary? Laughing at socialism,
you reptile?" . . .

"I'll go at once and give the grain to the pigs! Better they
should have it than you, you parasites!"

"To the pigs? Seed grain?" In two bounds Nagulnov reached
the door, pulled his pistol from his pocket, and struck Bannik on
the temple with the butt.

The hero of this clash, the village activist Nagulnov, for
whom Sholokhov feels great sympathy ("dear to my heart"),
says later:

"You say he brought in the grain? Well, it worked, then! Forty-
two poods of seed grain: that's not to be sneezed at. If every
counter-revolutionary was to hand over forty-two poods after one
blow with a pistol, I'd spend all my life going around hitting
them. After what he said, he deserved more than he got! He
ought to be glad I didn't tear his legs from his arse!"

Almost all the villagers were forced into the kolkhoz,
which was named "after our dear Comrade Stalin." What
used to be Gremyachy Log was thus turned into the Stalin
kolkhoz. All the villagers, both those who had been dispossessed and those who had not, began to grind their
teeth:

"Things are so bad that if there was any organization to join I'd
get on my horse and begin to let the Communists' blood flow."

"These are hard times, hard times," Yakov Lukich assented.
"But if that was all, we'd still have to thank God . . ."

"War? God grant it! Smile on it, St. George the victorious!

This very moment if you like! As it is said in the writings of the apostle . . ."

"We'd go out with staves, as the Vioshenka men did in 1919."

"I'd disembowel them alive . . ."

Atamanchukov, who had been wounded in the throat during the civil war and whose voice in consequence was inarticulate and thin, like the sound of a shepherd's pipe, remarked:

"The people have become very devils. They'd bite with their teeth."

And there was cause for teeth-grinding. There was no one to whom one could turn for protection. Timofei, the son of the dispossessed Frol, told upon his return from the regional town "of his harsh reception by the Public Prosecutor, who, instead of considering their complaint, had wanted to arrest him and send him back to the district."

As the dispossessed Titok puts it: "I won myself a comfortable life, I defended the just government . . ." And so the villages and *stanitsas* grew troubled. An uprising was imminent. But the Cossacks were loath to lead it; they remembered the bloody reprisals after every anti-Bolshevik attempt since 1918. Even the most zealous enemies of the Soviet government were uncertain. Ostrovnov, the middle farmer, thinks:

Perhaps . . . I ought to have put up with life in the collective farm for a year or two. Maybe the government will break up the farms within a year, when they see how badly things are going with them. And then I'd begin to live like a man again.

For years the farmers put up with the taxes, the continual deceit, Soviet legitimized lawlessness. The one thing they could not stomach was the attempt to take away what little freedom they had, which allowed them to remain independent farmers, not hired kolkhoz laborers. The uprising would certainly have erupted if Stalin had not made some concessions in his article "Dizzy with Their Success." The farmers were taken in. Here is what the Cossacks, already organized for rebellion, say to one of their leaders, the ex-officer Polovtsev, after reading Stalin's article:

"I said a newspaper's come from Moscow and in it is printed a letter from the chairman of all the Party . . . that is, the secretary of all the Party, Comrade Stalin. Here is the paper, dated the 4th of this month. . . . We read it aloud among ourselves a little before you arrived and—it works out that this paper's separated us from you. It's clear now that we—the peasants, that is—have got another road to take in life.

. . . . .

". . . owing to this article in *Pravda* we've decided not to revolt. Your road and ours have completely separated now. Our village authorities have been stupid; they've driven some of us into the collective farm, they've unfairly treated many middling peasants as kulaks, and our government didn't understand that you can only frighten girls, but you can't treat all the people like that. The chairman of our Soviet tried to muzzle us so much that we weren't allowed to say a word against him at a meeting. They tightened up the girths so well that we couldn't breathe; but a good master loosens the girths round his horse when going over sand or along a heavy road and tries to make it easier for her. Well, we did think, of course, that the order had come from the central authorities to squeeze the fat out of us, and we understood that this propaganda had been started by the Central Committee of the Communists, and we said the windmill sails don't turn without wind. And so, you see, that's why we decided to rise and join your Alliance. But now it comes out that Stalin's going to remove from their positions all those local Communists who drove the people forcibly into the collective farms and closed down the churches for no reason whatever without being asked. And it appears the peasant's going to have an easier time; they've loosened his saddle-girths. If you want to, you can join the collective farm, but if you want to, you can remain an individual peasant. And so that's how we've decided.

. . . . .

"Once the master himself has come to our defence, why should we crawl off to others? They took my vote away from me for no reason whatever and wanted to exile me. But I've got a son in the Red Army, and so I shall get back my right to vote. We're not against the Soviet government, but against our own village disorders. But you wanted to turn us against the government. No, that won't do!"

So "the master himself came to their defense." Polovtsev tried to rouse the people, but in vain:

"The Cossacks have refused to revolt in Tubyanskoye and in my own district too. Stalin has won them over with his article. There's the man I'd like to lay my hands on now. I'd—" There was a gurgling sound in Polovtsev's throat, the muscles worked beneath his cheekbones, and the fingers of his sinewy hands crooked and pressed into the palms until the joints stood out. Sighing deeply and hoarsely, he slowly extended his fingers and smiled on one side of his mouth. "What a people! Scum! Fools, bearing God's curse! They don't realize that this article is a shameful fraud, a manoeuvre. And they believe it like children. Oh, damn them! They're the scum of the earth! For the sake of high politics the fools are played like fish on a hook, the reins are slackened so they shan't be choked to death, and they take it all in good faith. Well, all right! They'll understand and be sorry, but then it will be too late."

The collective farms began to disintegrate, but the government continued to deceive the people. The mechanism of this deception is exposed in the novel. While permitting the peasants to leave the kolkhozy, the authorities give orders that they shall have no cattle or land, thus forcing them to choose between starvation or a "voluntary" return to the collective farms. Sholokhov elaborates upon this:

When Davidov received the notices, he attempted to argue with them, advised them to think it over, to wait a little. But they stood to their guns and at last he waved his hand:

"All right, citizens, but remember that when you ask to be taken back into the collective farm we shall think twice whether to accept you or not."

"We're not likely to ask to be taken back. We hope to manage to live without the collective farm again. You see, Davidov, we managed somehow to live without it before, we didn't swell with hunger, we were masters of our own goods, strangers didn't show us how to plough, how to sow, we were never under slave-drivers, and we think we shall live without the collective farm and not regret it." So Ivan Batalshchikov answered for them all, smiling into his twisted chestnut whiskers.

"And we shall manage to get on without you somehow. We shan't cry and get thin over it. Fact! It's easier for the horse when the woman's off the cart." Davidov retorted.

"And it's better we should part friends. Glass against glass, and separate with no offense done. May we collect our cattle from the brigade?"

"No. We shall raise that question in the management committee. Wait until tomorrow."

"We haven't got time to wait. You in the collective farm can start sowing after Whitsun, maybe, but we must go out to the fields. We'll wait till tomorrow, but if you keep our cattle a day longer, we shall take them ourselves."

There was a direct threat in the tone of Batalshchikov's voice and Davidov flushed a little with anger as he replied:

"I shall see how you'll manage to take anything from the collective farm stables without the management knowing! In the first place we shan't hand them over, and in the second, if you take them, you'll answer for it in court."

"For our own cattle?"

"At the moment they're collective farm cattle."

The novel makes clear that this was not the work of the local government representatives. This is what the district representative tells the kolkhoz chairman:

Bieglikh, a firm and resolute man, only smiled. "Then you go at them in your turn," he replied. "Of course by rights we ought to return their property, but the Regional Committee takes the attitude that it is to be given back only in exceptional cases, observing the class principle."

"Which is?"

"Well, you ought to understand that without any 'which is.' Give them back to the poor, but promise the middling peasants they'll have theirs in the autumn. Now is it clear?"

"But won't the same thing happen as with hundred per cent collectivization, Bieglikh? The District Committee took the attitude that we were to drive for a hundred per cent at all costs and as soon as possible. And we went dizzy. If we don't give the middling peasants their cattle back, that means that in fact we're putting pressure on them, doesn't it? What will they plough and sow with?"

"It's not for you to worry over that. Your concern is not with the individual peasant, but with your collective farm. What are you going to work with if you hand back the cattle? And besides, it's not our proposal, but the Regional Committee's. *And as soldiers of the revolution we have to submit to it without reservation.* How do you think you're going to fulfil the plan if fifty per cent of your cattle goes back to the individual peasants? No talks and no discussions! Hold on to the cattle tooth and nail! If you don't fulfil the sowing plan you'll lose your head!"

As he was seating himself in his britzka he casually remarked:

"Altogether, things are difficult. We've got to pay for the distortions, brother, and someone will have to be made a scapegoat. That's the system."

While the activist Makar Nagulnov, who had been punished for "deviations," is quite right when he says:

"But I consider that the Regional Committee is also deviating."

"How, for instance?"

"Like this: why didn't they issue orders that the collective farm members who resigned were to be handed back their cattle? Isn't that compulsory collectivization? Of course it is! Here you've got people leaving the collective farm and they're to have neither cattle nor implements. It's clear that they've got nothing to get a living with, nowhere to go; and they'll be crawling back to the collective farm. They'll squeak, but they'll crawl back."

"But the cattle and the implements have gone into the farm's indivisible fund."

"Don't play the fool, Comrade Davidov! All the lands close to the village have been taken by the collective farm, so our land will be a good way off, won't it? You won't give us our cattle back, so we've got to sow with our own hands or with cows, and then will you give us distant land? That's the sort of just government we've got!"

Davidov argued, and explained that he could not allot them land just wherever they wanted it, for he could not break up the stretch of collective farm land or cut wedges out of it and so violate the arrangements made in the autumn. The former members went out grumbling, but in a few minutes another crowd had poured in, shouting as they crossed the threshold:

"Give us land! What do you call this? What right have you got to hold back our land? That means you're not going to let us sow! And what did Comrade Stalin write about us? We shall write and tell him you're not only refusing to give us back our cattle, but the land, too. You're robbing us of all right to exist. And he won't praise you for this business!"

"Yakov Lukich, allot them land beyond the Rachy pond tomorrow morning," Davidov ordered.

"Is that virgin land?" they roared at him.

"It's fallow. How do you call it virgin land? It's been ploughed, only it was a long time ago, some fifteen years back," Yakov Lukich explained.

And at once a boiling, stormy shout arose:

"We don't want tough land!"

The affair ends with a minor rebellion, with the beating up of the "activists," and finally, of course, with the arrest and deportation of the "inciters." That the question of collectivization was a matter of politically enslaving the

Russian village and had nothing to do with improving the economy is shown very clearly in Sholokhov's novel. When the spring sowing begins, the villagers are herded to a community meeting and the kolkhoz chairman announces:

"I raise the question sharply: those who are for the Soviet government will go out to the fields tomorrow; those who're against, they can chew sunflower seeds! But those who don't go out to the fields tomorrow—we, the collective farm, will take their land from them and sow it ourselves."

It is not sowing that is at issue here. Sholokhov himself showed earlier in the novel that the individual farmowners were all excellent farmers and managers who worked day and night. They need no propaganda worker's orders; they know themselves when and how to sow. The orders are specifically addressed to the individual farmers. That they *obey* the order is what is at issue, and the lawlessness of the largest slaveholding country in the history of mankind permits the chairman of each kolkhoz to exercise unlimited power over the life and death of the villagers. Where can they turn for protection when the law upholds only the rights of the "active element"?

Ostrovnov asks Polovtsev, the White officer:

"You're a well-read man, you've studied books, tell me what's going to happen now. Where shall we get to with these collective farms?"

"To Communism, brother! To the true and genuine! I've read Karl Marx and the famous *Communist Manifesto*. D'you know what the end of the collective farm business will be? It will start with the collective farm, but it will go on to the commune, to the complete abolition of property. Not only your oxen, but your children, will be taken away from you to be brought up by the State. Everything will be in common: children, wives, cups and spoons. You'd like to eat vermicelli and goose giblets, but they'll feed you on sour beer. *You'll be a serf tied to the land.*"

"But supposing I don't want to be?"

"They won't even ask you."

. . . . .

"You served in my company, Lukich . . . Do you remember how, in Yekaterinodar, I think it was, when we were retreating, I had a talk with the Cossacks about the Soviet government? Even then I warned them, you remember? 'You're bitterly mistaken, my boys!' I said. 'The Communists will squeeze you, will twist you into a ram's horn. You must wake up, or it'll be too late!' Wasn't I right?"

Polovtsev certainly was right and those who believed Stalin's article and were herded into the kolkhozy a year later must often have recalled the words of the man whose leadership they rejected. Of course, it didn't come to "communal wives" and never will, but all the rest of Polovtsev's prophecy came true, all of it. Serfs tied to the land. Collective farmers.

Yes, serfs and their overlord, the chairman. Sholokhov depicts the system of kolkhoz government established by Stalin which has existed unchanged to this day. How is the kolkhoz chairman nominated?

. . . The District Party Committee, in agreement with the district co-operative, proposed the committee's representative, Comrade Davidov, as chairman of the collective farm management committee.

The chairman of the neighboring kolkhoz, The Red Sunbeam, is also one of 25,000 mobilized workers sent out by the Party. One flatterer says to the chairman of the Stalin kolkhoz: "The people have entrusted you with the management of our kolkhoz." In Leninist terms, the Party is indeed the people—their personification. But how do the people themselves feel about it? Ustin, a collective farmer, begins an argument with chairman Davidov:

"Don't shout, Chairman; you won't frighten me with your shouting and thundering. I've served in the artillery. Well, supposing we agree you're working for the general good. But in that case why strain the people's sinews by making them work day and night? That's where the plan comes in. You're trying to earn the praise of the district authorities, and the district are doing the same with the region; but we have to pay for it all. D'you think the people don't see through it? They see, all right, but how can they get away from you officials? Take you, for instance, and others like you. We can't remove you from your positions can we? No! And so you do just anything that comes into your head. But Moscow's a long way off; Moscow doesn't know what games you get up to here. . . ."

. . . . .

"Ustin Mikhailovich, when I was elected Chairman did you vote for me?"

"No, I didn't. Why should I have voted for you? You were brought to us like a cat in a sack. . . ."

"I came of my own choice. . . ."

"That makes no difference, you came like a cat in a sack. So why should I have voted for you, when I hadn't any idea what you were like?"

"But are you against me now?"

"What else could I be? Of course I am."

"Then raise the question of removing me at the next collective-farm meeting. As the meeting decides, so let it be. Only, you must give sound arguments for your proposal, otherwise you'll regret it."

"I shan't speak. You needn't be afraid, there's plenty of time for that. But while you are our chairman, tell us what you've done with our rest days."

But the matter will never come before the general meeting. Davidov immediately brands the collective farmer who has opposed him as a "counter-revolutionary":

"No, I'm not going to strike you, Ustin. You needn't hope for that, you White! But if you'd come my way ten years back things would have been different. Then I'd have sent you sick for ever, you counter-revolutionary!"

. . . .

"He's not a fool, he's an open enemy of our collective farm. We've had to fight men like him and we'll go on fighting them without mercy."

This is an old method of Lenin's: the liquidation of those whose opinions differ from his.

The people of course realize the situation and cry out during the kolkhoz rebellion:

"We've got our own government now!"
"A people's government!"
"Boo him, boys!"

. . . .

"Stop threatening us with your weapon, Comrade Nagulnov, or it will be the worse for you! Who are you going against? Against the whole village!"

"Don't come any closer! Not a step farther! Don't call me comrade! Once you've started stealing the State grain you're a counter-revolutionary. I won't let you tread the Soviet government underfoot!"

The bread which the collective farmers had brought in "for safekeeping" the day before has already become the state's.

The kolkhoz chairman, the secretary of the party nucleus, and a few Party activists are literally set as prison guards over a mass of collective farmers deprived of all rights. They have quite a job to do. They have to manage everything, drive the people on, crush the "counter-revolutionaries," report to the District . . . "It's going to be a beautiful life!" says the fanatic Nagulnov about the kolkhoz. "The chickens ought to be collectivized as well!" Sholokhov depicts fanatics like this with great literary power. It would be ridiculous to accuse them of greed, laziness, or immorality. No, in this sense they are clean men, but they are, nevertheless, worse than the plague. They bring death to all that's living. Like Makas Nagulnov, the most fanatic of all, they see the glimmer of "world revolution" somewhere in the distance. Nagulnov says:

"At once I'm back in the days of the civil war, back in the trenches, comrade. We must dig ourselves into the ground but we must draw everybody into the collective farm. Always a step nearer to the world revolution."

When the peasants begin to slaughter their cattle before joining the collective farm, Nagulnov exclaims:

"Siemion! I'm sorry for you. What have you got such a lazy brain for?" Then he almost shouted: "Can't you see we're done for if we can't manage the sowing? Don't you realize that? We simply must shoot two or three of the reptiles for this business. We must shoot the kulaks. It's their work! We must ask the higher authorities for permission."

"You fool!"

"There you are again with your 'fool'!" Nagulnov gloomily drooped his head. But he threw it up again at once, like a horse feeling the rider's knees, and shouted: "They're all slaughtering! We've come to a time of position warfare, as it was in the civil war. The enemy's rising all around us; and you? It's such as you who'll ruin the chances of the world revolution. It'll never come through you, you slow-wits! All around us the bourgeoisie are torturing the working people, are blowing up the Red Chinese in smoke, are beating up the blacks, and here you are being tender to the enemies! Shame on you! It's a terrible disgrace! My blood runs cold as I think of our own blood brothers that the bourgeoisie abroad are torturing! I can't read the papers because of it. All my inside turns over when I look at them. And you—what do you care about our blood brothers that our enemies are leaving to rot in prisons? You've got no pity for them!"

And then: "He thinks he's killing a bullock, but in reality he's stabbing the world revolution in the back."

These were the kind of people who shot "the enemies of the people" in the Lubyanka cellars and became guards in concentration camps.

"Wherever the Party sends a man, that's a man's job. Supposing, for instance, they say to me: 'Nagulnov, go and chop off some counter-revolutionary's head,' then I'll go with pleasure. Supposing they say: 'Go and hoe the potato plants.' I shan't like it, but I'll go. If they tell me to go and help the milkmaids milk the cows I shall grind my teeth, but all the same I'll go. The unfortunate animal may try to get away from me, but I'll milk her to the best of my ability. Damn her!"

And all this to produce an "earthly paradise," an anthill where each will be exactly like his neighbor:

"Wait till we break down all the frontiers, and I shall be the first to shout: 'Marry yourselves off to the women of foreign blood!' Everybody will get mixed up and there won't be the scandal of one man having a white body, another having a yellow, a third having a black, and the whites reproaching the others with the colour of their skin and regarding them as lower than themselves. Everybody will have pleasantly swarthy faces, and all alike. I've often thought about it at night . . ."

How are such fanatics made? Here is the portrait of Kondrat Maidannikov, a middle peasant who enters the collective farm voluntarily, although he still longs for his own property:
property:

Kondrat had long since ceased to believe in God, and now he believed in the Communist Party, which was leading the toilers of all the world towards freedom, towards the sunlit future.

Formerly he had been occupied from dawn to dusk; in the morning he would feed the bullocks, cows, sheep, and horses and take them down to drink; at noon he would once more scrape up hay and straw out of the threshing-floor, afraid of losing a single stalk. And later he had to tidy up again for the night. Even during the night he would go out several times into the cattle-yard to see that all was well and to gather back into the mangers the hay trodden underfoot. His heart rejoiced in his farmer's anxieties. But now his yard was empty and dead. There was nothing to go out to attend to. The mangers stood empty, the wattle gates stood wide open, and not even a cock-crow was to be heard all through the long night. There was nothing by which to tell the time and the passing of the hours of darkness.

What is most terrible is that he is convinced of the necessity of destroying in his heart the love for his own farm, the desire for a free, independent existence. The secretary of the Party nucleus tells him:

"Yes, you're right there. Wait a little then, don't join yet. We'll fight relentlessly against all shortcomings in the collective farm; all the collars will be fitted to the right horses. But if you see your old bullocks in your sleep, then you can't be in the Party. You must come into the Party without any suffering over property. You have to come into the Party when you're clean all through and are driven by one thought of achieving the world revolution. My father was comfortably off, and he got me used to the farm from my childhood. But I wasn't in the least attached to it, the farm meant nothing to me whatever. I gave up a well-fed life and four yoke of oxen to be a poor labourer. So don't you join until you've got clean rid of that scab of property.

How right Orwell was in his brilliant novel, *1984!* The Communists of *Seeds of Tomorrow* may well illustrate Orwell's every premise. The fanatical urge for *power* which is the end, not the means, of their life, the vision of the "world-wide anthill," "the demi-god with a mustache," blind obedience to the Party, sacrifice of everything that is alive and full of joy, and, in return for all that, limitless power over all human beings. Power, only power—which is why those who are outside the Party must become slaves.

Of course, Lenin's and Stalin's Soviet Union never had and has nothing in common with socialism. The socialization of the "capitalists'" property was aimed directly at the abolition of power over the exploited proletariat mass. But, by a strange process, this power of the minority over the majority not only failed to diminish but has grown enormously. It appears that private property is the means to the attainment not only of power but also of liberty.

The enslavement of the masses under capitalism was due to the fact that the major part of society did not own property, and property gives freedom. The solution seems to lie in a general capitalization rather than in a general socialization. However, this is a debatable point since private and public property are both only forms of something more significant: slavery and liberty. In his novel, Sholokhov makes plain that the socialization of the land came as a result of the Party apparatus' desire for power.

Just as in Orwell's book—and in the Roman Catholic Church too—fanatics here cannot get along with women, whom they consider the greatest evil in the world. This suggests an affinity among all churches, including the Communist one. The thoughts of the fanatic Nagulnov run as follows:

"I've given up Lukeria, for instance, and I know that I'm feeling grand. No one interferes with me, I'm like a sharp bayonet with the point directed into the struggle against the kulaks and the enemies of Communism."

. . . . .

". . . my woman, my wife I mean, is as necessary to me as a tail is to a sheep. I'm all whetted for the world revolution. I'm waiting for it, for the beloved. But my woman's only a gob and no more. She's just by the way. Yet you can't get on without her, you've got to cover your shame."

. . . . .

"In a word: in my bachelor state my hands and legs are free and my head's clear. But although I never drank vodka when I was living with her I was sort of drunk every day. My boy, so far as we revolutionaries are concerned women are pure opium for the people. I'd have that written into the Party constitution in capital letters, and I'd have every Party member, every true Communist and sympathizer read that great saying every night before going to bed and every morning three times on an empty stomach. And then you'd never have any devils getting into the mess our Comrade Davidov is in now. Why, when you stop to think, Andrei, just imagine how many good men have suffered from the woman's accursed seed! You couldn't count them all. How much waste they've been the cause of, how much drunkenness; how many Party reprimands have been given to good lads because of them; how many men are sitting in prison on their account! It gives you the shudders to think of it."

. . . . .

"And do you think it's impossible, then? Those who'd made fools of themselves and got married I'd let live with their wives, but I'd pass a decree forbidding the youngsters to get married. What sort of revolutionaries will they make if they get used to hanging on to women's skirts? A woman is to us what honey is to a greedy fly. We get stuck at once. I've seen it in my own case, and I know only too well! I'd sit down of an evening to read, to develop myself, and my wife would lie down to sleep. I'd read a little and then lie down too, and she'd turn her arse towards me. Then I'd feel insulted by her position, and I'd either begin to swear at her or I'd light a cigarette, fuming at her insolence, and unable to get off to sleep. So I wouldn't get enough sleep, and in the morning I'd have a heavy head and would make some political mistake. I've had some! And as for those who have children, they're completely lost to the party. In a jiffy they've learned how to look after their babies, got used to their milky smell, and then they're done for! They make bad fighters and hopeless workers."

The words of an active Communist's mother about the three most zealous Communists in the village confirm that this is not an exceptional case:

"I feel sorry for you whenever I see you. Here's my Andrei jogging along on his own, and Makar, and you too. Don't you all feel ashamed of yourselves? Strong bulls like you going about the village, and every one of you a hopeless failure with the women!

A question might be asked: Is not destructive thirst for power identical with the uniting force of love, only turned in a different direction? Just as the destructive force of an atom's nucleus is the same thing as the uniting force, which becomes catastrophic only after the nucleus is split. Twentieth-century totalitarianism is very like the split atom's chain reaction. It is interesting, in this connection, to point to Lenin's first unhappy love, Hitler's passionate and tragic love affair, and Stalin's love.

The blame for a never before equaled enslavement of the Russian people and, later, of other nations who submitted to a totalitarian regime is not negligible. Deception can only be practiced on one who allows himself to be deceived; one can only enslave a person if he submits to slavery. Thus, the slaveowner and the slave are two sides of the *same coin*.

This is also brought out in Sholokhov's novel. Those who do not become reconciled to Communist dictatorship lose their heads but not their souls. They remain free. It is significant that although Sholokhov was on the government's side, with his whole soul, he nevertheless involuntarily gave a truthful description of the "joyful hatred" expressed by the enemies of the Soviet government. Take the arrested kulak, Titok, for instance:

"A gun." Titok glanced sidelong at Nagulnov and threw his coat open. The roughly planed stock of a rifle with the barrel sawn off short looked like a white thigh-bone.

"Give it here!" Makar stretched out his hand. But Titok calmly pushed it away.

"Not me!" he said, and smiled, laying bare his black, tobacco-stained teeth beneath his drooping whiskers. He stared at Nagulnov with sharp, ferrety, yet merry eyes. "Not me! You'll take my property, and even my last rifle? A kulak's always got a gun, so they say in the newspapers. Without exception he has a gun. Maybe I shall get my daily bread with it, don't you think? The village correspondents may find me. . . ."

And here is how Sholokhov describes the arrest of Polovtsev, the Cossack officer:

Outside was another civilian, with hair greying at the temples. He was not so irreproachably polite and self-controlled as his younger comrade. When he saw Polovtsiev he stepped forward, blinking rapidly and turning pale with hate, and said: "You reptile! You'd crawled a long way. . . . So you thought you could hide away from us here, in this warren? You wait: I'll talk to you in Rostov. You'll do a dance or two for me before you die."

"Oh, how terrible! How you frighten me! I'm trembling all over like an aspen, I'm trembling with terror!" Polovtsiev said ironically, stopping to light a cheap cigarette. But from under his brows he looked up at the Cheka-man with sneering, hateful eyes."

. . . . .

"What do you think you can frighten me with? You're too naïve! With tortures? That won't come off: I'm ready for anything and can stand anything."

The collectivization all but stamped out the most talented and capable segment of the population. In its wake came an everlasting Soviet tune about the necessity for "remoulding the character" of the kolkhoz population and teaching them how to work. The government tried to cajole and to threaten the collective farmers to work as they used to work on their own. But before the collectivization the peasant was a free landowner, and although he had hard times, he knew that his life, his standard of living, depended on and would be determined by his own efforts. The farmer in a kolkhoz is worse off than a laborer in a factory. His day's pay is ridiculously low. The local authorities have unlimited arbitrary power. To earn his living, a collective farmer has to perform double labor: on the kolkhoz fields and on his own private plot. Most collective farmers, therefore, dream of moving to the city and working in industrial plants. But this is very difficult, for the government does not grant passports to collective farmers. There is no doubt that for thirty-five years now collective farmers have been sabotaging work in the kolkhoz fields. At the same time their miniature private plots have yielded excellent harvests of vegetables and other produce.

The "remoulding of characters" is still not a success. That is the most gratifying circumstance in Russia today. It all began, of course, in 1930, with the events depicted in *Seeds of Tomorrow:*

In the old days, when we were individual farmers, you were a hard taskmaster, you were like a wolf. You never let go; you took on any job in order to get hold of an extra kopek wherever you could. But now you're working any old how, just to throw dust in our eyes.

Already an effort was being made to remould people's characters then.

"You're being stupid, Davidov! See them get the work on to its feet and then come back. It's no miracle to be able to plough, brother! A good commander oughtn't to be in the line, but ought to command intelligently; that's what I tell you!"

"Drop your examples, please. I've got to teach them how to work, and I will teach them! Fact! That's directing properly!"

But it met with no success:

"When will you learn to develop some initiative of your own? How long am I to go on helping you? Clear out!"

The farmers would be glad to leave the collective farms today and develop their own plots by their own initiative. But this is impossible and they can only work on their tiny private plots (from 0.25 to 0.50 hectares) during their odd hours of rest. Interesting to note, there no one teaches them correct working methods, and yet here is how these plots come out:

It's a pleasure to see how well cultivated is that little private plot which is the farmer's own property! And you will see no trace of ignorance or sluggishness; everything is carefully planned; at every step you will note not only an accurate, economical calculation but also the ability to adopt the necessary agricultural techniques, signs of genuine agrarian culture (*Novy Mir*, 1964).

In "The Torn Ruble," a story of kolkhoz life by Sergei Antonov published in 1964 in the magazine *Yunost*, the hero is a symbolic figure: a young man full of various crazy but interesting ideas which he tries—unsuccessfully, of course—to put to work on the kolkhoz-owned machines. He is subjected to the "moulding and taming" efforts of a "politically active" girl. The process works; the youth becomes quiet and obedient, but the girl realizes that what she has done is wrong and declares at a meeting:

"The forming and educating of an active fighter and builder of Communism is a long, hard job which not everybody can accomplish. It is much easier to press him into your own mediocre mould; that's what I did to him. Keeping him from falsehood, I shielded him from the truth. I can warrant that he has become very well behaved now; he will obey each and every one. Now if you sit him down he will sit just like that, if you place him in a standing position he will not budge from it. He's become calm— like a corpse."

Yet the thought does not occur, either to her or to the author, that "fighters and builders" cannot be formed artificially, that it is not a question of moulding but of liberation from all moulds, since a creative spark exists within every man and is inseparable from his urge to be free, so that the least violation of liberty kills art.

Long years of slavery have undoubtedly left terrible scars on the soul of the "Soviet man." One is reminded of a staggering book by Margaret Bubber-Neiman which contains the following scene from real life. Shortly before the end of the war the author, together with a dozen other women prisoners, was freed from a German labor camp. The women

We stood still, at a loss what to do in that shoving crowd. Nobody ordered us around any more, no siren forced us to rise, rush to roll-call or go to bed. After so many years of camp life, a sudden demand was sprung on us—that we decide for ourselves what to do. Not all of us were able to take this difficult step. As I learned afterwards, some of the women, unable to decide, returned to Ravensbrück. They fled from this complex freedom which demanded personal initiative.

What will become of "Soviet man"? Fortunately, social existence does not define a man completely. Society, the soil in which the seeds spring up, does not determine which plant shall stretch toward the sun. The seeds themselves do. In the Soviet Union the soil is unfavorable for any plant except thistles. Yet this does not mean that all the seeds are rotten.

Worst of all is the misunderstanding of what goes on in the "first country of Socialism." Recently I read the opinion of an American farmer who visited the U.S.S.R. He declared that "that country will become one of the wealthiest in the world as soon as the Russians *learn how to work.*"

Thirty-five years have passed since the events described in Sholokhov's novel. There ought to be great changes, it would seem. After all, Stalin is dead, Khrushchev has made his noisy exit, time and again the Party's Central Committee has adopted resolutions for reorganizing the kolkhozy and sovkhozy. And yet we find the following conversation, between the chairman of the Sunny Path kolkhoz and one of the collective farmers, in "The Torn Ruble."

A couple of days ago someone began spreading the rumor that they were going to take away the private plots and farm animals. Mitka grew uneasy, decided to sell his house and get rid of his plot. He consulted with his brothers. From early morning they sat calculating, counting and recounting on bits of paper, and arguing about what to do with grandmother.

"So you've decided to hang your bast [rope] shoes on the railroad signal, huh?" said Ivan Stepanovich, the head of the kolkhoz.

"I'll have to hang out my bast shoes; with you I didn't get the chance to earn enough brass for boots. I've sweated for a whole year, and still no money. It's enough to make you howl!"

"And all that time you have the kolkhoz choir singing: 'O gladness inconceivable!' " added the one who wore a tie.

"So it's rubles you're thirsting for?" asked Ivan Stepanovich, his anger rising. "Strengthen the kolkhoz and the rubles will flow in."

"How can you expect to strengthen the kolkhoz when you have a tendency to pay people with lectures instead of wages?" gloomily asked the hitherto silent oldest brother.

"What lectures?"

"I'll make it clear. I'm also from this collective farm. At first, when we were named 'Death to the Kulaks Kolkhoz,' life was bearable. You at least got some chow. But then when it was changed to 'Yezhov's Kolkhoz,' they began to train the kolkhoz farmers to work like dogs for nothing. We get the sowing done and as a reward they read us a lecture. We reap another lecture. But food they just don't give us. Well now, my dear kolkhoz boss, consider this: you might find a nitwit to do your work for nothing, but the earth simply will not go on producing grain without receiving anything in return. It also needs nourishment. It begs for manure. Fertilizer, that is."

"The law of conservation of energy," sternly added the one in the necktie.

In the same issue of the magazine a Party spokesman, A. M. Rumyantsev, in an article entitled "The Foreseeable Tomorrow," says such charming things as:

Half a century ago, tsarist autocracy was overthrown; the evil which it exuded for posterity and for the nation as a whole unfortunately seems purely abstract now to those born in the years of building socialism. Half a century ago a society was founded without capitalists, without economic reprisal or exploitation of man by man. The common people who had achieved all this gained enormous experience. They underwent spiritual growth. In the process of unprecedented, titanic labor they made, quite naturally, a few errors and miscalculations. That could not be avoided . . . But the people became aware of their mistakes, corrected them, and grew in wisdom and experience from year to year.

History bears witness to how easy it is to find numerous examples of criminal errors committed in the development of bourgeois society which either are never uncovered or come to the attention of the masses only after decades or even hundreds of years.

We the Soviet people cannot afford ourselves this "luxury." We keep to the truth; we are against falsehood. The inevitable result of overcoming mistakes and accumulating positive experience is the overall rise of the Soviet people's integrity . . .

Consider the essence and the consequences of those achievements of Soviet society, which seem simple on the surface; it has become commonplace that everyone has an opportunity to study or acquire a skill; it has even become compulsory to reach a certain level of education. Self-respect, based on the fact that the Soviet man is not alienated from the means of production and that he is not constantly at odds with some sort of "boss," is an integral part of each one of us . . . Such benefits as wealth, comfort, plenty are in our own hands. It is necessary to learn and keep on learning sensible and effective management.

You and I, we have something to lean on in solving these problems, the Communist Party. It is the avant-garde of the people, their brain trust . . .

This all-round free development of the individual is the goal of Communism. It is accomplished primarily through the power of the kolkhoz boss.

After this, can one help exclaiming, along with the hero of Nikolai Arzhak's story "This Is Moscow Speaking":

And what about the fat-faced masters of our destiny, our leaders and teachers, true sons of the people, receiving messages of congratulation from collective farmers of the Ryazan region, from metal workers in the Krivoi Rog region, from the Emperor of Ethiopia, from a teachers' congress, from the President of the United States, from attendants in public toilets. The best friends of Soviet gymnasts, writers, textile workers, color-blind persons, and madmen? What should be done with them? Should they be forgiven? What about 1937? What about the postwar insanity when the country was possessed of the devil, thrashed about in the throes of a fit, and became hysterical and began devouring itself. Do they think that once they have desecrated the grave of the Mustached One,* that's all that's required of them? No, no, no, they must be treated differently. Do you remember still how to do it? The fuse. Pull out the pin. Throw. Lie flat on the ground. Lie down! It's exploded. And now, a leap forward. As

* Stalin. The desecration of his grave is to be understood figuratively. The story was written before Stalin's body was removed from the Lenin Mausoleum.

you run, spray around you at belly level. A burst of machine-gun fire! . . . They're lying over there—cut to shreds and riddled with bullets. It's slippery. One's legs slip. Who's this? He's crawling along, dragging his guts along the plaster-strewn floor behind him. And who's this man, bedecked with medals, who accompanies the Chief on trips? Why is he so thin? Why is he wearing a padded coat? I saw him once before, crawling along a grade, spilling his blue and red stomach into the dust. And these people? I've seen them! Only then they had on belts with the inscription *"Gott mit uns"* on the buckles, caps with red stars. . . .

Regrettably, Mikhail Sholokhov can easily be numbered among "our leaders and teachers." A member for many years of the Central Committee of the Communist Party of the Soviet Union, Sholokhov during his lifetime paid Party-inspired homage to all the Party and government leaders who appeared and disappeared at the summit. This only goes to prove an old saying: "Great artists are often petty people," and that's too bad. Here is what Sholokhov wrote [in *Pravda*, after Stalin's death]:

Farewell, Father!

How suddenly and terribly we are orphaned! The Party has become orphaned, the Soviet people, the workers of the whole world.

Since the day of Lenin's death, humanity has not suffered such a terrible, immeasurably heavy loss. We have lost the father of all working people and a great grief has walked over the whole country on silent feet and imperiously invaded every home, every family.

During these days people weep in solitude, but they are not ashamed to weep in front of others. During these days the bright tears of children and women flow together with the hard masculine tears of those who passed through four years of war without having learned how to weep; who shed no tear on the battlefield; only ground their teeth. . . .

Pain and grief burn in our hearts! Let the sacred sorrow for the father, teacher, leader, and friend who has departed from us remain in them forever, but let our unfailing love for him dry the tears in our eyes! The most humane of men, he loved only those who were courageous, not the weak in spirit.

The words that were addressed to the people by the closest brothers-in-arms and friends of the great Stalin: "Dear comrades and friends!" are yet sounding on the airwaves, and already the answer of the multimillion Soviet nation is coming from everywhere like powerful waves of love and endless devotion: "We are with you always and everywhere, our own dear Central Committee of the Communist Party, our own dear Soviet government!"

When the leader falls on the battlefield, struck down by death, the cowards and those of little faith run in panic or linger, while the true warriors fight on even more sternly and fiercely, as if taking revenge for the leader's death on the enemy and on death itself! But when did our heroic people fail to be heroic fighters as well? Thus it is also during these mournful days: labor becomes even more intense in building projects, in the factory workshops, in the mines, and on the southern fields of our fatherland; even more frantically do the people tackle their jobs wherever they are laboring with the thought of Stalin; where they are creating, reforming, moved by the sole majestic idea—the idea of Communism.

And wherever we are—even if we are far from Moscow—we all see Moscow in our hearts right now: the Column Hall of the Union Building, the mourning flags at half-mast, the casket framed with green branches, and that face—every line of which, every tiny wrinkle of which, is so familiar, dear, and near to us, but at the same time already removed from us by death . . .

Father, farewell! Farewell, dear father, beloved until our last breath! How much we owe to you . . . There are millions of us and all of us are mentally saying farewell to you, slowly passing by your bier, struggling to implant your features in our memories, we bow low and give you filial kisses, escorting you on your last journey . . .

You shall always remain with us and with those who will enter life after us. We hear your voice in the rhythmical noise of the enormous power-station generators, in the sound of the waves of the seas, newly created by your will, in the measured steps of the unconquerable Soviet infantry, in the soft rustle of the foliage in the vast regions of forest conservation . . .

You are with us forever and always, dear father. Farewell!

This is the same man who took part in the baiting of Pasternak and put gifts at the feet of the "de-Stalinizer" Khrushchev. Thus, in a speech at the 20th Party Congress, he said: "First of all, we could not forget to say thank you to the chief creator of the Program, to our Nikita Sergeevich Khrushchev."

Talent, however, is a gift of God and fortunately, because of Sholokhov's powerful talent, the books of this Party-oriented writer tell us something quite different from what their author intended. As we have said, *And Quiet Flows the Don* is incomparably more significant in a literary sense than *Seeds of Tomorrow*. In *Seeds of Tomorrow*, Sholokhov the Party member often suppresses Sholokhov the artist. I do not mean that Sholokhov is insincere. I want rather to point out that the typical Party member's hatred for free men occasionally evokes an obvious false note from the writer. For instance, the behavior of Polovtsev, who is supposed to have betrayed the whole conspiracy to the Chekists, is highly unlikely. Sholokhov had already shown us the intensity of Polovtsev's hatred for the Soviet government, and his undaunted courage. Polovtsev's actions described on the last page of the novel—when he betrays his friends allegedly because "the game is lost; one has to pay for the losses"—are psychologically unsound. The Polovtsev of the early part of the book would not have uttered a word during the interrogations, if only out of hatred for the Cheka.

Equally unbelievable is the behavior of Yakov Lukich Ostrovnov, who starves his mother to death for fear that she might accidentally betray the conspiracy. Ostrovnov is earlier shown to be particularly devoted to his mother, whose permission and blessing he asks before joining an anti-Bolshevik organization. Moreover, he is described as a man of above-average intelligence—and the murder of his mother is senseless and even dangerous: the old women next door could have come into the house. Throughout the novel Ostrovnov is shown to be the kind of man who works from morning to night without rest. Then, all of a sudden he is supposedly "sipping vodka often" at the house of Khropov, a poor Cossack who has reasons to fear Ostrovnov because he gets the vodka for nothing.

The daring protest of a poor collective farmer, Ustin, against Chairman Davidov ends in the revelation that Ustin is an idler. All of this is reminiscent of Party spokesmen's accusations against political "criminals" which used to appear in Soviet newspapers. The same can be said of Sholokhov's explanations of some of his character's motives—which bear a strong resemblance to Party editorials. Here is how Sholokhov explains Ostrovnov's unwillingness to be the constant victim of legitimized robbery by the Soviet government:

Yakov Lukich had a good eye for business. He did not want the meat from his sheep to feed Red Army soldiers, or workers in some factory dining room. They were Soviet, and for the past ten years the Soviet government had burdened him with taxes and exactions and had not allowed him to develop his farming on a large scale, to grow rich and fatter than the fat. The Soviet government and Yakov Lukich were mutual enemies, at daggers drawn.

There is none of this in *And Quiet Flows the Don*. It is of course absurd to explain the literary value of *And Quiet Flows the Don* by claiming that Sholokhov found the notebook of some White Guard officer and copied the whole novel out of it. We rather suspect that this rumor originated in Soviet circles as a fabrication of some envious fellow Party member rather than among the émigrés. The émigrés should be glad that a Party-oriented author wrote a novel which is so truthful on the subject of the Civil War. And as we said at the outset, *Seeds of Tomorrow* as a report on the destruction of the Russian village is an unequaled literary document.

> *The master-builder of all Stalinist building projects was Death.*
>
> ALEXANDER TRUSHNOVICH

The problems of the peasantry and of the village have always been a stumbling block for Marxists, and in Russia, primarily an agricultural country, this was one of the most difficult problems facing the "dictatorship of the proletariat." If it was not an easy job to force the peasants of Central Russia into collective farms, it was even harder in the case of the Cossacks, whose tradition was one of freedom and a system of elected representatives.

The Party realized, of course, that, economically, collectivization would doom the country to a permanent food shortage. It is doubtful, however, that the Soviet government will ever voluntarily decide to abolish kolkhozy the way the Yugoslav Party did in 1948. To abolish the collective farms would mean losing total control over a large segment of the population. Therefore, the Party goes in the opposite direction. For instance, Khrushchev declared two years ago that in a couple of years bread and milk will be given away free of charge in the Soviet Union, an interesting demagogical speculation. Indeed, many things became free of charge under "socialist" rule: education, public health services, etc. And now bread and milk will be free as well. Something is not made clear in all this, however. Milk and bread, education and health services hardly come tumbling out of the blue free of charge; they are the fruits of labor. Do the collective farmers, doctors, teachers give their labor away for nothing and live on air instead of food? Of course not. The question, then, is not whether one must pay for education, but once again, how totalitarian dictatorship can be strengthened. As long as a man pays for his education, his bread, and his milk with his own money, with his earnings, he remains comparatively independent of the government. But in a system where everything is "free," the power of the Party becomes absolute. For then the government determines how much a man is paid for a day's work, who is to be educated and who is not. In this sort of "free" system, the government takes from the laborers the fruit of their labor and redistributes it freely among those whom it chooses. This is exactly what Dostoevsky's Grand Inquisitor advocated as an ideal. The blindness with which Westerners blissfully praise the "free" benefits of totalitarian societies is astonishing. This state of affairs is what the talented contemporary Russian poet Bulat-Okudjava has in mind in his song, "The Black Cat":

> Oh, he never begs or threatens,
> But his yellow eye burns bright.
> Each man brings him something tasty,
> Saying "Thank you very much."

The joys of "free" living are experienced more keenly by the kolkhozniks than by other segments of society. But if totalitarian dictatorship attains a fairly pure form on the kolkhozy, it is carried to its ultimate conclusion in the forced-labor camps. In these camps—as well as in prisons—everything is without charge: food, clothing, bed, and even health and educational services. Essentially, the camp is a prototype not only for the kolkhoz but for the commune as well.

If collective farms are still not able to stand on their feet, are things any better in industry? Is the Soviet system justified here? Didn't totalitarian Germany have the best rockets, the best military techniques? Even enslaved, poverty-stricken China has developed an atom bomb. Gagarin flew up into the sky; there are atomic power plants in the Soviet Union.

How quickly people forget history. Before World War II, instead of Gagarin, there was Chkalov, who flew over the North Pole. And instead of the atomic power plants, the Dnieper Hydroelectric Station amazed the world.

And then, at the 20th Party Congress of the CPSU, Khrushchev admitted that millions of innocent people who had been sitting in concentration camps during those years had perished. Which should attract our attention, Gagarin or the concentration camps? Are the camps and forced labor really justified by successes in industry and technology? If they are not justified by the collective farms, why should they be justified in other areas of life?

Recently in *Komsomolskaya Gazeta* (the January 20, 1966, issue) there appeared an article entitled "A Word about Progress" by P. L. Kapitsa, member of the U.S.S.R. Academy of Sciences and a famous Soviet scientist, in which he staunchly declared that although "their number of research workers is approximately the same as ours [the United States and the U.S.S.R.], they now perform one third of the scientific research in the world and we only one sixth, twice less than they."

This is the same story as with the collective farms. Is it owing to the merits of the Party that Russia has turned from a backward country into an advanced industrialized country? Why, naturally.

But here is what the facts reveal (as given to us by N. Rutich in *Posev*, 1960):

If one discards the propaganda that is contained in almost every one of the Party reports (particularly well illustrated by Stalin's speech at the 15th Party Congress) which try to prove that pre-revolutionary Russia had been a "wasteland" or at least a backward country, then one comes to the realization that, in fact, the rebuilding of industry went extremely slowly.

It is enough to remind oneself that it was not until 1928 that the mining of coal as well as the manufacture of steel and cast iron reached the 1913 level. Not until that time did the first large building projects of prerevolutionary times as well as those begun but cut short by the revolution start to take shape.

We should remind ourselves that during the twenty-five years between 1887–1912 the tempo of the development of Russian industry was such that if it had not been for the October coup d'état, Russia would certainly have become the most advanced country in Europe by 1928, leaving her 1913 records far behind. It is enough to mention that during the twenty-five-year prewar period mining grew by 520%, metallurgy by 388%, the chemical industry by 600%, etc.

Using these numbers as our point of departure, it is easy to conclude that the level reached in 1937 with such colossal strain on every resource and with so many casualties could very well have been reached by 1928.

Which should we believe, then, the worldwide Sputnik show, or Kapitsa and Rutich? Let us recall the giant collective farms, the Red Chinese bomb.

It would be interesting to know how much more the Soviet Union spends on spaceships than on the needs of the population, as compared to the United States, and what the Red Chinese atomic program costs the people. But dictatorship is ever based on mass hypnotism—which a grandiose Sputnik show maintains. The Party never grudged funds for such purposes.

Of course, only a totalitarian state would use such enormous sums for purposes that are contrary to the population's basic needs. It would be a catastrophe if the United States should begin to change into a totalitarian state in order to match the Soviet Union's hypnotic methods.

I often hear the opinion that the Russian people are

supposedly unable to live without the threat of the knout and that, although Party dictatorship is unacceptable to European peoples, it is necessary for the Russians. Because in the country's long history a democratic Russia existed only for six months, from February to October 1917, it is difficult to refute these allegations. At times it seems shameful to be Russian. But totalitarian enslavement of the Russian people is now ceasing to be solely Russia's national problem. The Communist messianic idea of the labor-camp anthill is endangering the whole world. And it is *more dangerous than German Fascism,* because Nazism was an openly declared evil. It is quite a different thing with Communism. Communism proclaims humanitarian ideas, "calls everyone to a better life." Sholokhov gave a vivid picture of this better life in *Seeds of Tomorrow* and therein lies his undeniable merit. It is particularly important to reveal the unchanging essence of phenomena that occur in various totalitarian states under different, often opposing, guises. In this sense, the book of the latest Russian Nobel Prize winner is particularly noteworthy. However, it demonstrates something else too, the fact that if the Russian people let themselves be tricked in 1930, after all they went through, nobody in Russia will be taken in any longer by Party lies. But the West is very easily taken in. Even now one notices something which at first glance seems paradoxical: that the most convinced anti-Communists are to be found, not in the West, but in Russia.

How can one read without disgust, for instance, the account of "The Troubles of an American Communist," by Saul Pettit, in the New York *Herald Tribune,* about a certain Herbert Aptheker, the Director of the New York Institute for Marxist Research and a well-known theoretician of the Communist Party of the United States, whose greatest problems consisted in being unable to land a teaching position in an American high school after his graduation from

college, and after the war, in which he advanced to the rank
of captain, in having had this rank taken away from him. In
spite of this, Herbert Aptheker lectures on Communism in
American universities and no one stops him. This is permitted to him—a Communist! And yet he dares to talk of
"troubles." This is what breeds disgust! How can one talk
about such "troubles" to a man who has lived under a
Communist dictatorship?

The roots of that nightmare which Party terminology now
calls "personality cult" go back to Lenin himself. The Lenin
collectivization plan was very conscientiously fulfilled by
Stalin. The totalitarian dictatorship dates its beginning to
the moment the Bolsheviks seized power in October 1917. It
is ridiculous to credit Lenin for the comparative liberties of
the NEP system, which he was forced to allow in spite of his
"dictatorship of the proletariat" ideology.

Just two weeks after the seizure of power, the first Soviet
coalition government (the Bolsheviks and their short-term
allies, the left-wing Social Revolutionaries) fell apart as a
result of Lenin's demand that all the "bourgeois" newspapers
be banned. This took place on November 4, 1917. Several
days later *The New Life,* the newspaper edited by Maxim
Gorky, published an open letter by Lozovsky, Secretary of
the Bolshevik Union in the All-Russian Council of Trade
Unions, who resigned his Party membership in protest
against Lenin's policies. Here is that interesting letter, which
shows that Stalin had been a "faithful follower of Lenin"
after all:

I feel it is impossible to keep silent for the sake of Party discipline when I realize, when I sense from the depth of my soul,
that the tactics of the Central Committee are leading to the
isolation of the proletarian avant-garde, to a civil war within the
working class. . . . I cannot . . . be silent about the administrative fury of the VRK representatives, such as Lt. Colonel

Muraviev, who issued the order for mob law and for the confiscation of enterprises—an order worthy of the Tsarist generals that Shchedrin used to depict. I cannot keep silent . . . in the face of the stamping out of all press media which hold differing opinions, in the face of searches in private homes, arbitrary arrests, persecutions and baitings which arouse a muffled protest among the populace as a whole and give the working masses the impression that this regime of the bayonet and the saber is in fact that same dictatorship of the proletariat which the socialists have been preaching about for decades. . . . I cannot . . . ignore the smouldering discontent of the working masses who fought for a Soviet government only to find that it has become, as a result of a combination that is completely beyond their comprehension, a purely Bolshevik government. I cannot . . . acquiesce to a personality cult or make the holding of a ministerial office by this or that person a condition for political agreement, thus prolonging the bloodshed even for a minute. . . ."

It is by reading things of this sort that we come to the realization that the only hope for liberating the world from the totalitarian dictatorship of the Communist Party lies precisely with the Russian people, who have experienced to the full the "Leninist collectivization," "mighty building projects," and their "heroic Party." Only when the remains of the man who imposed bondage on Russia are carried out of the heart of the country he enslaved, only when the city of Peter shall bear once more the name of its founder, only then shall it become possible to say without shame, proudly: "I am a Russian!" Only after all neighboring nations cease looking forward with fear and horror to "Sovietization" and "collectivization" and cursing the Russians, then, perhaps, Lenin will be forgiven too.

But until then:

> Still no face appears, no cry is given;
> Linked by fetters which October won,
> Scarlet banners flare up like the living
> Human torches Nero burned for fun.

These four lines are from a poem by Evgeny Golovin, a young Russian, which appeared in the underground magazine *Sphinxes* in 1965.

Particularly significant is the concluding quatrain of the poem:

> Since our Fathers' sanity had left them,
> We shall find the joy of all mankind
> Where the mausoleum rises from the pavement
> As if it were made of clotted blood.

[1966]

PASTERNAK'S *DOCTOR ZHIVAGO*

*   *   *

A FIRST READING of this long novel leaves a poor impression. One is actually astonished by the superficiality, not to say the carelessness, of the writer, whose effort appears to be rather a sketch for a novel than a finished work.

What, then, does one find in *Doctor Zhivago?* The novel is a chronicle of events in the material and spiritual life of a Russian intellectual, starting with his childhood before the 1905 revolution and ending with his death in 1930. To the main body of the novel is appended an epilogue set in the post-World War II era and a selection of Zhivago's poetry.

Interwoven into the chronicle are myriad episodes, miniatures of war and revolution, as well as brief character sketches and descriptions of nature. Much of the novel is devoted to the thought of Zhivago himself and, in discourse, reveals his and others' opinions on revolution, Marxism, poetry, philosophy, and related topics. It is quite apparent that the bulk of the philosophy set forth is that of the author himself, not his characters. Ideas expressed in a literary work, including those most central and significant, are really only colors used by an artist to bring people to life in a literary portrait.

Unfortunately, Pasternak failed, on the whole, to put his own philosophy into the mouths of live human beings, except in certain particular cases, which only succeed in proving the indefensibility of his ideas as he conceived them. Tolstoy has said: "The artist is like the biblical Balaam who, wishing to curse, offers a blessing." In this essay, we shall analyze the novel from an aesthetic point of view, a point of view we hold to be universal, and we shall assume that any ideological sins (referring to fundamental ideology, of course, not to Pharisaism) are sins against art. We shall refer to the writer's philosophical ideas only to explain the contradiction which we find at the base of Pasternak's and Zhivago's personal ideologies, something we would not have been constrained to do had the author remained an artist throughout.

Many sins of an elementary nature which spring to the eye at first reading are not banished by delving more deeply into the novel. The aesthetically sensitive reader, gripped by the more significant and crucial passages, cannot but be vexed by an inability to say exactly why he finds this novel so moving. If he is honest with himself and persistent, he will, upon rereading, discover its true value and come to realize that it is precisely those significant, crucial passages which are almost completely worthless, being, as they are, obstacles thwarting the reader's effort to put his finger on the essential meaning both of the novel and of the haunting poetry; of passages which, at first reading, seem meaningless and carelessly written.

The structure of the novel is, to put it mildly, naïve. The main characters meet one another accidentally: in Moscow before World War I, at the Galician front, in the Urals, in Siberia, again in Moscow. All this reminds us of the "light" novels of Mamin-Sibiryak. Were it not for the fact that an obvious artistic convention—and only a convention—underlying these many "accidental" and unconvincing meetings provides a symbolic meaning—"the criss-crossing of human destinies"—we would be inclined to think that the author intentionally ignored "external," in order to emphasize "internal," composition of the work. Pasternak has no dramatic talent.

His dramatic entanglements do not compare at all with his soaring descriptions of nature. Nearly all his characters are pale and invisible, each speaking the same language as the next, except for various representatives of the common people, who speak in an overly folksy way. Episodic sketches of war and revolution (with the exception of the scene in which the partisans execute the men who betray them) are historically and realistically, rather than artistically, true and cannot compare with the full-bodied portraits of civil war in Sholokhov's *And Quiet Flows the Don* or Babel's *Red Cavalry*.

To comprehend Zhivago's odyssey, one must have a thorough understanding of modern Russian history: the actions of Siberian partisans, Kolchak's forces, White armies, the February and October revolutions, and so on. It is perhaps true that the author intentionally avoided differentiating between important historical events in order to stress the novel's central theme that revolution—all revolution—is a cosmic disaster, a disaster which lops the human off the human being and kills man's most valuable attribute: artistic creativity.

Coming to an analysis of the main vehicle for this theme, Dr. Zhivago himself, let us first of all divest him of Pasternak's personal reflections and analyze him as he is drawn in the pages of the novel. One arresting scene vividly demonstrates the author's art rather than his "sermonizing": Lara's monologue over her lover's coffin. This scene is raised to a high artistic level, but the content of many, many monologues in the novel is that of a sermon:

"At last we are together again, Yurochka. And in what a terrible way God has willed our reunion. Can you conceive of such misfortune! I cannot, cannot. Oh, God! I can't stop crying. Think of it! It's again so much in our style, made to our measure. Your going—my end. Again something big, irreparable. The riddle of life, the riddle of death, the enchantment of genius, the enchantment of unadorned beauty—yes, yes, these things were ours. But the small problems of practical life—things like the reshaping of the planet—these things, no thank you, they are not for us."

The art of this passage lies in the inability of Lara, faced with the coffin, to express herself in any other way. But in practically every other place in the novel where someone is revealing his ideological position and attitude toward life—whether Dr. Zhivago himself; or the lady librarian of a small town in the Urals; or Zhivago's uncle, Nicolai Nicolaievich; or the father of Zhivago's wife, Tonya; or Lara—everyone sounds like everyone else. The author relies on "Zhivago wrote" or "Lara said" as the sole means of differentiating among the speakers and writers. Thus, we are confronted not with art but with "sermonizing," proselytizing, and to point to the content value in this preaching is artistically irrelevant.

"Sermonizing," then, a rather coarse tendency to propagandize, is the fundamental shortcoming of the novel.

Zhivago is an intellectual who symbolizes the failure of the Russian intelligentsia in the revolution, or rather the failure of what the author considers to be the most important part of the intelligentsia. While it is interesting to compare Zhivago with Gorky's "typical petit bourgeois," Klim Samgin, as individual characters, it is naturally out of the question to compare Gorky's whole brilliant epic with Pasternak's novel, at least from any artistic standpoint. Samgin and Zhivago are comparable because they come from the same social milieu and live in the same historical period. Along with these similarities, there is also a difference between the "typical" intellectual Samgin and Dr. Zhivago. Zhivago is a poet, a creator, and if, on this account, he cannot "typically" represent those who are "only" intellectuals, he does symbolize—and this was precisely the author's intention—all poets and creative artists. This is the only real difference between Zhivago and Samgin, although it may also be noted that Samgin is, in all instances, more intelligent and honest with himself than Pasternak's character.

For Zhivago, prerevolutionary life was all poetry, love, and philosophy. Like the majority of Russian intellectuals, he indulges in fantasies—but nothing more—about revolution; he practices medicine, he publishes poetry, he marries. In the depth of his soul Zhivago is convinced that revolution is something to discuss over a cup of tea, and little else. When his idyllic civic life is suddenly smashed to pieces, when he is forced to abandon his carefree immersion in poetry and philosophical meditation and steal wood to keep his family alive in famished, freezing Moscow, he curses the revolution, Marxism, and all who have militantly destroyed his peace and happiness—not the peace and happiness of the Russian people, mind you, but his own. It does not occur to him that the revolution might not have happened had all Russians been able to enjoy his life of ease and tranquillity. While fleeing from starving Moscow to the Urals, he damns all revolutions throughout history:

But revolutions are made by fanatical men of action with one-track minds, geniuses in their ability to confine themselves to a limited field. They overturn the old order in a few hours or days, the whole upheaval takes a few weeks or at most years, but the fanatical spirit that inspired the upheavals is worshipped for decades thereafter, for centuries.

Zhivago often contradicts himself. In an earlier passage he compares the growth of the Roman Empire from Hellenistic roots with the development of the Bolshevik state out of the enlightenment of nineteenth-century Russia. Thus, it is not at all clear to him whether the cause of revolution is "one-track-mindedness" or enlightenment. If this is not all that important, it at least proves Gorky's dictum: "The petit bourgeois likes to philosophize, just as the idler likes to fry fish." Here is the philosopher, Zhivago, on Marxism as a science:

"Marxism is too uncertain of its ground to be a science. Sciences are more balanced, more objective. I don't know a movement more self-centered and further removed from the facts than Marxism. Everyone is worried only about proving himself in practical matters, and as for the men in power, they are so anxious to establish the myth of their infallibility that they do their utmost to ignore the truth."

Zhivago's actions, however, are important. Although he sincerely hates Bolshevism, he flees from all active struggle against it and tries to live through the "period of cosmic disaster" by philosophizing about love and Christ in the beds of two women, Tonya and Lara. Even here he does not succeed. The Red partisans carry him off and force him to minister to their wounded. The essence of the doctor's character is revealed in one chapter in which he accidentally finds himself in the firing line during an attack on the partisans by White troops, mostly schoolboy cadets. All Zhivago's sympathies are on the side of "the children who are dying heroically." The idea of joining them flashes through his mind but is immediately rejected—that would be endangering his life. Bored with lying idly in the line of fire, he starts shooting sporadically at a tree and, because the cadets are running helter-skelter across the field of fire, he kills one of them accidentally and wounds two others. Let us not forget that all the while he is "spiritually" on their side.

When he finally manages to get away from the partisans, he quits the practice of medicine altogether and flees contact with people, taking refuge in Lara's love. After her departure, he returns to Moscow, lives there with and has children by a woman he meets quite by chance and whom he does not love, completely disintegrates morally, and finally dies, leaving behind his poetry and his notebook.

Thus Zhivago, who talks unceasingly of his love of mankind, shoots cadets with whom he sympathizes, out of boredom. Zhivago, who prates about belief in Christ, ceases to offer his doctor's skills to those around him. In agonizing times of hunger and national suffering he retreats from people to a loveless marriage. And at the same time he haughtily limits his view of those closest to him:

"The only bright and vital thing about you is that you are my contemporaries and friends!"

Zhivago's declarations on love and Christianity and his pride at belonging to an "elect" reminds us somehow of Dostoevsky's "You are guilty before all because you could have been a light in darkness but were not." The doctor's Christianity is only a caricature of Christianity.

On the other hand, we must stress that Pasternak is an artist, and despite all his sympathy for Zhivago (let us note it would be wrong to identify Pasternak and Zhivago completely), despite ideas common to both author and hero, despite the many passages in which art gives way to "sermonizing," he nevertheless draws a sharply defined, even brilliant, portrait of the main character in a way quite contrary to his intention. For, paradoxically, Pasternak's desire to show that revolution kills the *human in man* turns into a demonstration that the *human in man* kills conformity. The tragedy of Zhivago, his moral death, lies not in his opposition to the Bolsheviks, who are winning, or in his ill-luck to have to live in a time when no one can just stand on the sidelines and sing songs, but in his serving Reds while hating them, in his shooting Whites while loving them, and in his fleeing and fleeing and fleeing, obstinately refusing to come to grips with the fact that there comes a time when not to resist is to be no longer a man. True, only a man can create poetry, but Zhivago wants to do this and nothing more.

Pasternak's "sermonizing" is a rebellion against all revolutions. Zhivago holds that it is important, not to prepare for life while rearranging it, but to live. This affirmation conceals a basic contradiction in the author's theoretical (fortunately, only theoretical) attitude toward life and history. To get to the wellspring of this central concept of Zhivago's, we must refer to all of Pasternak's reflections and observations, which all too frequently have no organic relationship to the subjects who are made to utter them. They are justifiable, and then only to a certain extent, when they appear in Zhivago's notebook.

Pasternak's philosophical observations can be summed up as a curious mixture of pantheism, Christianity, Berdyaev, and Nietzsche, influenced occasionally by the Hegelian view of history, by Dostoevsky, and also by Tolstoy's attitude toward nonresistance to evil. Let us give a few illustrations:

Gregariousness is always the refuge of mediocrities, whether they swear by Soloviev or Kant or Marx. Only individuals seek the truth, and they shun those whose sole concern is not the truth. How many things in the world deserve our loyalty? Very few indeed. I think one should be loyal to immortality, which is another word for life, a stronger word for it. One must be true to immortality—true to Christ!

After Christ's coming, there are not nations, only persons.

. . . Man is made up of two parts, of God and work.

Now what is history? It is the centuries of systematic explorations of the riddle of death, with a view to overcoming death.

With birth you were resurrected.

Consciousness is a poison when we apply it to ourselves. Consciousness is a light directed outward, it lights up the way ahead of us so that we don't stumble. It's like the headlights on a locomotive—turn them inward and you'd have a crash.

I was once a great revolutionary but now I no longer think anything can be done with force.

Pasternak is not really an original thinker. Moreover, his views are untenable. Revolutions are not "cosmic disasters." They are part of the "work" with which man builds history in answer to the enigma of death.

The author's thoughts and judgments on Soviet society, while artistically unsuccessful and pertaining only to this one specific historical period, are nevertheless interesting:

Men who are not free, he thought, always idealize their bondage. So it was in the Middle Ages, and later the Jesuits always exploited this human trait. Zhivago could not bear the political mysticism of the Soviet intelligentsia, though it was the very thing they regarded as their highest achievement, or as it would have been called in those days, 'the spiritual ceiling of the age.'

The greatest misfortune, the root of future evil, was the loss of faith in the value of one's own judgment.

Your health is bound to be affected if, day after day, you say the opposite of what you feel, if you grovel before what you dislike and rejoice at what brings you nothing but misfortune. Our nervous system isn't just a fiction, it's a part of our physical body . . .

Although victory had not brought the relief and freedom that were expected at the end of the war, nevertheless the portents of freedom filled the air throughout the postwar period, and they alone defined its historical significance.

Among the most interesting ideas in the novel is a judgment on the poet Mayakovsky:

I've always liked Mayakovsky. He is a sort of continuation of Dostoevsky. Or rather, he's a Dostoevsky character writing lyrical poems—one of his young rebels, the "Raw Youth of Ippolit or Raskolnikov."

We feel this to be one of the most incisive impressionistic criticisms of Mayakovsky ever set down.

We have noted that the better-than-average artistic qualities of Pasternak's prose are less obvious, and therefore harder to pinpoint, than the shortcomings of the novel, which, as we have said, are: untenable ideas, proselytizing, absence of dramatic talent, and the general structure of the book.

Yet, however clumsily the writer delineates character and however pale the characters themselves and undramatic the drama, all this cannot blur the transfixingly poetic passages on love and nature. Nor are these passages the only ones to reach poetic heights, for when Pasternak does not put his thoughts in the mouths of his characters, his remarks on man (the human condition) attain depth and artistry.

We may cite one example of this. Returning from the front to a starving Moscow, Zhivago is given a wild duck, with which he and his wife and friends make a meal. As they eat, they suddenly realize they have lost their appetite:

And so it turned out that only a life similar to the life of those around us, merging with it without a ripple, is genuine life, and that an unshared happiness is not happiness, so that duck and vodka, when they seem to be the only ones in town, are not even duck and vodka.

A brief passage. But what depth is hidden in this sketch. ". . . Duck and vodka . . . are not even duck and vodka." This observation says incomparably more than endless philosophical or religious ramblings.

Or, we may cite the relationship of Zhivago and his wife, Tonya, a relationship which at first glance, seems wholly undeveloped. The author does not describe anything obvious: a first kiss, the wedding, or any sort of spiritual or physical contact between them. Yet, in one short reference, we "feel" the doctor's love for Tonya, we learn why he loves her and how this love differs from his love for Lara. At first Zhivago and Tonya are only friends who have grown up together. One day a curtain catches on Tonya's shoulder. Her father observes that she looks like a bride. Tonya blushes and looks at Zhivago. When we see them next, they are man and wife.

Another example is the incident in which Zhivago laughingly overturns a sleigh in which he, Lara, and her daughter are riding. In that winter scene filled with the laughter of the three as they pull themselves out of the snow bank we sense the love Zhivago and Lara share in a more meaningful way than if Pasternak had delved into their intimate relations.

Pasternak's indictment of revolution, his enumeration and analysis of the disasters which follow in the wake of revolution, is rendered unnecessary and superfluous by his description of Zhivago's return to Moscow after the civil war is over.

Never in his life had he seen such dark-looking rye, rusty, brown, the color of old gold. Usually, when it is harvested in time, its color is much lighter.

These flame-colored fields blazing without fire, these fields silently proclaiming their distress, were coldly bordered by the vast, quiet sky, its face already wintry and shadowed by ceaselessly moving, long, flaky snow-clouds with black centers and white flanks.

Everything was moving slowly, regularly—the flowing river,

the road running by it, and the doctor walking along the road in the same direction as the drifting clouds. Nor were the rye fields motionless. Their surface was alive, they were astir with an incessant crawling that suggested something foul and repellent.

Never had there been such a plague of mice. They had bred in unprecedented quantities. They scurried over the doctor's face and hands and inside his sleeves and trousers at night, when he was caught by darkness and forced to sleep in the open, they raced across the road by day, gorged and teeming, and turned into squeaking, pulsing slush when they were trodden underfoot.

Shaggy village curs, turned wild, followed him at a respectful distance, exchanging glances as if to decide on the best moment to fall on him and tear him to pieces. They fed on carrion, did not disdain mice, and eyed Yurii Andreievich from afar, moving after him confidently as though waiting for something. For some reason they never ventured into the wood and, whenever he came near one, gradually fell back, turned tail, and vanished.

The woods and the fields offered a complete contrast in those days. Deserted by man, the fields looked orphaned as if his absence had put them under a curse. The forest, however, well rid of him, flourished proudly in freedom as though released from captivity.

The quality of passages like this leads us to believe that Pasternak would have realized his purpose had he concentrated on descriptions of nature. Fortunately, there are many of these, each such a jewel that we want to cut them all out of the book and frame them like pictures. They are so alive and vivid we can virtually smell the landscape in: "The snow yellowed in the afternoon sun and into its honeyed mellowness poured the orange syrup of an early twilight." And where Pasternak fails to reveal the essence of characters through dramatic conflicts or interior monologues, he succeeds by describing their contacts with nature:

Lara walked along the tracks following a path worn by pilgrims and then turned into the fields. Here she stopped and, closing her eyes, took a deep breath of the flower-scented air of the broad expanse around her. It was dearer to her than her kin, better than a lover, wiser than a book. For a moment she rediscovered the purpose of her life. She was here on earth to grasp the meaning of its wild enchantment and to call each thing by its right name, or if this were not within her power, to give birth out of love for life to successors who would do it in her place.

"The Poems of Yurii Zhivago," at the end of the novel, neither add to nor detract from the main body of the work. Zhivago's poetry differs to a certain extent from Pasternak's. The author seems to achieve in the poems what his character strives to achieve in the novel:

. . . All his life he had struggled for a style so restrained, so unpretentious that the reader or hearer would fully understand the meaning without realizing how he assimilated it. He had striven constantly for an unostentatious style, and he was dismayed to find how far he still remained from his ideal.

I cannot agree with the widely held opinion that Pasternak's poetry is difficult to understand because of its complexity. His poetry is difficult, yes, but difficult because it is simple. Simple truths are the hardest to understand. Take the first stanza of the poem "False Summer":

The leaves of currants are coarse and woolly.
The house shakes with laughter, the windowpanes ring.
There's great chopping within it, and pickling, while pepper
And cloves are put in to lend tang to the brine.

"The leaves of currants are coarse and woolly . . ."—this is musical, rhythmic, with no deep meaning, just descriptive. But as we read the stanza through, we are possessed with a strange harmony, a harking back to some naïve, half-forgotten memory, and the "cloves are put in to lend tang to the brine" lingers. We read the stanza again. Now it is descriptive only in a superficial sense; the "cloves" are no longer only cloves but something more significant, familiar and half-remembered, yet curiously remote. Suddenly our feelings crystallize into a thought: childhood. Childhood: tinted dawns with obligatory glasses of milk, the tragedy of a broken plate, cherries decorating one's ears and . . . that exciting, important autumn activity, pickling things for the coming winter and putting in the "cloves." Or in the poem "Winter Night":

> As during summer midges swarm
> To beat their wings against a flame,
> Out in the yard the snowflakes swarmed
> To beat against the windowpane.

This we remember too: the window and the snowflakes. Pasternak's poetry is flight back to childhood. This is one of the most striking characteristics of "The Poems of Yurii Zhivago," especially those poems which deal with the seasons and love and Christian themes.

Despite the excellence of the poetry appended to it, *Doctor Zhivago* is not a great novel. I cannot agree with such critics as Marc Slonim, M. Jones, A. Gajev, and others who maintain that Pasternak's novel artistically equals Tolstoy's *War and Peace*. But, compared to the average performance of Soviet writers following the dictates of socialist realism, and considering that writers of the stamp of Vsevolod Kochetov were lauded as masters of Russian prose in the 1950's, we must admit that *Doctor Zhivago* is a novel unequaled in its time.

[1962]

RUSSIAN MODERNISM

I paint the world not as I see it but as I think it.
                                    PABLO PICASSO

                    *   *   *

THE twentieth-century was born in mid-nineteenth-century Russia.

The twentieth century's first man is Dostoevsky's "man from the underground." Nearly a century has passed since this nameless (nameless because "I" is all of us, as Viktor Shklovsky lucidly observed) "man from the underground" shouted: "$2 \times 2 = 4$, that's not life, gentlemen, but the beginning of death." Since then, wars and revolutions, proletarian Internationals, death camps, Einstein, Freud, and Lenin have thundered by; the "underground man" has many times been proscribed, stifled, driven "underground," persecuted by Zhdanovs and Rosenbergs, ignored by "serious scientific minds"—all to no avail.

The cry from the "underground" is ever louder, and if yesterday it was heard only in the books of Kafka, the paintings of Malevich and Kandinsky, and the symphonies of Stravinsky, today it bellows from each new book, painting, symphony. Improved social organization, higher standards of living, and the unmatched development of technology only amplify this cry.

Modern art is the art of the "man from underground." But we can immediately add that when modern artists of all types claim Dostoevsky as their teacher, it is like the contemporary misanthropes who point to Molière as their teacher. All Dostoevsky's creative effort is a battle with the "underground man," an effort to answer the question of this Russian Hamlet.

What is this man's essence? He lives in a prison of reason. More precisely, he does not live; he only thinks. For the shackles on his thoughts do not permit active participation; in fact, they permit no movement of any kind. "Because, if you think it through, you have to admit it's not worth lifting a finger." It is more important to know why he should lift his finger than actually to lift it. That is his damnation. Since the world is not rational, one why leads to innumerable others, until the ultimate limit of an unshatterable wall of natural laws is reached to which even reason itself must submit. Thus, the laws of nature become man's prison. But as we probe deeper, we find that it is not laws of nature, that is, of reason, but the question *why* which confines the "man from underground," because *why* is the ultimate goal.

Knowledge—the purpose, the very goal of life—this is the "underground man's" essence, his prison, and his original sin. For those who regard thought as only one of life's elements, thought does not enslave, and revolt against reason is senseless. The revolt of the "underground man" is a slave's revolt. How could Marx be a slave of thought? Remember his words on that subject? "It is not essential that the world be understood, but that it be changed." All Marxism grows out of this idea. Knowledge is a means, not an end.

Dostoevsky, similarly, while struggling with the "underground man" within him comes to this conclusion: "It is more important to love life than to know it." This is the Christian myth. But these answers do not satisfy the "underground man" because they require faith, that is, *credo quia absurdum,* which he so passionately desires but cannot acquire because $2 \times 2 = 4$. The progress of mankind and the "paradise on earth" to come are related to the "man underground" in exactly the same way as "life after death" and the "everlasting joy of heaven." Both Marx and Dostoevsky reply to the sick man's query "How can I be cured?" with the answer "By being healthy."

Revolt against reason, flight into the unconscious ("flight" because we are dealing with the way back, as in the legend of the prodigal son), everything that characterizes modern art, is the revolt of slaves. At the end of this road home is the total surrender of Beckett's *Molloy*: "As far as I'm concerned, I've always preferred slavery to death or killing." Every revolution, whether spiritual or social (and that really means life itself), is inimical to the "underground man" because, in the final analysis, it is senseless and irrational. How is it possible for anyone who thinks this way to man any sort of barricade?

Even if I managed to reach a higher stage of development, I would also ask you from that vantage point to account for all the victims of life and history, for all those victimized by chance, for superstition, for Phillip II's inquisition, and so on. Otherwise, I should hurl myself headlong from that higher stage. I do not need happiness, even as a gift, unless I can feel that everything is well with all my blood brothers. Some say disharmony is a precondition for harmony. This may be useful and a calming thought for megalomaniacs but not for people destined by their very lives to express the idea of disharmony.

It is not difficult to recognize in these words the "underground man's" closest relative, Ivan Karamazov. What is most interesting, however, is that these words were not written by Dostoevsky but by Belinsky. His letter to Gogol is well-known. This is the critic whose very name has for decades assaulted the "man from underground" (wherever the "man" is identified with Dostoevsky himself or is Dostoevskyan). But this is Belinsky in a private letter. As we can see, Doestovsky is not "guilty" for the philosophy of the "man from underground," even if he is often accused of it by Soviet theorists.

In this connection, one is staggered by the spiritual color-blindness not only of Lunacharsky but of those who oppose his ideas as well; Merezhkovsky, for instance. That same "voice of truth and reason," that is, $2 \times 2 = 4$, which Dostoevsky seeks to bury and which Lunacharsky so fervently seeks to resurrect is actually Lunacharsky's most dangerous enemy at a later date, as it is for Vorovsky and other thinkers of their persuasion. Very likely, had he lived in the twentieth century, Dostoevsky would have been a fanatical Stalinist. It is not an accident that he was friendly with Pobedonostsev, one of nineteenth-century Russia's darkest figures. Gorky cut deep when he said that Dostoevsky, transformed into a judge of the world, would be the Grand Inquisitor. This insight into the main problem of Dostoevsky—the most complex conundrum of the twentieth century—is amazingly rare among so-called "progressive" Russian thinkers (Dobrolyubov, Chernyshevsky, Mikhailovsky, and a few others) and probably contributed much to Gorky's vacillation between Lenin on the one hand and the restorers of God, Bazarov, and an early Lunacharsky, on the other.

How is it possible to create and not believe in any sort of creativity? How is it possible to speak to anyone and to believe, that is, to "know," that this is senseless? For, indeed, the primary and basic characteristic of modern art is that it is a monologue, directed not at others but at itself. It is the voice of a lonely man in the utter desolation of an "inner world," an inner world that is the only reality.

In the drama of the future the whole presentation will be different. First of all, the difficulties of the dénouement will be set aside. The new hero has a past—reminiscent—but no present; neither wife, nor sweetheart, nor friends, nor occupation. He is alone; he communes only with himself or with imaginary listeners. He lives a life apart. So that the stage will represent either a desert island or a room in a large, densely populated city, where among millions of inhabitants one can live alone as on a desert island. The hero must not return to people and to social ideals. He must go forward to loneliness, to absolute loneliness.

Everyone will recognize the theater of Beckett and Ionesco in this vision of the theater of the future. There is no present. There are only memories. Speakers speak pensively in an unheeded stream of words, in ultimate desolation. What is amazing is that the above was written by Lev Shestov over half a century ago, and in Russia at that, when the Russian theater was dominated by Ibsen and Maeterlinck, Chekhov and Gorky.

The artistic direction of an idea is based on some kind of philosophy, however far the artist himself may be from any well-developed *Weltanschauung*. It is impossible to deny the close ties between positivism, Darwin's theory of evolution and naturalism, the rationalism of the eighteenth century (that is, the "religion of reason") , and classicism. In the same way, all modern "isms," however different from one another they may appear, belong to a stylistic structure based on the philosophy of the "man from underground" (whose precursors were, naturally, Plotinus, Pascal, Kierkegaard) or, to go one step further, on the philosophy of Shestov, Berdyaev, Rozanov (the Russian Nietzsche) , and the ideologues of the so-called "second idealistic offensive" after 1905.

It is no accident that the collected works of Shestov are being published today in Sartre's France, the France of existentialism and abstract painting. What is existentialism but a watered-down and primitively simplified version of the "second idealistic offensive"? True, there is an essential difference between Russian thinkers and Sartre, Camus, or Heidegger. Whereas the Russian thinkers evince strong belief in the possibility of overcoming man's alienation, wherein lies their greatest contribution, the Western European existentialists essentially merely register and "clarify" this alienation. The best example is Camus's *The Myth of Sisyphus*. But the Soviets made no reference at all to the philosopher Shestov or the modernist Remizov, in the latest edition of the Soviet Encyclopedia. Thus, the story of the Grand Inquisitor in *The Brothers Karamazov* has been repeated. But, as always, in vain. Shestov and Berdyaev were resurrected in Pasternak's *Doctor Zhivago*.

Here in Yugoslavia, Shestov was translated for the first time toward the end of 1960 and that from a few pages of an Italian book, Gaetano Picone's *A Panorama of Contemporary Ideas*. There is no sense in ignoring Shestov, Berdyaev, Sorel, Unamuno. Kafka, Faulkner, Beckett, Ionesco, Honegger, Klee, Chagall all say about the same thing, but in a language that does not tolerate discussion. It is time to bring the "underground man" out into the sunlight. Left "underground," he is more dangerous. Today's Molloy will tomorrow be the first to join the ranks of a new SS, because for Molloys of all kinds this is the only solution. Better Satan than a horizon inscribed "zero, zero, zero," as in Beckett's *Endgame*. The "underground man" has posed a question and the answer has not yet been found. But to pretend that we don't hear the question is to thrust our head into the sand.

However paradoxical it may seem, Marx, with his dialectical materialism (which is, as we know, Hegel's "spirit of objectivity" set back on its feet; that is, $2b \times 2a = 4$ substituted for $2a \times 2b = 4$), is the real father of modern art. And—however much this may enrage Lukács—Marxism gave birth to existentialism, just as Hegel is the father of Schopenhauer and Kierkegaard, and Breton, who shouted "Stop jesting, Voltaire," is a direct descendant of Voltaire. It is not an accident that the thinkers of the "second idealistic offensive" —Struve, Berdyaev, Bulgakov and others—were, along with

Lenin, the participants of the first Marxist front in Russia. It is amusing to listen to Sartre bleating about the synthesis of Marxism and existentialism. Surely it is difficult to maintain that the synthesis of cat and mouse would produce a rhinoceros.

For the past several years the Soviet Union has permitted a gradual rehabilitation of two modernists, Leonid Andreyev and Andrei Bely, and we may assume that sooner or later Alexei Remizov will have his day and that ultimately Lev Shestov will too. In his memoirs, Ilya Ehrenburg clears the path for Remizov, who is only Shestov translated into literature.

For nearly four decades now the Russian modernists have been banned in the Soviet Union and, due to a variety of circumstances, are virtually unknown in the rest of the world. What do the names Remizov, Zamyatin, Bely mean to us? Little or nothing. How many realize that, fifteen years before Kafka, Alexei Remizov in his novel *The Pond* wrote a famous scene that is found in *The Trial?* Ten years before Joyce, Andrei Bely developed many of the things which later made Joyce the classic of modern literature.

In 1901, Leonid Andreyev wrote *The Wall.* The form and theme of this story are very similar to Beckett's works. Fyodor Sologub in his novel *The Little Demon* in many ways anticipates Sartre by nearly half a century.

The twentieth century was born in Russia. This is an unknown fact.

In the last decade of the past century, Russian literature experienced something which today we call the "disintegration of realism." This process lasted until nearly a decade after the October Revolution, when it was bureaucratically quashed. Symbolism burst into bloom, Nietzsche and Ibsen were translated. Maeterlinck's stream of works and the strong current of Russian literature overflowed in several directions which often ran counter to one another. So-called "critical realism" still had a place, novels were still written in classical form, but the great new talents, Chekhov and Gorky, no longer succeeded in producing conventional narrative novels or realistic characters. And they did not strive to do so, either. "I have been reading your [*Lady with a Lapdog*]," wrote Gorky to Chekhov in 1905. "Do you know what you are doing? You are killing realism. And soon you will kill it for good. . . . Moreover, it all seems to lack simplicity, i.e., it just doesn't seem real."

In the literary and intellectual fabric of that era, one thread stands out prominently in an otherwise conventional pattern, the thread of Russian modernism.

The three great prose writers associated with Russian modernism are Bely, Andreyev, and Remizov, all born in the decade 1870–1880 (joined later by Zamyatin, who was born in 1884). All three were hyperintellectuals given to philosophy, rationalism, and mysticism, and like the "underground man," all three burned with desire to believe but could not. It is exceedingly instructive to delve into the artistic achievement of these first modernists, inasmuch as modernistic literature, only now coming into its own, has clearly identifiable roots there.

The most important progenitor of modern Russian literature is Andrei Bely (pseudonym for Boris N. Bugaev). His novel *Petersburg* marks a crossroads in the history of Russian prose. Bely, which in Russian means white, has a symbolic meaning, for white is the color of the apocalypse. To the sense of alienation and loneliness, which the Russian modernists felt hovering over themselves and over life itself, was joined an awareness of a mysterious force, of the impending apocalyptic end of the world. We take little risk in presuming that this "mysterious force" is really the "wall" of natural law and reason, Hegel's "spirit of objectivity." While the external world still exists in Bely's novel, it continually meshes with an internal world. The second is important and real; the first is unreal, fantastic, grotesque. When the external world intrudes into the internal, the irrationality of the external world provokes the grotesque. Let us not forget that for all "underground people" reason—the "wall"—is the only reality (just as, for the medieval world, *universalia sunt realia*). All the main characters see cogitation as their principal task. In fact, it is their only "proper" life. External events serve only to set internal processes into motion. Bely brilliantly described the sensation of thinking as feeling (entirely of the body) stimulated by certain thoughts. Man's attitude toward the internal world is the same as his attitude toward the external world.

For the past few hours fragments of thoughts had floated before his eyes like shimmering sparks, like the gay stars of a Christmas tree. They showered continuously, from dark to dark, passing through the place lighted by consciousness. The figure of a contorted clown appeared; then a gaudy Petrushka rushed past at a gallop—from dark to dark—passing through the place lighted by consciousness. It glittered, an objectively kinetic image; when the thoughts merged together, his consciousness sketched a shocking, inhuman meaning into them. "I'm a scoundrel . . ." Nikolai Apollonovich spat out in disgust.

But his father had also come to that conclusion.

No, no!

These swarming thoughts were autonomous. He did not think them: they conceived themselves; they thought, sketched, and formed themselves; they thumped in his heart and drilled in his brain; crawling out of the sardine tin, they rose above it. He had hidden the sardine tin . . . apparently . . . in the table drawer, and escaped from the accursed house to roam the streets.

The oppressive confluence or, rather, the pyramid of events, bore down on him.

The pyramid is the delirium of geometry: a delirium for which there is no instrument of measurement . . . a delirium which—possibly—may only be measured by means of figures.

Thirty zeros are a real horror, but remove the digit before them, and all the thirty zeros perish. Zero alone remains.

There is no horror in this unit, it is a mere trifle. But a unit plus thirty zeros is a monstrosity . . . it hangs entirely on this single unit, this tiny, thin stick . . .

Yes—it was as a human unit, that is, as a gaunt little stick, that Nikolai Apollonovich had lived, completing his course in time—

—Nikolai Apollonovich, in Adam's garb, was a mere little stick; ashamed of his meager figure, he had never ventured into a Turkish bath—

—no, never in all eternity!

And now, upon this little stick had fallen all the monstrous weight of a number exceeding a milliard milliard; and from within him an inexpressible feeling was surging, swelling out of eternity—

—in the same way that a belly swells from expanding gas, a complaint from which all the Ableukhovs suffered—

—through all eternity.

Whereas for the realists nature, the "external world," was humanized, the modernists reversed the process: the "external world"—or, more precisely, the symbols of the "external world," the thoughts and metaphors—merely expresses the ongoing condition of "internal reality." Carl Jung very likely made a serious error in his dual classification, extroversion and introversion. For example, we note that Andreyev, Mayakovsky, and Aragon are introverted at one point in their lives, extroverted at another (this is especially true of Andreyev), depending apparently on whether they believed in the "external world" or not. Surrealism is, in essence, only "internal" naturalism. From its ancestor it even inherited the famous "experimental method." Experiment in art is as meaningless as mathematical proofs of the existence of God. There is nothing more amusing than the spectacle of Lifshits and other theoreticians of his stamp all trying to prove that reason plays too big a part in creativity and cutting down the surrealists instead of using them as illustrations of their assertions.

Petersburg, the title of Bely's novel, is symbolic of rationalism and reason. Even in Dostoevsky's works, leading characters who live in St. Petersburg (as in *White Nights*) often regard the external world of the city as unreal, fantastic, because they are, or will become, "underground men."

Let us cite a passage from Remizov's novel *The Pond,* published in 1908:

The door squealed open.

Two men, wearing black cloaks and black half masks, with thin, golden rapiers swinging at the hips, entered the cell, gripped him silently under the arms and led him from the jail.

They walked for an age through unknown narrow streets, turning into side-streets which became blind alleys, going back on their tracks till they came out onto a wide plaza jammed with people.

The crowd blocked all exits; people seemed to creep and squeeze over one another. An idle horse-drawn streetcar rocked with hysterical forced laughter and the driver, wrinkling his yellow face and braking for all he was worth, cackled and giggled unceasingly.

Beyond the patchwork crowd a bright blue sky was wrapping itself in the shining net of a burning sun and was floating, rather than flying, lower and lower.

He could not reach it as he stood on the high scaffold and looked out over the swarming crowd; the hangman struck him on the neck and his head fell onto his chest and his gaze rested on the terrible, tender spot.

A great deal has been written about an identical scene in Kafka's *The Trial.* But with Remizov this is still a dream; for Kafka, it is reality. Ties to the external world are not yet entirely severed in *The Pond,* and that is why we see more clearly the active crystallization process brought to completion by Kafka. Remizov's principal characters, like all "underground men," "know" that the external world exists but they do not believe in it and that is what makes it unreal and fantastic. In Kafka, Beckett, and other modernists, time is paralyzed, nullified. In Remizov we can still discern how time stopped, because the writer is still trying to write a narrative novel in the classical sense but constantly breaks the thin thread of his story—a thread which serves only as a tie to the external world, just as in Bely—with visions and dreams. For the principal character of the novel the world becomes more and more the internal world, and the powers of the subconscious (or superconscious: we still don't know here which is the master and which the servant) are symbolized in the living persons of the two hangmen.

It is of interest to determine exactly when time stops. The main character commits a crime. He rapes the girl he loves, and a few pages later, time stops. Let us recall what Raskolnikov says to his mother and sister after he commits his crime: "And everything all around me seems not to be happening here . . . it's as if I were looking at you from a great distance." The crime has cut the threads that tied him to the people he loved. The world has become unreal and time has stopped. In reality, only time exists, a dead time. Thus we come to a paradox: the more incomprehensible and horrible the world, the more petrified and dead the internal world, so that analysis (only possible when an object moves either very slowly or not at all, as in a post-mortem) becomes the basic modus vivendi (Joyce, Proust) while at the same time the external world moves with frenzied speed.

Because fear of the outside world is irrational (the ties that made this world seem close and comprehensible are severed), it paralyzes time. It is hardly a coincidence that most modernists are émigrés, that is, people alienated because of circumstances. And this gives rise to an interesting phenomenon: most of the artists and thinkers of the twentieth century are of Jewish origin. When Paul Éluard says, "It is necessary to kill all feeling and sensitivity in man," he calls to mind Spinoza's *"Non ridere, non lugere, neque detestari, sed intelligere."* The phenomenology of Husserl, grandson of Spinoza, is nothing more than modernism in philosophy. And Spinoza, according to Lev Shestov's penetrating analysis, is "the man who killed God."

Just as Remizov's *The Pond* is not a portrayal of the Russia of his time, so also Kafka's *The Trial* is not a vision of a future totalitarian society and the complete alienation that accompanies it, but a rather realistic portrayal of spiritual processes in a man who has quit fighting and who is therefore punished with the death of the soul. The inversion of the crime and the punishment in the works of Kafka is more apparent than real. One cannot be more mistaken than to call Kafka *Homo religiosus*. All his works illustrate how he loses his battle to find faith. Kafka knew this, and that is why he ordered his writing burned after his death. Fear is the absence of faith and faith is not rational. (Let us remember the fearlessness of the fanatically faithful, like the early Christians, the Protestants of Luther's time, and the revolutionary, Pavel Korchagin, in Nikolai Ostrovsky's novel *The Making of a Hero*.)

$2 \times 2 = 4$ leads to a crime punished by the death of the soul. Doubtless, the happiness of future generations is more important than the life of an old woman; doubtless, it is "more practical" that Sonya Marmeladova become a prostitute rather than let her brothers and sisters starve. But in the wake of these rationalizations on the part of Raskolnikov and Sonya comes the dreadful punishment: exclusion from life and the impossibility of love. (Dante, like Dostoevsky, put those deserving the severest punishment at the bottom of hell, where they were condemned to be incapable of love.) Raskolnikov sacrificed a living soul to an abstract idea: the "I" of an old crone. Sonya sacrificed her own "I." It turns out that man, far from being able to own another's soul, does not even possess his own soul. To allow oneself to be violated is as great a crime as the violation itself, and therein lies the key to Kafka's "inversion" of crime and punishment. The one who punishes, the Freudian superego (we very much doubt that it is the "collective unconscious"), does not ask us whether or not something is rational, but demands the strictest obedience to orders. Reason and the conscious cease to shackle and imprison us only when they are subordinated to the subconscious, the irrational. The end does not justify the means: all modern art tells us that. The end, the purpose of life is life itself, and not knowledge of life. The means is often the end. The trend toward problematic philosophy in twentieth-century literature itself speaks of spiritual decay. Let us recall Plato's words: "I deem that the true votary of philosophy is likely to be misunderstood by other men; they do not perceive that he [the philosopher] is always pursuing death and dying . . ."

Modern art is the art of the Homunculus in the second part of Goethe's *Faust*. Homunculus (the "man from the test tube" or the "underground" or Plato's "cave") knows all and can do nothing. Hamlet dies the instant he awakens and begins to live; Homunculus, the instant that, in his over-powering desire for life (Venus), he breaks his test tube. Will Homunculus of the twentieth century manage to survive if he finds the strength to break his glass "wall," his test tube, his $2 \times 2 = 4$?

One of the basic characteristics of all "isms" is an absolute perfection of form naïvely called "formalism." In literature this shows up in ornate language, neologisms, and other devices. The result is that thoughts and words (symbols of thoughts) become the only reality, so that the enrichment of the word content becomes the enrichment of existence itself. Therein lie the roots of the *fabula* (more accurately, what has replaced the *fabula* of the classical novel), which through association has become the so-called "stream of consciousness" in modernistic works, as in Joyce's *Ulysses*. Thought, word, the metaphor, become the only reality. So we understand Breton completely when he says that "the word has ceased to be a means of communication." A passage in Leonid Andreyev's story *The Red Laugh* (published in 1904, a decade before Kafka) contains an example of complete catharsis and uses an approach that served as a basis for Kafka's *Metamorphosis:*

Those children . . . Their mouths, resembling the jaws of toads or frogs, opened widely and convulsively; behind the transparent skin of their naked bodies the red blood was coursing angrily— and they were killing each other at play. They were the most terrible of all that I had seen, for they were little and could penetrate everywhere.

I was looking out of the window and one of the little ones noticed me, smiled, and with his eyes asked me to let him in. "I want to go to you," he said.

"You'll kill me!"

"I want to go to you," he said, growing suddenly pale, and began scrambling up the white wall like a rat—just like a hungry rat. He kept losing his footing, and squealed and darted about the wall with such rapidity that I could not follow his impetuous, sudden movements.

"He can crawl in under the door," I said to myself with horror, and as if he had guessed my thoughts, he grew thin and long, and waving the end of his tail rapidly, he crawled into the dark crack under the front door."

"Like a rat" becomes the rat itself!

It is interesting to follow the distortion of form and the

"disintegration of realism" in the creative work of Andreyev. He used "realistic," "symbolist," and expressionist styles nearly a decade before the appearance of expressionism in German and other Western European literature. The form of his works, even the language and sentence structure, depends on whether or not at any given moment he believed in the revolution (the so-called "Red myth"). Characteristically, he wrote his best story, the brilliant and realistic *The Seven Who Were Hanged,* at a time when, far from trying to create a masterpiece, he wanted only "to shout as loudly as possible: Don't hang them, you beasts!" as he said in a letter when the revolutionaries of 1905 were to be dealt with by the tsarist regime. The artist's fight gives birth to realism and *fabula*. The artist surrenders and modernism is born. At that instant when words again became a means of communication, the gifted writer Andreyev created a work of genius. Kaiser is right: the death of the storyteller is the death of the novel. Or as Rozanov said about contemporary Russian literature at the close of the nineteenth century: "Man is dead; only his trousers remain"—just as Nietzsche said, "God is dead." Naturally, only the death of faith is meant in each case. The disintegration of realism is the result of the disintegration of personality, which in turn is nothing but personal surrender.

The description of a schizophrenic in the Medical Encyclopedia exactly matches the description of Andrei Bely's style in the well-known Soviet Literary Encyclopedia: "Rhythmic speech, neologism, associative thinking [the 'stream of consciousness'], feeling of catastrophe, mysticism," etc., etc. Schizophrenia is total separation from the outside world, the ultimate degree of "alienation." During wars and revolutions and similar events when man, whether he wants to or not, is forced to fight, the number of new cases of schizophrenia is reduced to an incredible minimum. Or, to cite Blondel: "All spiritual disease is a result of the separation from the environment—physical, social, spiritual." Fighting reestablishes the severed ties.

Here is an interesting passage from the story "The Wall" (1901):

Time did not exist for us. There was no yesterday, no today, no tomorrow. The night never left us, not resting beyond the mountains to return again, strong, shiny black, and still. Because of this it was everlastingly tired, breathless, sullen and full of meanness. Sometimes when it could no longer tolerate our clamor and moaning or could not see our sores and our misery, its black, heaving chest boiled with stormy fury. It growled at us like a chained man-beast, with its fiery fearsome eyes angrily blinking, showering light on the black, fathomless precipices and the gloomy, haughtily silent wall and the pitiful band of trembling men. The men pressed themselves to the wall as if it were a friend, begging its protection, but it was ever our enemy. The night, outraged by our pusillanimity and cowardice, would begin laughing menacingly, bobbing its grey, spotted belly, and the ancient, bald mountains would join in this satanic laughter. Somberly amused, the wall echoed it resonantly, playfully dropping stones on us which crushed our heads and flattened our bodies. These giants calling to one another were enjoying themselves, and the wind whistled a wild melody. We lay prone, listening with horror how deep within the earth something enormous was turning and twisting, vaguely knocking to be let out.

Then we all begged: Kill us!

But though we died each second, we were immortal like the gods.

At last, the senseless transport of fury and gaiety would pass and the night would sigh heavily, spitting damp sand at us like a sick person. We joyfully forgave it, laughing at its exhaustion and weakness like children.

Then we would dance in circles, couple by couple, and I, a leper, would find a temporary darling for myself. It was so merry, so enthralling. I would embrace her, and she would laugh, and her teeth were so white and her cheeks rosy-rosy. *Pozobleu-pozobleu.* It was so enthralling.

One can not understand how it happened, but happy smiling teeth started chattering, kisses became as sour as vinegar, and with a scream not quite yet devoid of joy we would start biting and killing each other. And that darling with the white teeth was beating me on my sick weak head, clinging to my chest, reaching into my very heart with her sharp little claws, beating me, a leper, who was so miserable, so miserable. This was more terrible than the anger of the night itself or the heartless laughter of the wall. I, the leper, would cry and tremble with fear, and slowly, so nobody would notice, I would kiss the wall's vicious feet, begging it to let me alone, let me pass into that world where there are no mad people killing one another. But base as it was, the wall would not let me pass, and then I would spit at it, beating it with my fists, and yelling at it: "Look at this killer! It's laughing!" But my voice choked, my breath stank, and nobody would listen to me, a leper.

Time stands still, the attempt is futile and senseless, the wall is the same as in *Notes from the Underground.* "Time is out of joint."

Here is Andreyev himself on surrealism, in 1908, at a time when no one in Russia had heard of Freud, and predating André Breton's *Manifesto of Surrealism* by sixteen years:

Just as a brave, talkative, determined man, when in the company of quiet men, deadens their inaudible voices—similarly reason, when man is awake, deadens all other voices reaching indistinctly out from the secret depths of the body. And only during sleep, when reason powerlessly crosses over the precipices of absurdity, losing the thread of logical thinking, do they resound loud and imperative, often with as much sense as the great master reason itself.

A passage from *The Pond* puts this line of thought into practice that same year:

Everything approached and drew away as if flowing before one's eyes . . . there . . . the washstand penetrated the bed, and the chair's legs were crawling over the floor . . . suddenly they made an infernal circle and the circle was jumping around in circles . . .

From some foggy stifling distant place furious voices cried out and thrusting a blazing knife into the darkness crept away . . . and Nikolai pictured himself crawling after them on an intolerably green field over mounds of living bodies . . . into the pitch darkness . . . into despair.

Here is another example from Bely's *Petersburg:*

Weightless, bereft of sensation, suddenly deprived of gravity, of every physical sense, he fixed the space of his eyes (he could not say positively that his eyes fixed it, because all bodily sensation had left him); he realized, too, that he no longer had any parietal bones, that in their place there was a gap; Apollon Apollonovich saw in himself this round gap which formed a blue circle. At the fatal moment when according to his calculation the Mongol, who was imprinted in his consciousness but was now no longer visible, was about to reach him, something resembling a roaring wind in a chimney rapidly began to pull his consciousness through the blue parietal breach—into infinity.

A scandal (his consciousness noted its occurrence, but he could not remember when): the wind blew Apollon Apolionovich out of Apollon Apollonovich.

Apollon Apollonovich flew through the round breach into the darkness above his head which was somehow like the planet earth, and there he was scattered asunder into sparks.

There was primordial darkness; and the consciousness struggled within it—no universal consciousness, but a very simple one.

The consciousness now turned back, releasing two perceptions: they descended like two arms. What they perceived was a sort of shape (very like the bottom of a bath) filled with stinking filth; the perceptions splashed about in this bath of filth; soon they had become stuck to the sides of the bath. The consciousness now fought to get out, but something heavy weighed down the perceptions.

Then the consciousness saw its habitation: a little yellow old man, whose bare heels were pressing against a rug.

The consciousness, it seemed, was the little old man himself; as he sat on his bed, the little old man listened to the distant clatter.

And then Apollon Apollonovich suddenly understood: his journey through the corridor, through the salon, through his head—had been only a dream.

And no sooner did this thought occur to him than he awoke: it had been a double dream.

Russian modernism exerted a strong influence on budding post-October literary life, on that constellation of brilliant prose writers: Boris Pilnyak, Isaac Babel, Alexander Malishkin, Yuri Olesha, all of whom perished tragically but who, with the exception of Pilnyak, have now been rehabilitated in the U.S.S.R. We will give an example of this influence by first citing a passage from Alexei Remizov's novel *The Pond:*

He went past the soldiers who were marching along to music. The swelling copper sounds poured into him, making him huge, turning him into ringing copper. He was dashed along the street, ringing.

Now compare with it this passage from Yuri Olesha's famous novel *Envy* (1927):

The band marched along and, beyond it, Valya was floating. The sound of the instruments held her up in the air. She was carried by the sound. She went up and down, over the trumpets, depending on the height and strength of the sound.

Passages like this are legion.

Similarly, Pilnyak is a direct descendant of Andrei Bely.

His prose contains many passages which seem to have been simply copied out of *Petersburg*. We quote Bely first:

The Nevsky Prospect is rectilinear (speaking among ourselves), because it is a European prospect; every European prospect is not simply a prospect, but (as I have already pointed out) a prospect is European, because, h'm . . . yes . . .

. . . Other Russian cities offer little more than piles of little wooden houses.

Petersburg differs impressively from them all.

If you insist on affirming an uncouth legend that Moscow has a population of a million and a half, then you will have to admit that the real capital should be Moscow, because only capitals have a population of a million and a half. If you believe this uncouth legend, then Petersburg is not the capital.

Petersburg, St. Petersburg, or Peter (it is all one), is also part of the Russian Empire.

Now comes Pilnyak:

Peter means stone, and the throne city, Saint-Peter-Burg is Holy-Stone-City. But the meaning can be given in one word: Saint-Peter. Burg is defined by three words: Holy-Stone-City; there is more than one meaning and Saint-Petersburg is therefore a fiction. The perspectives of the avenues of Saint-Peterburg tended in the very end to be transformed from prospects into metaphysics.

Bely:

There was neither Earth nor Venus nor Mars: only revolving rings. Then a fourth planet was shattered, and an immense Sun was being compressed into a new world. Mists drifted past; Nikolai Apollonovich had been thrown into infinity; distances flowed by.

Then he was on earth again; the sword of Saturn hung in the air, and the continent of Atlantis had been destroyed. Nikolai Apollonovich was now a depraved monster. Afterwards he was in

China . . . then he had been reincarnated as a Russian noble-
man . . .

Time had completed its revolution: Saturn's reign had returned.

Time had stopped moving; everything was perishing.

. . . . .

"What is our chronology?" . . .

"We haven't any, Kolenka. Our chronology, my dear, is simply
zero . . ."

Pilnyak:

Anyway, there was no moonlight; anyway, there was haze and
there was also fog, darkness, and obscurity. It was hailing. How
should I not tell inexpressibly how in snowstorms, in the snow, in
the howling of the wind, in the snowdrifts, in the roar and the
whirlpool I, nearsighted, snow sticking to my glasses, the glass
frosted over; I can't see without them or rather I can see only
some of green haze, snow is striking my open eyes, out of the blue
haze snowflakes suddenly appear, falling more and more thickly
as if there were more than there really were, and one has to keep
one's eyes closed, and one has to stretch out one's hands, and the
houses, the church, the wind, the snow bend over you. More and
more.

Suddenly

emerges

absolute quiet, silence, motionlessness, immobility—immobility
in a furious rush. This is the theory of eternity. This is for me the
revolution, China creeps here also, and the woman with the
Mordvin face; suddenly, around the corner, a roar and whistling
—suddenly the stone woman with the Mordvin face.

The study of Russian modernism (the importance of
which cannot be overstressed) is unusually difficult because
most of the works themselves are not available (we have only
the collected works of Leonid Andreyev) and because his-

torical and theoretical treatments of that period are lacking. In the huge tenth volume of the *History of Russian Literature,* published by the U.S.S.R. Academy of Sciences in 1954, which deals with the period of the "disintegration of Russian realism," Bely is barely mentioned, and Alexei Remizov not at all!

Modern art tells us that there exists a kind of inner slavery which is not directly dependent on the outside world (a drastic example of the severed tie between the inner and the outer world: schizophrenia), and in this is its great, invaluable contribution. It is not impossible that the future liberator of mankind from "inner slavery," from $2 \times 2 = 4$, will be able to repeat about Remizov, Andreyev, Kafka, and others what Marx said of Balzac: "From them I learned more about man's soul than from all the worthless pages of social, individual, experimental, depth, etc., psychology." Thought, idea, belief, love, suffering, our "I" are no less real than automobiles and rockets. Perhaps there will come a time when it will be possible to investigate with precision instruments Job's claim that his suffering was greater than the sand of all the seas. Perhaps the day is not far off when all the current wrangling between idealists and materialists will seem as amusing as the disputes of medieval scholars about how many angels could dance on the head of a pin. When today much of this argument is called "idealistic mysticism," it behooves us to recall that the French academics called the inventor of the phonograph a charlatan. The "unnatural" and the "supernatural" both belong to nature. Lightning did not become less lethal the instant men knew that it was "only" an electric charge of a certain voltage and had nothing to do with Zeus. There is no essential difference between a confession in church and psychoanalytic therapy. Modern art has revealed much that is "unnatural" in our nature.

Perhaps the day will soon dawn when we will understand the following aphorism of Lev Shestov's: "Men of genius generally have idiot children. Thus the astrologers gave birth to astronomers and the alchemists to chemists."

It is clear that in this somewhat condensed essay we have put forward some heretical thoughts and ideas (without which it is impossible to write about modern literature). They are heretical because of the attitude they express toward the "high degree of knowledge and science which is modern man's present social development," and other things in that vein. Because we know this, we feel it fitting to call on Goethe, who expressed a brilliant thought: "Only that which is fruitful is true."

Dixi et salvavi animam meam![1]

[1961]

[1] I have spoken and I have saved my soul. [Trans.]

EVGENY ZAMYATIN: THE CHAGALL OF RUSSIAN LITERATURE

On the occasion of the publication of North, *selected short stories by Evgeny Zamyatin, in Belgrade (1963)* in *Serbo-Croatian*

> *A gray, nonexisting, frozen sun in fog and from left and right, from above and below, a dove beyond the house in flames*
>
> "The Dragon," 1917

*   *   *

AT LAST we have Zamyatin in translation.

Belgrade's *Nolit* is continuing a long tradition of publishing the world's avant-garde writers. Zamyatin, one of the greatest writers in twentieth-century literature, has been all but unknown to our reading public. This is understandable when one realizes that for more than three decades now even Russian readers have had no access to the works of this literary giant, who, consequently, has had no welcome in the socialist world as a whole.

Between the wars his early novel, *Where the Devil Said Goodnight,* was translated in Yugoslavia and published along with two stories, "Mamay" and "Yola," in the series "A Thousand Best Novels." After World War II, two sketches appeared: "The Dragon" [Zagreb, 1954, in an anthology of

Soviet prose] and "The Eyes" [Zagreb, 1961, in a student literary journal]. But that was all. Now we have an excellent selection of Zamyatin's stories decently translated by Mira Lalić. This collection represents a great event on the Yugoslav literary scene, comparable only to Gorijan's translation of Joyce's *Ulysses* and Milica Nicolić's translation of Andrei Bely's *Petersburg*. So we are afforded at least a portion of the output of a great triumvirate: Zamyatin, Bely, and Andreyev. Among the Russian modernists, only that colossus, Alexei Remizov, is missing.

In discussing Zamyatin, we must refer to the first decade of the twentieth century, which gave birth to modernism in Russian literature, a period—the most important and least known as far as Russian prose is concerned—which set a style and trend continued by Zamyatin, Boris Pilnyak, and Isaac Babel after the revolution. These three writers, whose works may be called the quintessence of Russian modernism, have been the dominating influence on such later Soviet writers as Alexander Malishkin, Yuri Olesha, Konstantin Fedin, Leonid Leonov, and others, down to Boris Pasternak. Indeed, this same influence, rooted in the prerevolutionary era, can be seen in works produced by young Soviet writers in our day.

When modernist literature was outlawed in the early 1930's, not only were young Soviet modernists no longer to be mentioned, but the very founders of twentieth-century Russian literature—Andreyev, Remizov, and Bely, without whom none of the great works of Soviet literature known today would have appeared, including Sholokhov's *And Quiet Flows the Don*—were put under a pall as well. That is why the rehabilitation in the U.S.S.R. of certain post-revolutionary writers is now being followed up by the rehabilitation of their teachers, the prerevolutionary modernists.

Official Soviet rehabilitation of Russian modernists began in 1957. Already a good many of the writings of Andreyev and Babel have been issued, as well as a more limited selection from Bely. The rehabilitation of Pilnyak and Zamyatin is a question of time. One recently published collection of modern Russian literature even includes Dmitri Merezhkovsky, hitherto anathematized. Remizov and Lev Shestov have also been referred to.

In Yugoslavia, works by Isaac Babel, Leonid Andreyev, and Boris Pilnyak have been appearing regularly. Last year the translation of perhaps the most important novel in Russian twentieth-century literature, Bely's *Petersburg,* was made available. And the gap created by the absence of Remizov is soon to be filled since a Belgrade publisher has selections from his prose in preparation.

Yevgeny Zamyatin was born in 1884 and was by profession a naval engineer and later a professor at the Technical Faculty. He began his literary activity shortly before World War I. For his the novel *Where the Devil Said Goodnight,* a gloomy portrayal of Russian army life, he was persecuted by the tsarist regime. During the war he spent some time in England and wrote a great novel, *The Islanders,* a satire on bourgeois English society, in the style which was to become his hallmark.

After the revolution and during the civil war he brought out some of his best work, including the short story "Mamay" (1918). Four years later, in 1922, he finished a play *The Fires of St. Dominic,* an allegorical satire on inquisitions of all types; and in 1924 he published abroad the novel *We,* a cutting portrait of a mechanized, totalitarian society to come, very much like the pessimistic descriptions which Huxley, Orwell, and others were to offer many years later. In *We* he greeted the revolution not as "the last proletarian" revolution, and declared: "What number is the greatest? . . . Which is the last revolution? There is no greatest number.

There is no last revolution." By this time he had become an
object of harsh official criticism and, in 1930, when the
bureaucratic apparatus was becoming crystallized, Zamyatin
found it impossible to publish anything. With the help of
Maxim Gorky, who went on his behalf to Stalin, he finally
obtained permission to leave the U.S.S.R. in 1932 and thus,
unlike Babel and Pilnyak, saved his life.

It is no exaggeration to say that Zamyatin's influence on
Soviet literature to come will be enormous, equaling perhaps
that of Gogol on nineteenth-century Russian literature. Zamyatin is not only the creator of a highly original satirical-
grotesque style with pronouncedly expressionist attributes,
not only a writer whose flow of language has an elastic,
almost tactile quality with restless, disharmonic, inverted
clauses that seem to mirror the spirit of our age. He is also a
superb artist-technician, which is not as unimportant as it
usually seems to be. His choice of words and metaphors is
that of an engineer, a technician of today, and thus fore-
shadows the "technical" terminology becoming more and
more current in popular speech and thought. For this reason
Zamyatin should appeal to present-day readers. While he
does not accept realism in his art, neither does he permit
decadent symbolism. He believes in movement from reality
to an inner world, and vice versa, and the greatness of his art
is the skillful transition across the frontier between them.

In 1923, Zamyatin wrote an important essay, "On Literature, Revolution, and Entropy." It is worthwhile citing part
of this essay here:

We can put a police officer or a commissar in the cart, but the
cart will still remain a cart. And literature will still remain the
literature·of yesterday, if we drive a real life—even "revolutionary real life"—along the well-traveled highway—even if we drive
it in a fast troika with bells. What we need today are automobiles, airplanes, winged flight, seconds, dotted lines.

The old, slow, soporific descriptions are no more. The order of the day is laconicism—but every word must be supercharged, high-voltage. Into one second must be compressed what formerly went into a sixty-second minute. Syntax becomes elliptical, volatile; complicated pyramids of periods are dismantled and broken down into the single stones of independent clauses. In swift movement the canonical, the habitual eludes the eye: hence the unusual, often strange symbolism and choice of words. The image is sharp, synthetic; it contains only the one basic trait which one has time to seize upon from a moving automobile. The lexicon hallowed by custom has been invaded by dialect, neologisms, science, mathematics, technology.

There is a rule, if you can call it a rule, that the writer's talent consists in making the rule the exception; but there are far more writers who turn the exception into the rule.

The business of science and art alike is the projection of the world onto coordinates. Differences in form are due to differences in the coordinates. All realist forms involve projection onto the fixed, plane coordinates of the Euclidean world. These coordinates have no existence in nature. This finite, fixed world does not exist; it is a convention, an abstraction, an unreality. And therefore realism—be it "socialist" or "bourgeois"—is unreal; immeasurably closer to reality is projection onto fast-moving, curved surfaces—as in the new mathematics and the new art. Realism which is not primitive, not *realia* but *realiora,* consists in displacement, distortion, curvature, nonobjectivity. The lens of the camera is objective.

A new form is not intelligible to all; for many it is difficult. Maybe. The habitual, the banal is of course simpler, pleasanter, more comfortable. Euclid's world is very simple and Einstein's world is very difficult; nevertheless, it is now impossible to return to Euclid's. No revolution, no heresy is comfortable and easy. Because it is a leap, it is a rupture of the smooth evolutionary curve, and a rupture is a wound, a pain. But it is a necessary wound: most people suffer from hereditary sleeping sickness, and those who are sick with this ailment (entropy) must not be allowed to sleep, or they will go to their last sleep, the sleep of death.

This same sickness is common to artists and writers: they go contentedly to sleep in their favorite artistic form which they have devised, then twice revised. They do not have the strength to wound themselves, to cease to love what has become dear to them. They do not have the strength to come out from their lived-in, laurel-scented rooms, to come out into the open air and start anew.

To wound oneself, it is true, is difficult, even dangerous. But to live today as yesterday and yesterday as today is even more difficult for the living.

When we read the post-October Soviet modernists, including Zamyatin, one thing becomes clear. Within the framework of modern expression, within the dimensions of disintegrated, modernistic form, there exist two currents flowing in opposite directions. One flows toward the absolutely abstract, the static; the other, toward the dynamic—the starting point of the latter being itself abstraction. Pilynak's *Mother Earth* differs little as far as form is concerned from Joyce or even from Samuel Beckett's *Molloy*. But whereas Beckett's world seems paralyzed, motionless, Pilnyak's is constantly on the move. Characteristic of Pilnyak, too, is his development of plot through association and through "interior monologues" and the insertion into his tales of fragments from old chronicles, citations from law codes, regulations, and precepts, just as modern painters use wire and old tin. But the difference is that everything in Pilnyak pulses and roars along in a frantic stream of life. The prerevolutionary modernism of Andreyev, Bely, and Remizov was moving toward absolute abstraction, and the world of their writing was growing less dynamic; Pilnyak, Babel, and Zamyatin, on the other hand, were moving in the opposite direction, toward realism. Had Russian literature not been bureaucratically stifled in the

1930's an exciting Russian realistic literature would be flowering now. But we should not forget that contemporary realism could spring only from abstraction, not from classical realism. Therefore it is Zhdanov's, rather than any Western, influence that is incomparably more important as a catalyst in bringing (a probable) future Soviet modernism into full bloom.

Abstraction, death of the soul, is a direct result of the alienation of the personality, the disintegration of the individual and society (when each no longer accepts the other), total introversion, withdrawal into the world of the ego, in which ideas, thoughts, and words become the sole reality. One of the causes of introversion is oppression. Every act of oppression is thus a direct agent of alienation and this alienation is reflected in art as abstraction. In Hitler's Third Reich, the leading example is Kafka.

If in the 1930's no attempt had been made to force integration in Russian literature by annihilation of the individual personality (which is exactly the essence of "socialist realism"), realism in art would be very much alive in the U.S.S.R. The integration of the individual and society cannot be achieved through violence and oppression. Only in an idealized communistic society, in which an integration of this kind theoretically exists, would "classical" art be possible; that is, the artist would not live in a dualistic world, in an "outer" and "inner" reality. "Socialist realism" is an attempt to destroy this duality, not through treatment and cure, but by amputating the "inner world" itself, an amputation which, fortunately, proved impossible. Impossible because, as Zamyatin puts it, "socialist realism is not realistic."

"Socialist realism" merely prolonged the dominance of abstraction in art. The modernism of Zamyatin, Pilnyak, or Babel is infinitely more "socialist" than any artificial realism. The greatest Russian literary critic and theoretician of this century, Viktor Shklovsky, wrote: "The modernists are turning the world topsy-turvy not to astound but to regain a sense of reality." Mayakovsky, who, together with Pasternak, founded LEF [Left Front, a literary group, and the name of their journal], which spoke for leftist, modern art, wrote after a visit to Pablo Picasso's studio in 1922: "Now I can banish fear. With Picasso there is no returning to classicism. His studio is variety itself, beginning with a realistic blue-pink painting in the oldest, most ancient style and ending with a construction of tin and wire."

We know "reactionary" romanticism in Chateaubriand and "progressive" romanticism in Byron. Perhaps the modernism of Zamyatin, Pilnyak, and Babel can be called "socialist" modernism. Let me insist: post-revolutionary Russian modernism differs from its Western counterpart, but not in form. It is moving from abstraction toward "life." It is dynamic. In any case, it is not the fault of artists living under socialism that they cannot produce "classical realism." Art is always the mirror of society, and modern art is no exception. A man cannot improve his looks by breaking his mirror. Quite the contrary, that only makes progress impossible.

Zamyatin's novels are the literary counterpart of Chagall's paintings. People fly in the air, flow about the room and collide with objects; small animals leap from people's eyes; there are endless such effects. Here is a sample from Zamyatin's *The Cave:*

A part of Martin Martinovich, who was putting dried potato peelings through a coffee grinder to make crêpes, was casting claylike grins at Masha; another part of him was a bird flying from freedom outdoors into a room and dashing itself blindly, senselessly against walls, ceiling, windows . . .

And Martin Martinovich, split in two parts, the one looking at an immortal organ-grinder, an immortal little wooden horse, an immortal ice floe; the other, panting, helping Obertishev count his logs . . .

Flattened, like a piece of paper, Masha was laughing on the

bed. Wound into a tight knot, Martin Martinovich was laughing louder and louder . . .

There is a tendency in Yugoslavia on the part of those commenting on Russian modernists to "justify" the errors and deviations of these writers and issue an appeal that they be forgiven for breaking a straight line in the stream of Soviet literature, with respect both to their content and to their style. Milica Nikolić, discussing Marina Tsvetayeva and Osip Mandelshtam in *Modern Russian Poetry* (Belgrade, 1961); Mila Stojnić, writing about Bely, Pilnyak, and Zamyatin in *Introduction to "Petersburg"* (Belgrade, 1962); the study *Russian Literature of the Twentieth Century* (Sarajevo, 1962) [all three in Serbo-Croation]; and Mira Lalić in the preface to her translation of Zamyatin (Belgrade, 1963), all seem to include the notion that we "should forgive Russian modernist writers all their sins and errors, that, in spite of their having gone astray, they still have a lot to give us," etc.

This is a totally wrong approach to these writers. If one excises all the "errors" and "mistakes" in content and style found in Pilnyak, Babel, Olesha, Zamyatin, Mandelshtam, Pasternak, and even Leonov, one is left with the same kind of standard Soviet writers whose names are listed by the hundreds in countless official histories of Soviet literature and who today are not read, whereas "heretics and sinners" remain popular not in spite but because of their ideological-stylistic "errors." And if it is so, why should their original, unique, historical and artistic attitude in life be called "erroneous"?

In either accepting or rejecting Zamyatin, Pilnyak, or Babel, we must understand one thing: that their very worth lies in their so-called errors. That is why they are read today. For, as Zamyatin himself wrote:

Errors are of greater value than truths: truth is machine-like, error is alive; truth reassures, error unsettles. And even if the answers are quite impossible, so much the better: to ask answered questions is the privilege of minds constructed on the same principle as the cow's stomach, which is ideally suited, as well we know, to chewing the cud.

[1963]

SOME RELEVANT
HISTORICAL ASSOCIATIONS

The "new" French novel and LEF: Shklovsky, Shestov

* * *

THE SO-CALLED "new" French novel, whose leading
representatives are Marguerite Duras, Claude Simon, Michel
Butor, Alain Robbe-Grillet, and Nathalie Sarraute, is being
written about and discussed all over the world. To define
briefly the practice and theory of the writers of the "new
novel," which does in fact represent a new literary trend, we
might say this: according to these writers, a novel is a way of
experiencing reality in which both writer and reader participate. In order to commit the reader as wholly as possible,
a certain transformation of the form of the novel, a shifting
of reality (Russian formalists would say a "detachment") , is
needed. The typically "phenomenological" doubt of the
author's ability or right to elevate himself above his material
conditions the reduction of the story line to a minimum. The
absence of elaborated characters or any attempt to identify
the literary work with the subject it describes are also required characteristics. There are no descriptions of inner life,
which is only hinted at through descriptions of objects and
events. "The novel as a search" is how the "new novel" is defined by its leading theoretician, Michel Butor.

Few people realize that the theory of the "new novel" is
not new at all.

From 1923 to 1925, in Russia, the literary group called
LEF was very active in promoting modern act. Most prom-

inent in this group, headed by Vladimir Mayakovsky, were the poets Boris Pasternak and Nikolai Aseyev and the theoreticians Viktor Shklovsky and Boris Arvatov. Essentially, LEF was continuing the traditions of prerevolutionary Russian futurism. From 1927 to 1928, the new LEF, consisting of the same people, was active. It later became *REF* (Revolutionary Front) and was suppressed by bureaucratic means after Mayakovsky's death in 1930.

LEF adherents advocated the theory of "thing-ism" (in Russian, *veshchizm*) ; that is, they called for the focus of an artistic work to be the description of an object, not the description of a person. "The task of a writer is to describe events, not people," wrote Boris Arvatov. LEF denied writers the right to create characters and plot. It advocated a "literature of fact," as opposed to a "literature of inventions," and sought the maximum participation of the reader in understanding reality through a work of art.

This is, word for word, the French "new novel." Unfortunately, LEF did not produce any important prose writers. Alexei Remizov, among Russian writers, most closely approximated the LEF theory. He did not belong to the LEF but in an early and, for him fairly atypical novel, *In a Field Azure* (translated in Yugoslavia between the wars) , he completely fulfilled the requirements of the LEF theoreticians. Thus, we can say that he was the originator of the French "new novel." Since Remizov was translated and read in France, the possibility is not excluded that this great Russian writer directly influenced contemporary French literature.

After the revolution, in addition to LEF, a so-called School of Formalism flourished. Paralleling and closely associated with the development of Russian futurism, it concentrated on literary criticism and the theory of literature. Its main representatives were Viktor Shklovsky, Roman Yakobson, Yuri Tynyanov, Boris Eichenbaum, V. Zhirmunsky, A. K.

Vinogradov, and B. Tomashevsky. To start, between 1916 and 1919, the "formalist" group was called OPOYAZ (Society for the Study of Poetic Language). After the revolution, it operated within LEF and within another important literary group, The Serapion Brothers. At the beginning of the thirties, because of bureaucratic pressure, the "formalists" evolved first into "forsovts" ("formal-sociological" approach to a literary work) and later disappeared completely from the field of criticism and theory of contemporary literature. Most of the theoreticians of the formalist school turned to problems of artistic creation in previous eras (at least one century back); the others devoted themselves to writing historical novels. Tynyanov wrote *Death and Diplomacy in Persia*, a novel about Griboyedov, and *Kukhlya*, a novel about Küchelbecker (both translated in Yugoslavia). Viktor Shklovsky wrote *Marco Polo*. Roman Yakobson, who is second only to Shklovsky in importance among the formalists and is one of the outstanding linguists of our century, emigrated to the United States, where the traditions of the Russian formalists were continued in the so-called "new criticism." After 1956, when conditions again became favorable for the development of critical opinions, several books by Viktor Shklovsky, the founder and leader of the formalist school, were published.

In discussing Shklovsky, we are involuntarily reminded of Lev Shestov, the great Russian existentialist philosopher, who is less well known as a literary critic and as the founder of so-called "philosophical criticism." The leaders of the school of formalism, and indirectly LEF (hence the "phenomenological" theory of its prose), were under his influence. The purpose of art, according to Shklovsky, is to "transform the known into the unknown"; the purpose of philosophy, "not to appease men by explaining the world, but to disquiet them by pointing out the relativity of every explanation."

"There are no miracles, everything is a miracle," wrote Shestov. "The task of man in this world is to pose to every answer his own question," said Shestov. Resignation, passivity, explanation mean death.

Lev Shestov (1866–1938) was attached to no group. He devoted himself to philosophy and to philosophic criticism of literature and is one of the most important Russian critics of all time. Yet he is little known. His studies on Tolstoy, Dostoevsky, Turgenev, Chekhov, Nietzsche, and Shakespeare represent the highest peak of modern thought. He produced his most important works between 1900 and 1910. In chronological order, they are *Shakespeare and His Critic Brandes, Good in the Teachings of Tolstoy and Nietzsche, Dostoevsky and Nietzsche, All Things Are Possible, Beginnings and Ends, Potestas Clavium, On Job's Balances—Wanderings through Souls.*

Shestov's work anticipated all of contemporary Western European thought, including Heidegger, Jaspers, French and Spanish existentialists, even Ernest Bloch.

Unlike Western existentialist philosophers, who are inclined to pessimism, Lev Shestov possessed an immense tragic optimism and an endless confidence in this world into which we have been "thrown." He had confidence, not in man, but in the cosmos. According to him, alienation disappears the moment man realizes that nature, "the outside world," even death, are not enemies of the individual. In the *Myth of Sisyphus,* Camus wrote that Shestov "only toward the middle of his life began walking with enough assurance through a desert, all the realities of which he turned into rocks."

In fact, the desert through which Shestov walked is no longer desolate. In his footsteps walk innumerable modern thinkers today. The awareness that we (and not just each individual "I") are all "strangers," in Camus's sense, that we have been "thrown into this world" leads us by a strange dialectic back to social reality. Not to be aware of alienation is the ultimate in alienation.

In his studies of Plotinus, Pascal, Bergson, Solovyev, in his polemic with Husserl (his "brotherly enemy," as their relationship was described by Gaetano Picone), Shestov advanced the opinion that although awareness of alienation, awareness of the dream in which most men spend their lives, indeed opens a way to an awakening, the awareness itself is not awakening. Only the act of the individual, not social consciousness, leads to freedom, to life. The awareness of life itself is not yet life. This point of view links Shestov directly both to Marx, whose basic tenet is that "it is essential not to understand the world, but to change it" (or rather, to attempt to change it), and to Bergson, who wrote in *L' Évolution créatrice:* "Thus, to strive to understand in any other way but through reason is absurd; but if one honestly accepts risk, then action will perhaps cut the knot tied by reason, a knot which it cannot untie."

In 1909, in *All Things Are Possible,* Shestov, with the foresight of genius, predicted an "anti-theater" almost half a century before the appearance of Ionesco and Beckett.

Sartre's literary essays were translated last year in Yugoslavia; a few years ago, Heidegger's essay "On the Substance of Art" was published. Today, reading Sartre and Shestov, one can't help being amazed by the limitations of Sartre's thought in comparison with the all-embracing, biblically clear thinking of the Russian philosopher, which a half century ago reached a point that Sartre and Heidegger have not even approached.

Sartre, Heidegger, Camus, and many other existentialist thinkers and artists are translated and read in Yugoslavia. They are written about, they are discussed and argued against, so that a philosophy of the absurd, whatever our attitude toward it, is present and undoubtedly has considerable effect. How paradoxical, then, that hardly anyone in Yugoslavia knows Lev Shestov.

For the first time in history, Western Europe, which otherwise has been skeptical toward Slavic philosophers, has recognized a Russian thinker. Yet we, Slavs ourselves, came to know him through the French and the Germans.

How ironic that for years official Soviet philosophers and critics of the "cult of personality" ignored and kept silent about the very thing that Russia had given the world, *modern thought,* while at the same time attributing to their people, often undeservedly, all kinds of innovations in science and art. Fortunately, LEF has now been rehabilitated. Viktor Shklovsky is being published again, and Lev Shestov's name is openly mentioned.

[1962]

AT THE CROSSROADS:
NOTES ON CONTEMPORARY
RUSSIAN PROSE

*　　*　　*

ANYONE WHO carefully follows Soviet literary develop-
ments cannot fail to notice that Russian literature today is
standing at a crossroads with branches leading in several,
and opposite, directions. This raises two significant questions:
In which direction will the torrent of young talents turn?
Will measures undertaken to direct the stream of Russian
literary development obtain results opposite to those intended?

One thing is indubitably clear since the appearance at the
turn of the century of those modernistic trends which resulted in a break with nineteenth-century traditions: Russian
literature has never been so seriously and critically chal-
lenged to reconsider prevailing values as it is today. A certain
spiritual liberalization of the literary atmosphere after 1956
has strongly affected the existing situation. Great prose
works—as the most complex form of literary creation—are the
deepest reflections of contemporary events.

To the student of contemporary Russian prose the most
striking fact perhaps is that "socialist realism" is no longer
reflected in contemporary writing, even though it continues
as the only officially sanctioned method of artistic expression.
The older generation of Soviet writers, most prominent
among whom are Mikhail Sholokhov and Leonid Leonov,
has played an increasingly less active role in the literary life
of the country. The age group represented by such writers as
Konstantin Simonov and Vera Penova has, of late, produced

works which are anything but apologetic and which usually come to terms with the recent past. To the efforts of the youngest literary generation (Dudintsev, Bondaryev, Tendryakov, Nekrasov, Ovechkin, Voronov, Solzhenitsyn, Kazakevich, Kazakov, to name the most representative) we unhesitatingly affix the label "critical realism," noting that this implies all the virtues and shortcomings of nineteenth-century Russian realism. Only such third-rate writers as, let's say, Vsevolod Kochetov (*The Zhurbins, The Brothers Yershov*) continue to hold to the strictures of socialist realism as conceived and advocated by Andrei Zhdanov.

Several unique and important elements are at work in the quickening ideological-aesthetic fermentation now characterizing Russian cultural life which will doubtless exert considerable influence upon future literary trends in Russia. There is, first of all, the widening acquaintance of Soviet writers, and of the Soviet reading public, with Western literature. Works by Faulkner, Thomas Mann, Hemingway, Salinger, Adamov, Sartre, and Camus have recently been translated. The importance of this cannot be overestimated, especially when we remind ourselves that for decades Soviet readers have been all but totally isolated from world literature. It is the plain truth that the works—and even the names—of James Joyce, Virginia Woolf, D. H. Lawrence, T. S. Eliot, Ionesco, Beckett, Franz Kafka, and many other representatives of modern literature are still completely unknown to Russian readers. But this only means that the fermentation will be prolonged.

The second significant element is the rehabilitation, starting in 1957, of the pre- and post-October founders of Russian modernism whose names have been anathematized for more than three decades, and their consequent reintroduction to the public. These, of course, are that great modern artist Leonid Andreyev, who created modern Russian prose; Andrei Bely, whose novel *Petersburg,* published last year in Yugoslavia, is the most significant book in twentieth-century Russian literature; Isaac Babel, Alexander Malishkin, Viktor Shklovsky, etc. But here, too, the process has not run its course, for as yet the Soviet public is ignorant of the achievements of such writers as Boris Pilnyak, Evgeny Zamyatin, Lev Shestov, Marina Tsvetayeva, and that greatest of Russian historical novelists, Mark Aldanov.

Third among important new elements is the unprecedented growth of interest in Dostoevsky, especially among the younger generation, a fact which provides a comment on the direction of present reading interests and which is all the more evident because of the long neglect of this great writer's works in official criticism and commentary. Over the past several years, about twenty books have been published by Soviet essayists and critics which discuss Dostoevsky's work, but the writer's complete works have thus far not been issued.

The fourth notable element is the sudden great popularity of several writers who until now have been outside the mainstream of Soviet literature and who, moreover, cannot be called "realists": Konstantin Paustovsky, Yuri Olesha, Alexander Grin, and Mikhail Prishvin. This interest is paralleled by an enormous, and also unprecedented, rise in popularity of half-forgotten, but nevertheless important, nineteenth-century writers, such as Leskov and Melnikov-Pechersky, whose work is penetrated with deep mysticism.

Thus, the Russian reader today is avidly interested in nearly everything but the works of the socialist realists.

Such is the spiritual climate in which the young Soviet literary generation is emerging, the so-called *shest'desyatniki* (men of the sixties) in whose hands lies the future of Russian literature. The most important among these new critical realists are Vladimir Dudintsev, somewhat older than the rest

(*Not by Bread Alone,* 1956, a novel) ; Vladimir Tendryakov ("Three, Seven, Ace," 1960, a short story) ; Yuri Bondaryev (*Silence,* 1962, a novel), and Alexander Solzhenitsyn (*One Day in the Life of Ivan Denisovich,* 1962, a novel about Stalin's forced-labor camps). Boris Pasternak's *Doctor Zhivago,* written in 1958, stands in complete isolation from the mainstream of literary events in Russia—although from the point of view of artistic quality it represents undoubtedly the greatest achievement of postwar Russian literature. Since to date it has not been made available to the reading public in Russia, it is of importance for literature outside the Soviet Union only.

The *shest'desyatniki* of Russian prose have several common features, the most important being an uncompromising, critical attitude toward reality. The heroes in their works—like the writers themselves—in most cases went off to war as twenty-year-olds and, upon returning to civilian life, came into conflict with their environment, courageously accepted the struggle, and, in most cases, lost. Casting about in contemporary Western European literature to find a writer spiritually and stylistically congenial to the more prominent young Soviet prosaists, we can single out Erich-Maria Remarque, who, as Soviet statistics show, is (hardly surprisingly) the most popular foreign writer in the Soviet Union today. For the problems dealt with by the *shest'desyatniki* are typically existential: relations between individuals and society and individuals and history.

Despite the fact that Dudintsev's *Not by Bread Alone* was condemned by official criticism after it had created somewhat of a sensation, it is evident that the most talented among the *shest'desyatniki* have taken exactly the same path chosen by Dudintsev, so that any analysis of his novel is also largely an analysis of the works of the "men of the sixties." A variant of the clash with his environment which Dudintsev's hero, Lopatkin, experiences occurs repeatedly in the creations of the younger authors.

The central idea in *Not by Bread Alone* comes out in a dialogue characterizing the essence of what is happening throughout the vast country. One of the novel's main characters, Drozdov, portrayed as a typical intelligent bureaucrat, says to his young wife, who represents the rising generation: "You once told me that I go to extremes. But extremes cannot exist for a man who is building a strong material base. Because this base is what comes first. The more I build it, the stronger our country becomes. This is not Turgenev, my dear." His wife replies: "You're missing the point. The base is the relation of people to matter, not matter itself."

The clash between the builders of the "base" and the young: this is the essential conflict of Russian prose today. One can already maintain that prototypes of both the bureaucrat and his antagonist which have sprung to life in recent Russian prose will live for a long time in Russian literature, just as, throughout the whole of the nineteenth century, Russian writers were developing prototypes created by Fonvizin and Griboedov.

In Yuri Bondaryev's novel *Silence,* we are confronted with archetypes of unscrupulous, social-climbing Party members such as Uvarov and fanatical priests of the "cult of personality" such as Sviridov. At one point Uvarov, commenting on the novel's young hero, Sergei, remarks: "Sergei is a Decembrist, and this is not the time for Decembrists." This shows clearly how the aspirations of the young are in revolt against the status quo and how conservatives are ever prone to use the same old clichés noted nearly fifty years before by Maxim Gorky when he wrote of the petit bourgeois: "The eternal slogan of the petit bourgeois is: 'Our time is not the time for great accomplishments.' "

In his novel, Bondaryev comes to grips with the most acute

problems in the life of his country. The novel's hero tells his father, an old Communist Party member: "Men like Uvarov and Sviridov undermine the cause of the Party and faith in justice. And you know all this but you keep silent, offering the international situation as your weak justification or making other excuses. Look, as an old Communist, tell me, why do you tolerate Bykov? You don't think that we're bribing some of these rascals, yes, bribing them so they won't be on our backs all the time, and that we smile, we keep our traps shut, we greet each other politely and all the while we know everything?"

Silence is interesting from another point of view in that it reveals a different road along which Russian literature might travel, the road of modernism. The influence of modern literature is quite obvious, for instance, in the following excerpt: "He saw black, hairy, spider-like planes soundlessly circling above him: their shadows, with grasping, greedy claws, were floating against the factory smoke-stacks and diving into the canyons of the streets. He could see clearly that they were not planes but gigantic spiders, but at the same time they were planes too, and now they were tracking him as he ran through the town."

We might call the art of the talented young writer Vladimir Tendryakov a kind of "neo-realism" similar to the technique employed in postwar Italian films. In the story that brought him acclaim, "Three, Seven, Ace" (Zagreb, 1962), Tendryakov starkly describes conflict among a few simple individuals in a primitive part of modern Russia. The basic idea is that changes in the social order by no means solve all human problems.

Solzhenitsyn, in spite of the world-wide public attention given his novella *One Day in the Life of Ivan Denisovich*, is, unfortunately, on the whole, probably not a "born writer." What he has written thus far is extraordinarily talented reportage, and it is likely that the moment he has described all that has happened in his life, his pen will dry up. It is enough to compare his story with Dostoevsky's *Notes from the House of the Dead* to discover the difference between them. For Dostoevsky, every real-life occurrence in the world of forced labor serves as a point of departure for analyzing human existence. For Solzhenitsyn, it is the essence and aim of his work.

We must mention also the possibility that a number of works "written for the drawer" exist and may eventually see the light of day. This indeed happened in 1956 when Evgeny Shvarts's satiric drama, *Shadow,* certainly one of the outstanding works for the Soviet stage, appeared in print; it had been written in 1940.

In any case, it is certain that Russian literature today is alive and taking its place on the world literary scene just as it did in the decade following the revolution. A bigger question, however, is whether Russian writers will follow the same road along which the *shest'desyatniki* have traveled or whether they will turn into the road followed by such writers as Andrei Bely or James Joyce. Considering the complexity of the process of fermentation alluded to earlier, as well as the various factors at work within it, and taking into account that their action and influence are just beginning to make themselves felt in the world of Soviet letters, it is obvious that the process will have to continue for some time before one can hazard a prediction about what will eventually evolve.

[1963]

THE MISSION OF *NOVY MIR*

*   *   *

SPIRITUAL LIFE in the Soviet Union is developing apace. Important new voices are being heard in every area of human endeavor. While it is a truism that every spiritual revival incorporates its own convulsions, conflicts, and temporary retreats, it would seem that the forces propelling the Russian renaissance onward are strong enough to resist all efforts to kill it, those efforts being hopeless attempts at stopping history's wheel. At any important juncture of human development, in any "starry moment" of human existence, generally one group of people sharing the same ideas, speaking with a common voice through a journal or magazine, comes to the fore to force a pathway through what until then seemed an impenetrable barrier blocking the way ahead.

Such a progressive voice is raised today in the Soviet Union by the literary journal *Novy Mir,* the organ of the Writers' Union, whose editor, the well-known poet Alexander Tvardovsky, has contributed as much to Russian literature through his courageous editorial accomplishments as through his verse.

Founded in Moscow in 1925, *Novy Mir* can now take pride in the fact that many important Soviet literary works, some of which have since become classics, first saw the light of day in its pages. In 1928, the journal published the second part of Maxim Gorky's great epic, *Life of Klim Samgin.* From 1927 to 1941, it brought out Alexei Tolstoy's trilogy, *Road to Calvary.* In 1929–30, Alexander Malishkin's *Sevastopol* and Leonid Leonov's *Sot* appeared in the journal, and from 1937 to 1940 it issued the fourth part of Mikhail Sholokhov's

And Quiet Flows the Don. Among the important postwar works that appeared in *Novy Mir* are *Not by Bread Alone* by Vladimir Dudintsev (1956) ; *Silence* by Yuri Bondaryev; *One Day in the Life of Ivan Denisovich,* by Alexander Solzhenitsyn (1962) ; a short story by Solzhenitsyn, "For the Good of the Cause" (1962) ; and Tvardovsky's own satirical poem, *Tyorkin in the Other World* (1963).

Three poets of the younger generation, Yevtushenko, Rozhdestvensky, and Voznesensky have been published in *Novy Mir.* The journal was the first to offer a critical review of the achievements of the great Russian modernists Andrei Bely, Evgeny Zamyatin, and Boris Pilnyak, a review in which Alexei Remizov's name was mentioned for the first time in many years. Despite weaknesses, especially frequent trite phrases on the advantages of realism, the review's central theme makes it a milestone in Soviet letters. And to *Novy Mir*'s distinctions can be added its protest against the mutilation of Boris Pasternak's poetry, which had come out with numerous "corrections" and abridgments in a 1962 edition.

It was normal that *Novy Mir*'s general stance should lead to retaliation on the part of literary conservatives. In 1954, the journal was attacked for "ideological deviations," but subsequently it gained the full support of Nikita Khrushchev. As the months went by, *Novy Mir*'s general interest and quality increased.

Recently, three important contributions provoked widespread reaction in the Soviet press: a long, courageous, honest, and exceptionally humane essay by V. I. Lakshin, "Ivan Denisovich: His Friends and Enemies," in which Lakshin harshly and uncompromisingly opposes all who sought to belittle the significance of Solzhenitsyn's story and who tried to minimize the tragedy of millions of innocent victims who perished in Siberia or were buried alive in Stalin's concentration camps; an article rehabilitating the émigré writer Ivan

Shmelyov; and finally (this quite unexpected, even for *Novy Mir*), an appreciation of the great modern thinker Teilhard de Chardin—offered to Russian readers for the first time.

Novy Mir stirs up resistance—witness the many attacks penned against Dudintsev's *Not by Bread Alone;* Ilya Ehrenburg's serialized memoirs, *People and Life;* Solzhenitsyn's "For the Good of the Cause"; and against the editor-in-chief Tvardovsky himself. These attacks came out in the literary journal *October,* a mouthpiece for the most conservative elements in Soviet culture, of which the critic D. Starikov and the novelist Vsevolod Kochetov are leading exponents.

Alexander Tvardovsky (born in 1910) came into prominence immediately after World War II with the appearance of his long poem, *Vasily Tyorkin* (1945), about an ordinary Soviet soldier, a simple man of the people, no hero, but touchingly human and honest. In 1963, Tvardovsky published a sequel, *Tyorkin in the Other World* (written 1954–1963), in which the soldier goes to the "other world" after his death in battle. The poem tells of Tyorkin's adventures in this "other world."

At the beginning of the poem the author begs the reader not to see in the poem "forbidden ideas" that would seem to threaten the very foundations of the Soviet system. He also apologizes for not putting his hero in a more up-to-date setting, among cosmonauts or in a modern factory, but, as he says, "cannons are pulled to the front lines with their barrels pointing backward."

The poem makes clear that the "other world" is, in fact, the U.S.S.R. during the time of the "cult of personality." It is divided into socialist and bourgeois "other worlds," with an impassable border between. Tyorkin, who arrives in the socialist "other world," is told that here, in "our world," in our life after death, all is progressive and good because it has a scientific basis, whereas the bourgeois "other world" is rooted in reaction. Tyorkin is introduced to the advantages of "our other world": its all-pervading discipline, which is absent in the bourgeois world. In "our" world we have orderly procession; in "their" world, they have a rabble. In "our" world we have organization and, what is most important, everyone plays a leading role. Of course, there are a few shortcomings: for instance, too many people are employed by the System, the Network of Organs, and the Committees (the Committee for Eternal Building is an example), but it is impossible to reduce their number. The Commander-in-Chief can only transfer them from job to job or retire them with pensions larger than their salaries. This Commander-in-Chief is none other than he whose name was uttered by dying Russian soldiers: Stalin. Supreme power is vested in a Special Department which knows everything and has spies everywhere. Tyorkin's comrade-in-arms and friend, now employed by the Special Department, apologetically tells him that despite their old friendship he will have to inform on Tyorkin because of his will to live, a capital crime in this "other world." Since contentment reigns in this "other world," no one is allowed to complain, and Tyorkin is in despair because, although there are impressive buildings and art galleries everywhere, he can't find a decent place to eat or a bed for the night. Food exists only on paper, because all menus are fictitious—which reminds Tyorkin of life on earth with its fictitious "working days" in the concentration camps at "Kolyma, Magadan, Vorkuta, Narym," where endless lines of inmates march through the years in tomblike silence. Tyorkin finally concludes that even the front line in 1941 was better: at least there was the hope that one could save one's life, but in "our other world" there is no such hope. He escapes and returns to earth.

Tvardovsky's poem reminds us of Evgeny Zamyatin's prophetic novel, *We* (written in 1922), for which its author was anathematized. In both the poem and the novel there is a "United State" led by a "Great Benefactor." Everyone lives by the clock. There is no free choice of activities. "State Science" cannot be criticized. Citizens voluntarily spy for the Special Department. Discipline is total. In a word, a real "other world."

After Tvardovsky's poem appeared, Starikov—the same critic who at one time attacked Yevtushenko—denounced its author in *October* [1963], in an article entitled "Tyorkin against Tyorkin." Quite unintentionally, Starikov granted Tvardovsky the highest compliment a writer can receive, for, in Starikov's words, the poem "is a cannon that fires not only into the past but into the present as well." We need only recall Maxim Gorky's statement that a genuine artist, even when his work is a historical novel, writes only for the present. Starikov reproaches Tvardovsky for "making fun of our society and discipline" and yet not criticizing the things that "hinder the building of the future": lack of self-control, negligence, gossip.

So critically absurd and comic are many of Starikov's attitudes and assertions that one cannot help laughing. "Tyorkin is an individual," writes the critic, "and as such, irritates one and all with the necessity for his biological existence." And this, while commenting on Tyorkin's desire to find a place to eat and sleep! Starikov ends by saying that the poem is more a political polemic than a piece of literature. This assertion reveals a subtle ideological change, for until then all adherents of socialist realism, such as Starikov, had pleaded for a political struggle against pure literature.

The severest storm to hit Soviet public opinion was whipped up by *Novy Mir*'s first issue of this year [1964], particularly by Lakshin's article on Solzhenitsyn. *Literatur-*

naya Gazeta reported that Lakshin was sharply attacked at meetings of the Moscow branch of the Writers' Union. The weekly magazine *Ogonyok* in a short, harsh editorial warned: "Do not believe Lakshin. He artificially creates enemies of Ivan Denisovich." Then *Literaturnaya Gazeta* printed a front-page editorial denouncing Lakshin for seeking "in to-day's healthy social and political atmosphere" to accuse the critics of the famous Solzhenitsyn story of being sympathetic toward the "cult of personality."

These combined reactions to the Lakshin essay, unusually severe as they were, only strengthen our belief that his allegations are justified and that the attitudes which he so intelligently opposes in fact exist. What is the controversy all about? Who was insulted and why?

We know that when *Novy Mir* published *One Day in the Life of Ivan Denisovich* in 1962, it was with the complete, and public, approval of Khrushchev. For the first time in Soviet literature, a literary work brought up an extremely sensitive subject in the history of the first socialist state; namely, the fact that concentration camps had existed for years, camps which, if compared with Dostoevsky's *House of the Dead*, make it look like a pleasant sanatorium. Despite the fact that the story was widely acclaimed and was nominated for the annual Lenin Prize, a great many Soviet critics attacked it.

These attacks boil down to a condemnation of Solzhenitsyn for not having given a balanced picture of the historical period, especially with reference to the "cult of personality," which, according to the critics, was positive in many respects. The hero of the novel, a former collective farmer, now a Red Army soldier, and later a prisoner, was "indifferent to everything good or bad going on in Soviet society" (V. Surgunov in the journal *Moscow*). Ivan Denisovich is criticized for his individualism, for "being resigned to his situation," for not opposing the oppression of the Soviet system. The hero's tragedy is condemned as "the tragedy of loneliness" (N. Sergovantsev in *October*). In short, the critics agree that Ivan Denisovich is not a positive hero of Soviet times.

In his long essay, Lakshin countered the critics and, in a detailed, subtle analysis, denied their accusations one by one. "The whole system of concentration camps into which Ivan Denisovich was thrown," wrote Lakshin, "was created to crush and ruthlessly annihilate all sense of law and justice in man, to bring to bear in all things, large and small, an extra-legal arbitrary rule which made even an impulse toward revolt totally unthinkable. The camp authorities never for a moment allowed the inmates to forget that they had no rights whatsoever and that their sole appeal was to arbitrary rule. Of this they had constant reminders: Lieutenant Volkovoi's whip, with which he flogged men in solitary confinement; no rest on Sunday; and constant work, work, work." Any protest was senseless, for it could accomplish nothing. Lakshin continues: "It was not the punishment that was bitter but the complete futility and absurdity of protesting against it." This is why even Senka Klavshin, who had heroically led an uprising in Hitler's Buchenwald, had his spirit broken in the Soviet camp and, because he saw no solution, became sunk in apathy.

Lakshin submits therefore that to censure Ivan Denisovich for not "protesting" is worse than hypocritical. "To die purposelessly is stupid, senseless, and unnatural," he writes. "Ivan Denisovich, having opted for life, even the miserable pain-racked life of the camp, stuck to his decision not only to survive at any price but to accept the challenge that destiny had flung him and unashamedly to preserve his self-respect." We can easily understand how the inner lives of Ivan Denisovich and every other unhappy lodger in a "Siberian hell" were reduced to a single *idée fixe:* to make sure that the tiny crust of bread, his evening meal, was not stolen. World affairs were of no concern in this setting. "Thus," continues Lakshin, "to reproach Ivan Denisovich for not resisting, for not defending his rights, for resigning himself to his prisoner's lot, and for not thinking about how he fell into such misfortune is to demonstrate—to use Chernyshevsky's famous line—'a vulgar lack of sensitivity.' "

In his detailed analysis of the novel, Lakshin stresses the solidarity that held Ivan Denisovich and his comrades together and strengthened them in their common misery, and refutes the allegation that the tale is imbued with "the tragedy of individualism." He writes: "It is crystal clear that this is a tragedy not of 'individualism' but of honest Soviet men who became victims of a cruel exercise of power and arbitrariness."

Contradicting attempts on the part of the critics to play down the importance of the existence of concentration camps, Lakshin seizes upon a digression of one of the prisoners to affirm, in his own words, that the real life of Russia was being lived in the camps themselves, not outside, where marchers paraded through the illuminated streets of noisy cities to honor the aviators who had flown over the North Pole, where triumphs of work and plan fulfillment were endlessly celebrated. Noting that the events in the novel take place on a day in January in 1951, Lakshin writes: "I don't know about others, but as I was reading the story, I was persistently plagued by one question: what was I doing then, what was my life like? . . . At that time, thirteen years ago, in the month of January our newspapers were discussing the progress of works on the Volga-Don Canal; the speeding up of the steel-casting process; the enlargement of kolkhozys; the transplanting of several varieties of Georgian tea in the northern regions; the approaching elections; the Korean War; the Alisher Navoi jubilee, the Hockey Cup finals. . . . But how was it I was told nothing of Ivan Denisovich? Can it really be I was not aware that on that silent, bitterly cold morning he and thousands of others were marched out by guards with dogs through the main gate of that camp and across snow-covered fields to their work assignments? . . . It is most difficult not to be obsessed with this thought."

Lakshin concludes with the observation that Solzhenitsyn's choice of Ivan Denisovich as our "guide through Hell" was a good one: a quite ordinary man who conveys to us the innate horror of the camp by describing what to him, in his state of misery, was a "happy day" in camp life. "We feel that he has lived in our literature for a long time, that without him our literature would have been deprived of something." All negative evaluations of Solzhenitsyn's novel—"no more than pinpricks deserving no attention but for the fact that they have recently become so petulant"—are, in Lakshin's view, frustrated in the literary-aesthetic sense and malevolent in the socio-political sense. They harbor an urge to minimize, nay, to forget the tragedy of Russian people. Lakshin continues: "*One Day in the Life of Ivan Denisovich* is only one year old. Yet it has provoked more argument, interpretation, and polemic than any other book published in the past several years. This book will not suffer the fate of those flash-in-the-pan sensations that flare into controversy and are then forgotten. On the contrary, the longer this book lives in our literature, the clearer its importance to that literature will become and the more fully will we understand how necessary its appearance was. This story will live a long time." So ends Lakshin's remarkable essay.

The popularity of editions of the works of the Nobel Prize winner Ivan Bunin and of excerpts from the writings of Dmitri Merezhkovsky, Zinaida Hippius, and Marina Tsvetayeva, all coming out with increasing frequency, is paralleled by a mounting interest in the work of other Russian émigré writers. Responding to this interest, *Novy Mir* printed a selection of stories by a talented émigré, Ivan Shmelyov. This was the first opportunity since 1917 for Russians to read his work.

Ivan Shmelyov (1875–1950) first appeared in Russian letters in the first decade of the twentieth century and was heralded for his novels *Citizen Ukleykin* (1907) and *The Man from the Restaurant* (1911), both of which are penetrating social analyses. During World War I he wrote stories portraying the inhuman side of that world slaughter house. After the revolution, when he had left Russia, he wrote his famous *The Sun of the Dead* (1923). Introduced by Thomas Mann and subsequently translated into many languages, this novel was in many respects the precursor of Pasternak's *Doctor Zhivago*. Both novels view the revolution not simply as social chaos but as a cosmic catastrophe. In 1933, Shmelyov published *Summer of Our Lord,* a collection of stories, some of which appeared in *Novy Mir*. Almost everything Shmelyov wrote was published in Yugoslavia between the wars.

The same issue of *Novy Mir* contained a review of Gian-Carlo Vigorelli's *Il Gesuita Proibito: Vita e opere di P. Teilhard de Chardin* [*The Forbidden Jesuit: Life and Works of P. Teilhard de Chardin*]. Written by I. Kravchenko, the review introduced the French Jesuit to the Soviet public for the first time. Teilhard de Chardin, like Lev Shestov, Nikolai Berdyaev, Emmanuel Mounier, José Ortega y Gasset, and Miguel de Unamuno, is one of the most original and important thinkers of our time. His works have been published in innumerable editions in all civilized countries and are moving ever closer to the center of Western European philosophical debates.

Teilhard de Chardin (1881–1955), the French Jesuit, scholar, paleontologist, geologist, anthropologist, philosopher, theologian, mystic, and poet, is, in Pasternak's words, "the most important, the most familiar, the most intimate thinker of our day." According to a leading French Marxist, Roger Garaudy, his great work "opened the door to a fruitful dialogue between Marxism and Christianity."

The French Jesuit spent his life leading an underground war against extreme conservatism in the Catholic Church. The Church itself looked with suspicion upon the original ideas of this remarkable father—which accounts for the fact that the majority of his writings were published after his death. They aroused as much enthusiasm and acclaim on the one side as they did criticism and resistance on the other.

This scholar lived and worked in all the continents of the world. He founded the Institute of Geobiology in Peking, traveled across Africa, made archaeological excavations in Spain, became president of the French Geological Society, and died in New York. He formulated a new interpretation of cosmic evolution according to which the evolution of man and human cultures is but a part of a general development extending to an imaginary point of existence called by him the "Omega Point." This development has four stages: preexistence, existence (life), thought, and life beyond. He presented his ideas in many books, the most important of which is *The Phenomenon of Man*. He first appeared in print in 1916, with an essay, "Life in the Cosmos," which has been called by critics "the awakening of Teilhard's genius." In Yugoslavia he was translated for the first time a few years ago, when his "Phenomenon of Christianity" was included in a collection, *The Panorama of Contemporary Ideas,* by Gaetano Picone (Belgrade, 1960).

Kravchenko, who introduced this great Christian and individualistic thinker to Soviet readers, laid special emphasis on the refusal of Catholic leaders to accept his teachings. It is clear that the Russian critic, in commenting on these teachings, both sympathizes with them and altogether fails to understand them.

[1964]

THE MORAL OF A POLEMIC

*   *   *

A POLEMIC proceeding in the Soviet press is being reported in journals around the world. The problems at issue are of the greatest importance to the past of socialist society as well as to its present and future—which means the future of mankind. The polemic centers on responsibility for a sociologic-psychologic-historic complex generally called "the cult of personality" and was set off by the publication of Ilya Ehrenburg's memoirs, which are still appearing in *Novy Mir*.

Actually, Ehrenburg's memoirs provide an excuse for raising questions of great import—not only with regard to the U.S.S.R. Their greatest significance lies in their frank exposure of the difficult years between 1930 and 1956, the first such exposure in Soviet history. In eight issues of *Novy Mir*, Ehrenburg developed the thesis that Soviet citizens were wittingly brought up in an atmosphere of lies, silence, and total conformity during the whole period from the final crystallization of Stalin's bureaucratic apparatus right down to the dictator's death.

Ehrenburg's thesis has been attacked in *Izvestia* by [Vladimir] Ermilov, a critic who alleges that Ehrenburg is insulting a whole generation of Soviet men and women who neither consciously shied away from the truth nor submitted to dictatorship but who, in fact, had complete faith in Stalin.

The two positions are unambiguous. Ehrenburg is speaking for those who *knew* what was happening in the U.S.S.R. and had no illusions about Stalin's personality but kept silent to stay alive. No doubt this kind of behavior was hardly heroic. On the other hand, Ermilov is the spokesman for countless honest Communists who *blindly* accepted Stalin's infallibility, often even when they were deported to labor camps in Siberia.

We must immediately stress the fact that both these points of view admit to no personal responsibility for "the cult of personality," but hold others responsible for it. Underlying the silence, lies, and craven submission on the part of those who *knew* and *understood* what was going on was the fact that all who would not or could not lie and obey lost their lives overnight. Maxim Gorky, Isaac Babel, Boris Pilnyak, Vsevolod Meyerhold, Mikhail Koltsov, on and on: the list of Russian artists and thinkers who fell victim to the cult is long indeed.

Those who *knew* say: "We had to keep silent." They imply that they certainly were not to blame and that in the absence of harsh persecutions, deportation to Siberia, not to say worse, they would have spoken out. The other side, partly as a defense, tell us: "We were sincerely, honestly, and courageously following him in whom we put our trust, and, had Stalin been different, everything would have been fine." They were not responsible either, and Stalin alone is to blame for not being what they believed him to be.

In a sense, both sides are right. Had there been no *blind* trust, it would have been impossible to create an atmosphere in which those who *knew* perished or were constrained to silence. In this sense, Ehrenburg is right. The generation supported by Ermilov made "the cult of personality" possible. But Ermilov is right, too, when he submits that this generation did not wittingly lie or keep silent. Thus, the polemic is carried on essentially between those who lacked courage and those who lacked good sense. Both sides hold Stalin chiefly, and each other partly, responsible.

It is precisely because of the existence of genuine hatred for Stalinism and "the cult of personality" that we should note that holding Stalin responsible for everything is a dangerous lie that should be combatted not so much for the sake of the past as for the sake of the future. Everyone shares the blame for "the cult of personality." Only those who perished in prison or in labor camps are innocent before history and humanity. Only those are guiltless who, trusting *their own* reason, had the courage to be nonconformists, knowing that neither the international situation nor the historical moment nor bright Communist hopes for the future could justify oppression and lies (the lies being a kind of oppression). They knew that there is no *useful* lie.

If everyone who knew had had the courage to disobey and speak out, perhaps the history of the U.S.S.R. would have been quite different. Furthermore, if all who followed Stalin, however bravely and stolidly, had trusted *themselves* instead of the "leader," the "cult" would never have come into being.

Ermilov assails Ehrenburg for insulting his generation in asserting that they were conformists submissive to lies. Actually, this generation was only deceived, says Ermilov; although the guilt of those who *knew* and kept silent is patent, he would have it appear that those who sincerely trusted Stalin were guiltless. But the root of the phenomenon of "the cult of the personality" is in that very trust in a "leader."

We know that the large majority of Germans sincerely and courageously believed in their Führer right to the end, but does their sincerity or their faith justify the crimes of Hitler's soldiery? Does strong conviction in his own righteousness excuse Eichmann?

What Ermilov is implying is that, had some other leader filled Stalin's shoes, the horrors of Stalinism would never have come to pass. This is probably right—we believe that if Lenin had lived some two decades longer, history would have taken a different course. But this in no way solves the problem of "the cult of personality." It merely avoids it. History provides examples of rulers who were revolutionaries in the full sense of the word and accomplished much for their peoples' progress. Peter the Great is one example. But does this example justify the social institution of monarchy?

The core of the whole problem lies in a question: How was it that the October Revolution—which was inspired and driven by a struggle against *sincere* faith in an imperial autocrat and other "infallible" and inviolable ideas connected to the ancient monarchy and the Orthodox Church— degenerated into a Stalinist Russia? The present and the future of socialism depend upon the answer to this question. This is why the Ermilov-Ehrenburg argument is so important. To blame Stalin for everything is neither *dialectical* nor *Marxist*. The fact that the generation of Soviets for which Ermilov is the spokesman trusted Stalin *sincerely* and *honestly* provides no excuse whatsoever.

A blind belief in a leader or a "cult" really transfers one's own personal responsibility for life, history, mankind, and the cosmos on to another's shoulders: a leader's, god's, the laws of nature, or what you will. Each time a man, whether out of weakness, stupidity, lack of courage, or whatever, stops thinking for himself and blindly places his fate in the hands of a leader he believes in, a cult is born. And it is totally irrelevant to wonder what might have happened had the leader been someone other than Stalin.

Doubtless, it takes great inner strength and courage to accept the idea that each of us bears a personal responsibility. It is not pleasant to think that we are responsible not only for ourselves but also for an infinity of bodies and minds yet unborn, which, in fact, we bear within us, and that no one can absolve us of this responsibility. It takes incomparably greater strength and courage to trust *oneself* and one's own judgment than to believe in some "higher" institution or personality. And that all the people believed in the infallibility of the "leader" excuses no one. Boris Pasternak made the following penetrating observation in his *Doctor Zhivago:* "The main misfortune, the root of all future evil, was the loss of faith in the value of one's own thinking."

The central problem facing the architects of socialism is not attaining a society controlled by a wise and humane "leader" but teaching people how to control themselves. Nothing good can come from oppression, since at the heart of oppression stands someone who makes decisions for others. This leads to a vicious circle.

One thing is undeniable: the conscious conformity of those who *knew* and the unconscious conformity of those who *believed* made "the cult of personality" possible.

We stress again that the polemic between Ehrenburg and Ermilov is of immense significance even though it unfortunately does not penetrate to the heart of the problem. Let us hope it represents merely the beginning of a public debate on the essence of Stalinism. This is of importance not for Stalin, who can no longer be judged, or for his victims, who cannot be brought back to life through official rehabilitation. But it is of importance for us and for those who will come after us.

[1964]

WHY WE ARE SILENT

*   *   *

WHY ARE most intellectuals in the socialist world silent about true conditions in their countries? And why is it that if they do speak out publicly, their critiques concern only peripheral aspects of society rather than the core of the matter—the systems under which they live? These questions, I think, must often be asked in the West. I would also guess that the average Western reader explains the silence in one of three ways: by assuming that people in the socialist countries are satisfied with things as they are, or that fear prevents them from speaking out, or that they are unable to get into print.

None of these explanations is correct. No society exists yet which satisfies all its constituents, and in socialist countries, as elsewhere, there are many people who have reason to be unhappy with the systems under which they live. As for fear of reprisals, we know from history that even the most ruthless terror has not succeeded in keeping people quiet very long. In the few instances where terror has succeeded, it was only because those who endured it were undeserving of anything better. Nor is it difficult to publish. All of the leading intellectuals in the socialist countries have frequent opportunities to expose their views in the Western press, particularly if they are critical of socialism. Nevertheless, even though Western intellectuals and journalists daily write sharp criticism striking at the very roots of capitalist society, both in their own and the socialist press, it is an extraordinary rarity when socialist intellectuals do the same—and the event instantly produces a sensational uproar.

No, contentment, or fear, or the inability to publish—these are not the answers. There is a deeper cause for the silence in the socialist world.

When Western intellectuals, from Sartre to Rolf Hochhuth, write critically of social conditions in their countries, the mere fact that they can speak out without danger of being arrested or losing their means of subsistence elicits respect in socialist countries for the society, and the country, that allows such free criticism. That is why writing of this kind by Westerners, regardless of whether it is published in the West or in the socialist press, cannot be successfully exploited here as a propaganda weapon.

The situation is almost exactly the opposite in the case of criticism of conditions at home by people who live in socialist countries. Since this is impossible in the socialist press, when it is published only abroad it becomes a powerful weapon against one's society and nation, a weapon that usually falls into the hands of those same forces at which a Hochhuth's criticism is directed. Thus, for most of us it is impossible to write critically in the Western press as well, despite the ample opportunity to do so. The socialist intellectual who expresses himself freely before the Western public begins to feel, somehow, like a traitor.

I believe this feeling has been experienced even by writers who, thanks to unusual circumstances, have succeeded in speaking the truth about their society in their own country. Pasternak, Dudintsev, and Solzhenitsyn must have felt this uneasiness. And this sense of treachery is a much more decisive factor in inhibiting free expression than fear of the reprisals to which socialist intellectuals submit themselves. For socialist criticism is employed not only as a weapon against the socialist states but also against socialism, and against all those oppressed by poverty or racial prejudice in the Western world. So we intellectuals of socialist societies feel like traitors when we speak the truth—traitors both to our countries and to all who fight for freedom in capitalist society. That is why the majority of us are silent.

At the heart of the matter lies a cruel paradox. Those who prevent us from speaking the truth here in the socialist world abet the repression of freedom in the capitalist world; whether they like it or not, they concretely strengthen reactionary forces of all kinds in the opposite camp. Similarly, those in the West who outlaw Communist parties, and engage in censorship and McCarthyism, *strengthen* Communist totalitarianism. It is as if there existed connected vessels of freedom. Pressure against freedom in one part of the world automatically causes pressure against freedom in all parts of the world; the struggle for freedom in one's own society is simultaneously a struggle for freedom for all humanity. And in this struggle socialist intellectuals are in a tougher, incommensurate situation because they are condemned to silence.

For us in Yugoslavia, the situation is especially complicated. We have, without doubt, incomparably more freedom than any other socialist state, and when we demand still more, we are rebuked not only by those who are in power in our country but also by Western liberals: "There you are, being ungrateful; you were given more than the others, now you want everything." But freedom, like life, cannot be parceled out. In addition, Yugoslavia's approach has in good measure been adopted by all European socialist countries, making the problem of freedom in Yugoslavia the problem of freedom in the entire socialist bloc.

Indeed, Yugoslavia has become a prism in which the fates of mankind are being refracted. While the U.S.S.R. is to a large extent liberalizing itself, while the youth of the socialist countries is growing closer spiritually to the best traditions of the Western democracies, American youth is moving toward the left, toward what socialism promises, toward the ideals of a material democracy and not merely a political one. These two trends are thus heading for each other; sooner or later they will meet. It is my conviction that Yugoslavia, which does not belong either to the Eastern or to the Western world, is where these two movements will converge. For exactly that reason, the question of freedom may be of greater importance in Yugoslavia than in any other country today. The fight for tomorrow's free humanity, in the economic and political sense, is not being waged in Vietnam, but in Yugoslavia.

I do not believe that the fundamental conflict of our day is between the socialist and the capitalist systems; rather it is the conflict between *democratic socialism* and totalitarianism —be it political totalitarianism, as in the socialist countries, or economic, as in the West. All the propaganda activities directed against the opposite social system, from one or the other side, only serve to throw sand in the eyes of those who fight for freedom on both sides. That is why the most reactionary Western circles are lavishly aided by the slightest encroachment on free expression in socialist society.

The ruling orders East and West, I believe, have common interests. Should the two worlds reach an understanding preserving today's conditions, the cause of liberty would not greatly profit thereby. It is a terrifying vision: a world totalitarianism in which people might well recall with longing the days when the truth about one system could be freely expressed within the framework of the other. Because Yugoslavia represents in many respects the synthesis, or more accurately, a potential synthesis of East and West, the fight for freedom of speech and opinion in Yugoslavia is simultaneously the fight against both political and economic totalitarianism—a struggle against the possibility of a synthetic politico-economic totalitarianism which would choke the life out of all mankind.

After Yugoslavia's tempestuous turn toward democracy in 1948, a turn which affected all other socialist states, Yugoslav society has today arrived at a critical point. The road may lead either backward toward a totalitarianism of the Soviet type, or toward a hitherto unattainable democratic socialism. A subtle yet determined contest is being waged between the status quo, the so-called *socialist democracy*, and the ideal of *democratic socialism*. The initial effects of this contest will be visible within the next year.

It would be a mistake, however, to think that Yugoslavs battling for freedom within the present socialist system are opting for a capitalist social order. On the contrary, they may be fiercer enemies of Western economic totalitarianism than those who currently hold the strings of power in socialist society. The difference between political and economic power is purely a matter of form, not of substance. Consequently, authentic democracy is most realizable in a society that is free from private ownership and that has succeeded in eliminating the possibility of any group assuming absolute political power. The last is where the socialist countries have so far failed, and why they are still less democratic than capitalist states.

Today Yugoslavia is on the way to realizing a unique experiment—an attempt at a socialism that is not totalitarian. I would not call this form of socialism Communist, for it is distinct from the Marxist-Leninist doctrine of the so-called "dictatorship of the proletariat"—that is, the dictatorship of one party—which leads automatically into political totalitarianism. Rather, I would call it Christian—not because the free democratic socialist society would profess the Christian faith, but because the *projection* of authentic *Chris-*

tianity into the socio-political sphere is democracy. Accordingly, any society that maintains the totalitarianism of one ideology, like Franco's Spain, cannot be called Christian even if the ideology is a Christian one.

Let us not forget that Adolf Hitler was a foremost anti-Communist, yet Hitler's actions helped prolong the rule of Stalinism in the U.S.S.R. for nearly two decades. It is impossible to fight oppression with oppression, or lies with lies. Oppression can be fought only with liberty, lies only with truth. I am not in sympathy with Communist ideas, but when the West starts persecuting Communists, I become a Communist. Every time the policeman's club strikes a demonstrator in the West, it invisibly but no less crushingly strikes all those who yearn for freedom in our half of the world. The Ku Klux Klan burns our freedom, too. The only way one society can help another society which is not free is by being free itself.

That is why the United States today, with its war in Vietnam, is performing a disservice to the cause of freedom in the *socialist* world. As the Russian philosopher Nikolai Berdyaev says: "Force cannot save anyone because salvation presupposes an act of freedom. . . . The devil triumphs when he is being warred against in an evil, devilish way. . . ." In contrast, when the West German magazine *Der Spiegel* succeeded in ousting Defense Minister Franz-Josef Strauss, respect for Western democracy was heightened in the socialist countries—where a similar incident is inconceivable. The suppression of the West German Communist Party, on the other hand, undermines the struggle for freedom in our society.

Judging from all the evidence, that cancerous wound of mankind, totalitarianism—in all its forms (Fascist, Communist, economic) —tends to appear *synchronously* in the European-American part of the world.

One need only compare the dates of the coming of dictatorship in Russia, Germany, Italy, Spain; the simultaneity of "enforced collectivization" and the economic crisis in the West; "Zhadanovism" and "McCarthyism" after World War II in Russia and America; and so on, to perceive that everywhere the process is the same, differing only in form and intensity. The difference, though, should not be lightly dismissed. It would seem to me that because totalitarianism is now most intense in the socialist world, it has the greatest number of active enemies there. It also seems to me that Europe has emerged from the hell of totalitarianism to find itself in purgatory, and will not allow a return to hell. Each victory of freedom in any country is, therefore, significant—because it testifies to a movement toward recovery of health in all of Europe. Freedom will perhaps penetrate deeper in countries that have survived the disease of totalitarianism than in countries that were not infected by it, or suffered it only mildly. Every experience enriches, even if the enrichment means rejection of the experience. (I am convinced, in fact, that Marxist ideology as a basis for totalitarianism will remain a danger longer in the Western than in the Eastern world.)

But eventually the disease must be overcome, if only because no totalitarian society will be a match for the Asiatic totalitarianism which is just being born. This will require a free, Christian Europe, united with a democratic (that is to say, Christian) Russia—just as the Stalinist U.S.S.R., after all, had to arouse the national Christian spirit of the Russian people to withstand Hitler's Germany. And the struggle for a democratic Russia is being carried on today in Yugoslavia.

What is the essence of that struggle?

Despite the numerous freedoms Yugoslav socialist society enjoys today, thanks to its doctrine of self-rule, there nevertheless hangs over us the unceasing possibility of a relapse into totalitarianism. This is because there is no practical way Yugoslavia could defend itself, should the power now in the hands of top Yugoslav Communist Party members fall into the clutches of a Stalinist. That it is impossible to criticize the real basis of the system without the approval of the executives of the system does not today represent a great tyranny—but this could prove catastrophic. For, in spite of self-rule, all channels of information and all permitted social organizations are under the control of the Union of Communists; in the last analysis, therefore, they are in the Party's hands. And every one-party system, whatever else may be said about it, is some kind of subspecies of Stalinism. It cannot be justified on the grounds that, in the specific case of Yugoslavia, it has been an unusually liberal one-party system, just as an absolutist monarchy cannot be exculpated because of the temporary appearance of a benevolent ruler.

Under the conditions that have developed in Yugoslavia, one thing vitally needed to insure future progress is a free press—an organ that is not controlled by the Communist Union. A second vital area of reform concerns ideological freedom—permitting the open expression of non-Marxist thought (whether individualistic or religious). A third necessity for advancement is free public association—the banding together of people who do not occupy influential positions in the ruling party.

Again, the situation in Yugoslavia proves that the struggle toward these goals is not between socialism and capitalism, but solely between the partisans of "enlightened (or unenlightened) socialist absolutism" and the supporters of democratic socialism. There can be no question of restoring capitalism, nor could the force be found to maintain it; and as I have said, the potential of democracy is incomparably greater in the socialist society than in the capitalist one. Certainly, the organization of an opposition—that is, creation of a two-party system—would not only *not* work against but would to a large degree facilitate the imposition of a genuinely social (as distinguished from an economically or politically private) power over the means of production and over material goods.

I think that Yugoslav society is already conscious of the need for the socio-political democratization of its *system of socialism.* At the same time, in the last two or three years there have been increasing signs that within the Communist Union, and outside it, there still exist a not inconsiderable number of people who are inclined toward totalitarianism. In a changed historical situation, but under an unchanged system, they would bring about a relapse into Stalinism. It cannot be stressed too often or too strongly, therefore, that the fight for freedom to criticize the present socialist system publicly, the fight against the *ideational totalitarianism of Marxist thought,* is a fight for the future of the entire European–North American population.

To be sure, like any war, this one for democratic socialism will have its victims. Unfortunately, liberty has never yet been won without cost. But today *free socialism* has its chance in Yugoslavia. This battle is being fought, consciously and unconsciously, in all areas of Yugoslav social life, in all hearts and minds. Alas, in our society one must still write and speak about it in veiled fashion—the notions of an organized opposition within socialism, of a school system secularized from Marxist dogma, and of openly non-Marxist thought in the press, still seem much too heretical and promptly provoke charges of reviving capitalism. Nonetheless, should the forces of democratic socialism emerge victorious, the remaining socialist states will follow Yugoslavia's example—and sooner or later, the modern capitalist states will too.

We in the socialist world are silent because we do not want to betray our countries, or provide fuel for the forces of reaction that oppose the fighters for freedom in the West. Above all, we want what the enlightened people of the West enjoy—free thought and a free press. Then we would no longer have to keep silent.

[1965]

THE UNSPOKEN DEFENSE

[EDITOR'S NOTE: This article was written by Mihajlov in September 1966 for presentation before the Zadar court, where he was on trial for attempting to start an independent magazine without ties to either party or government. He was not permitted to present his defense and it has not been published in his country. On September 23, Mihajlov was sentenced to a year in jail, and on April 19, 1967, he was sentenced to an additional four and a half years, less time already served. His defense, under the present title, first appeared in *The New Leader* for May 8, 1967.]

*   *   *

I WILL EXPLAIN and document those of my statements used by the prosecution in charging me with criminal activities. I beg the court to allow me to deal with the quotations taken from my articles in a somewhat different order than they appear in the indictment, where they are presented in a partially distorted manner and without consideration of logical and chronological facts. To avoid repetition, I will speak of my articles in the order of their appearance.

The earliest article of the three for which I am today accused is entitled "What We Want and Why We Keep Silent" and is presented by the prosecution as my second article. The article was published more than one year ago in the American magazine *The New Leader,* the organ of the American Labor Conference on International Affairs. It was later reprinted a great many times the world over, and especially in the press of Western socialists. No one can say this article is subject to the law invoked in the accusation against me: 'Spreading false information for the incitement of the people." The article is not subject to this law because it was read in Yugoslavia only by the editors of two journals who did not publish it, and by one or two friends of mine. Thus, in fact it did not reach the public at large. The same happened with other articles of mine about which I will speak later.

It is beyond comprehension that the indictment merely quotes one and a half sentences from "Why We Keep Silent" (which covered ten typed pages) and takes those out of context. Only the whole article can convey its true meaning, whereas the prosecution cuts one sentence in half and by so doing changes the meaning of both sentences cited to incriminate me. Using this procedure, one may accuse anyone who writes of anything at all.

I wrote "Why We Keep Silent" for the following reason. A year and a half ago my reportage from the Soviet Union, "Moscow Summer, 1964," created a geat sensation,[1] although it was nothing more than an ordinary report written in haste from my travel notes. Much reportage of this kind is published daily in the Western press. For me the question was why this simple reporting by a man in a socialist country should create such an outcry; or why Pasternak's *Doctor*

[1] Part I of "Moscow Summer, 1964" was published without incident in the January 1965 issue of the Belgrade literary monthly *Delo*. Part II, starting with a section entitled "Concentration Camp Themes," was published the next month and aroused almost immediate Soviet protest—apparently because of its blunt references to Soviet slave-labor camps and their legacy. On February 11, *Delo* was ordered banned; that same day Marshal Tito branded Mihajlov a "reactionary."

Parts I and II of "Moscow Sumer, 1964" then appeared as a special expanded issue of *The New Leader* for March 29, 1965. Part III, which did not appear in Yugoslavia, ran in *The New Leader* of June 7, 1965. The entire report, with a foreword by Myron Kolatch and an introduction, notes, and biographical sketches by Andrew Field, was subsequently published as a Farrar, Straus and Giroux–New Leader Book under the title *Moscow Summer*. [*The New Leader*]

Zhivago or Dudintsev's *Not by Bread Alone* should provoke a nearly world-wide historical uproar, while similar novels in the West often go unnoticed by the larger public; why a simple sociological study, *The New Class,* by Djilas, so agitated the world? The answer was clear: because such events are common occurrences in the West and rare in the socialist world.

In "Why We Keep Silent" I wanted to explain the reasons for that silence to myself and to others. I rejected the explanation that intellectuals in the socialist countries keep silent only out of fear. I further rejected the explanation that they have no opportunities to put their views before the world public. It is a known fact that every writer from a socialist country can publish his views in the world press, particularly if he is critical of his own society. I quote my analysis of the situation from my article. [Editor's note: Here Mihajlov quotes four paragraphs from the previous article, beginning with "When Western intellectuals . . ." (p. 329). We leave intact the final paragraph.]

At the heart of the matter lies a cruel paradox. Those who prevent us from speaking the truth here in the socialist world abet the repression of freedom in the capitalist world; whether they like it or not, they concretely strengthen reactionary forces of all kinds in the opposite camp. Similarly, those in the West who outlaw Communist parties, and engage in censorship and McCarthyism, *strengthen* Communist totalitarianism. It is as if there existed connected vessels of freedom. Pressure against freedom in one part of the world automatically causes pressure against freedom in all parts of the world; the struggle for freedom in one's own society is simultaneously a struggle for freedom for all humanity. And in this struggle Socialist intellectuals are in a tougher, incommensurate situation because they are condemned to silence.

The last sentence, taken out of context, is invoked in the accusation against me, yet this very trial proves the correctness of my assertions about the reasons for silence. The second sentence used, or more accurately half-sentence, comes from a paragraph beginning:

Judging from all the evidence, that cancerous wound of mankind, totalitarianism—in all its forms (Fascist, Communist, economic)—tends to appear *synchronously* in the European-American part of the world.

One need only compare the dates of the coming of dictatorship in Russia, Germany, Italy, Spain; the simultaneity of "enforced collectivization" and the economic crisis in the West; "Zhadanovism" and "McCarthyism" after World War II in Russia and America; and so on, to perceive that everywhere the process is the same, differing only in form and intensity. The difference, though, should not be lightly dismissed. It would seem to me that because totalitarianism is now most intense in the socialist world, it has the greatest number of active enemies there.

It is with the second part of the last sentence that I am incriminated in the indictment. Moreover, I am incriminated with an incorrect quotation because the prosecution has evidently employed the English translation in its entirety, not my original text, as proven by its use of *The New Leader*'s title for "What We Want and Why We Keep Silent."

I am also charged with calling the Yugoslav society totalitarian. I firmly believe I am right in calling it totalitarian. The primary characteristic of totalitarianism and totalitarian societies is the monopoly by one political party of all information media. In my "Draft of a Program for a Founding Conference in Zadar," which was illegally used by this court in a press campaign against me, I defined totalitarianism as follows: "Totalitarianism is an absolute monopoly in the socio-political life by *any* one ideology, religion, or political party." The Polish Marxist thinker Andrzej Stawar writes this about totalitarian societies: "Their common features are: the existence of a single party with a cult of its leader, ideological unification, etc." (*Selected Articles about Marxism*). The well-known British historian Hugh Seton-Watson writes in his book *Neither War Nor Peace*: "Totalitarian regimes will not permit any institutions or associations that are not directly controlled by them.... Totalitarian rulers deny all absolute standards external to themselves."

Accordingly, there exists a fully accepted definition of totalitarianism; the judgments do not differ. It always involves the unification of thought and social life in some single ideology. The prosecution is charging me with "equating the government of a workers' society and that of terror-ruled Fascist factions." This charge would be correct if the powers of the League of Communists were in fact identified with the workers. But that is precisely what I have refuted in my articles. It is unnecessary to document the monopoly on information in Yugoslavia. Throughout this case, nearly the entire press was bombarding me and my collaborators with the most perfidious libels, while we had no opportunity to reply, not even with a single word.

The best proof of the muzzled press in Yugoslavia was the Fourth Plenary Session of the League of Communists, held in June of this year [1966], which opened the way for criticism of the Security Services. Who was ever allowed to criticize Vice President Rankovic [head of the Security Services, ousted from office at the Fourth Plenary Session] or the Security Services until that session? Yet today our newspapers are overloaded with all sorts of criticisms and accusations against the same Security Services. Even Dr. Vladimir Bakaric had this to say in *Vjesnik* about the Fourth Plenary Session: "The Fourth Plenary Session of the Central Committee of the League of Communists of Yugoslavia has shaken us more violently and deeply because it has started to discuss problems which before no one dared to discuss. . . ." And of course just as before everyone was "unanimously" for Rankovic, now everyone is "unanimously" against him.

There is little need to demonstrate the destructiveness of an information-media monopoly in a given society. If not for such a monopoly, neither Hitler nor Stalin would have been able for years to keep the existence of the concentration camps from their people, or to hide their numerous other crimes.

Happily, in our country concentration camps did not exist. But it is evident that the life of our society has been greatly damaged by the Party's control of all information. No important measure taken by the League of Communists during the last twenty years has been subjected to any criticism whatever, with the result that the actual harm done by these measures has first become apparent several years after their enactment. To many it was obvious that certain programs would prove harmful, but they simply could not come out and oppose "the general line of policy."

Is it necessary to talk of the nearly complete economic destruction of our agriculture in the years of collectivization into so-called kolkhozy? Only now is Yugoslav agriculture starting to recover from that blow. Who was allowed in those days to publicly call attention to the damages inflicted upon the country by Party politics? And what about the "political factories," built for ideological rather than sound economic reasons and still a great burden on our economy? What about the interminable education reforms that have done so much to undermine the reputation of our secondary schools? All this could have been avoided if the monopoly of the press did not exist. Who ever dared to criticize anything of importance? Let us remember the case of Milovan Djilas and the consequences of his criticisms, even though he was vice president of the state.

Who can guarantee today that tomorrow the Central Committee's line will not be changed, and that a criticism which is now considered almost a criminal offense will not be "unanimously" acclaimed as correct? What guarantee exists that tomorrow a new Rankovic will not emerge? Who can today publicly criticize, say, the present new policy of the Central Committee of the Communist party in Yugoslavia? As long as there is an information monopoly it is possible to mislead the public. All our newspapers have written that I am "spreading national hatred" and that I am "getting money and orders from our enemy," but you can see for yourselves that I am being tried for the criticisms in my articles. What newspaper in Yugoslavia will write tomorrow that the Socialist Union of Workers in Zadar simply libeled me? For the court of public opinion is like any other court, and the principle of any court having pretensions to being even slightly democratic is that both parties to a dispute should be heard. The monopoly of information, no matter in whose hands it may be, is a priori undemocratic and carries within itself the possibilities for incredible crimes.

It is exactly this that I wrote about in my articles "Why We Keep Silent" and "Djilas and Yugoslavia Today." It is what I was referring to when I said in "Why We Keep Silent": "Despite the numerous freedoms Yugoslav socialist society enjoys today, thanks to its doctrine of self-rule, there nevertheless hangs over us the unceasing possibility of a relapse into totalitarianism. This is because there is no practical way Yugoslavia could defend itself, should the power now in the hands of top Yugoslav Communist Party members fall into the clutches of a Stalinist." That such a possibility could become a reality in our society was shown by the Fourth Plenary Session.

Naturally, in a society where the discussion of certain social matters is permissible during some periods and forbidden in other periods, depending upon the Central Committee's policy of the moment, a corrosive division is created between what is said officially and what concerns people privately. Let us recall some events that shook our whole country and about which the press was silent. What did our press write about the manner and number of persons arrested during the liquidation of Informbureau [the Yugoslav section of the Cominform] adherents in 1948–49? What did our press write about the Djilas case? Why did our press keep silent about the student demonstrations in Zagreb in 1959? Because only one party controls the country's information media. For this reason, when speaking about a one-party system, I have used the metaphor "schizophrenia of the body politic." I emphasize that it is used neither in mockery nor in ill-temper but in its objective meaning—that is, simply to describe a disease which manifests itself in the disintegration of the human personality and the splitting of man's consciousness. I used this metaphor intentionally to characterize the disease of our body politic: the separation of the public consciousness (and in our society this is represented by the press, radio, etc.) and that social consciousness which is present only in personal contacts between people. I believe this metaphor is quite accurate, and cannot see what is being alluded to in the charge that I was making false and untruthful assertions.

After all, I am not the first person who has called the one-party government an organism afflicted with schizophrenia. George Orwell wrote in 1945: "Totalitarianism is not so much an epoch of faith as it is an epoch of schizophrenia." Similarly, the Hungarian Marxist writer George Paloczi-Horvath wrote in 1956: "Do you realize what has happened to you? I have explained to you that they have brought you up in a way which has split you in two: one part for today and one for tomorrow. And do you know how doctors diagnose such a condition? Schizophrenia, and the splitting of the personality; a systemized, planned schizophrenia. You have yourself separated the personality into that which is conscious and that which is subconscious; into honest private individual men, and the ruthless, amoral builder of happiness. And what has happened to sóme personalities? The worst part of the split 'me' has swallowed the other part. You must realize that you cannot create a bright and happy future with a split personality, with two different standards for morals."

The indictment reproaches me for having written in one place "the so-called socialist society." The mere concept of socialism in our day is extraordinarily nebulous and, one must admit, in so many ways compromised. Hitler's Nazi party, the *Nationalsozialistische Deutsche Arbeiterpartei*, was, as we know, both a workers' and a socialist party. Mussolini considered himself a socialist and for many years wore a Marxist badge in his buttonhole. Hitler claimed that he learned most from Lenin and Trotsky. Stalin's U.S.S.R., with its exploitation of concentration-camp labor unequaled in history, also called itself socialist. China today calls itself a socialist country. Therefore, for the definition of socialism I will refer to the new Yugoslav Constitution, which specifies socialism as social ownership of the means of production, with no one having the right of monopoly of these means— that is, the right to usurp power over anything in our society.

I cannot consider a society to be socialist if one insignificant minority of 6 to 7 percent has all the rights, which is the case with the League of Communists, and the overwhelming majority of the population has no rights at all in the sociopolitical setup. We do not even have the rights given to Negroes in the United States--those of political association and the right to fight legally for their own constitutional guarantees.

Our society cannot be called socialist even if we take the definition of socialism given by the well-known Polish Marxist Leszek Kolakowski (who, by the way, is often translated in our country), in his article "What is Socialism?" He speaks thus of what Socialism is *not:* "The society which wishes that all its members hold the same views on philosophy, foreign policy, economics, literature, and ethics . . . the society which considers itself to be socialist merely because it has eliminated private ownership of the means of production . . . the society in which philosophers and writers say the same things as generals and ministers but always after the latter . . . the society which decides who may criticize and how to criticize . . . the society in which one man is unhappy because he speaks what he thinks and another is happy because he does not speak what he thinks . . . the society in which a man lives better if he does not think at all . . . the society which considers that people must be happier with socialism than with any other form of society. . . ."

Consequently, as long as a minority has all the civil rights and the majority has only restricted rights, I think it is absolutely appropriate to say that we are dealing with a so-called socialist society.

Realizing that the monopoly of information media is a result of the one-party system of government, that only political democracy can guarantee every other kind of democracy, and that our constitution makes possible an independent press, I came to the conclusion that the only way to end this discriminatory practice was to found an independent magazine. This discriminatory practice prevents the intellectuals in socialist countries and, of course, our Yugoslav intellectuals, from contributing to their societies by their independent thought. Last December [1965] I wrote in my "Draft of a Program for a Founding Conference in Zadar" of the possibilities for publishing a magazine openly in opposition and within the framework of the positive legal requirements in the Socialist Federal Republic of Yugoslavia. This Draft was an analysis of the current historical, socio-political, and legal realities in our country, and it was not intended for publication.

Apart from a few of my friends, I did not send the text to any home newspapers, nor did I give my permission for it to be published abroad. It was, however, published for the first time in the United States in June of this year, without my permission, by the American organization Freedom House. I first heard of this organization on the day my Draft was published, when Freedom House organized a conference to give moral support to the founding of the magazine. I did not give the Draft to the press simply because it was not written in the form of a newspaper article. I think it contains the same ideas that are to be found in my other two articles, which were written specifically for publication. In this Draft it is altogether clear that my aim was not to "incite the citizens," as the indictment charges, but only to found an independent magazine—which resulted in the registration of the magazine by my friends in August of this year. It is incomprehensible to me that such a step could have been called the spreading of false news by means of the press.

Analyzing the situation in our country, I came to certain conclusions that I brought out in my Draft. I asserted that ideological and economic liberalization, which is the aim of all the reforms, is not possible without political liberalization. My conviction is that a gradual political liberalization would lead to the loss of the totalitarian powers of the League of Communists. I am deeply convinced that with free elections—free in the sense that the right to campaign and run for office be given also to non-Communists—the Communist Party would not even obtain as many votes as it has members. But it is impossible to label this conviction as false, since the truth or the untruth of it can only be proved once it is realized. This is why I wrote that there cannot be anything but either a return to police dictatorship or liberalization in

Yugoslavia. This assertion from my Draft was also mutilated in the indictment; moreover, it was not indicated that more than half the relevant sentence was omitted. Naturally, the part where I discuss Yugoslavia's development favorably and contend that on the historical scale Yugoslavia is about ten years ahead of the other socialist countries is omitted.

The same thing happened with another quotation from my Draft, where the prosecution printed only the second sentence from one paragraph which interpreted the deleted first sentence. The missing sentence read: "It is possible to maintain the *status quo,* even for half a century as in the U.S.S.R., by police or party dictatorship alone, or, on the other hand, by raising the standard of living and liberalizing the economy through the concession of certain ideological freedoms while at the same time keeping the one-party system of government."

I further wrote: "It is just this last which is today taking place in Yugoslavia." In the indictment, however, we cannot see what it is that is happening in Yugoslavia because the first part of the passage is not brought against me. It is important to remember that my Draft was written in December 1965, when many prices were frozen and the economic reform had reached a crisis. This was a time when, according to the testimony of the Fourth Plenary Session of the Central Committee of the League of Communists, very strong factions supported by the most centralized alliance of all—the State Security Services—were stifling and obstructing reform by every possible means. It is understandable, then, that I came to the conclusion that the reform was compromised and would not bring great benefits until the society was politically liberalized. That I was entirely right in saying the reform had produced a drop in living standards is proved by the statistics published in *Borba* [official organ of the Yugoslav Communist Party] of September 14, 1966 which state that since the beginning of the reform the standards have actually declined by 32.8 percent.

At the time my Draft was written I could not foresee such an event as the Fourth Plenary Session and my prognosis and estimates of the economic measures taken by the government were pessimistic. But an evaluation of events is one thing and false information and assertion is quite another. False information would have been disseminated if I had written, for instance, that Yugoslavia made a secret agreement with, say, Indonesia, directed against Iceland, or that in Zagreb 50,000 people were arrested. What would happen if someone in England were brought to trial for expressing the view, in the press, that some government measures for economic stabilization will be a failure? Our Constitution guarantees "the right of every citizen to discuss the work of state bodies and autonomous social bodies and organizations dealing with subjects of public interest, and the right to express their opinions regarding such work" (Article 34, paragraph 2, point 6). Since I have expressed a negative opinion, is the Constitution to be interpreted as giving permission only for positive opinions on the work of all the government bodies?

My conclusion given in these articles—concerned with the success of the necessary economic measures and the one-party system of government—was that the reform, which had in view the struggle for an effective and rational organization of production based on a freer play of the economic laws, was not realizable until self-government as proclaimed in the Constitution was in effect in the real sense of the word. In our country (and that was the position when I wrote these articles) no authentic self-government existed; there were only the disguised powers of the League of Communists. The Fourth Plenary Session, or rather the reports in the press following it, brought to light that self-government was actually in practice merely a bluff.

The sentence referring to this bluff in "Djilas and Yugoslavia Today" has more than sixty words, which in the indictment, following the pattern of all other quotations, was cut down ridiculously to thirteen words.

That entire sentence reads as follows: "As long as there is no respect for the Declaration of Human Rights of the United Nations, which was signed by Yugoslavia, as well as for the Yugoslav Constitution and Yugoslav laws, and as long as there is no real possibility for the existence of a legal opposition of Social Democratic forces which would be under no control of any kind by the League of Communists, *to talk about social democracy, Yugoslav self-government* and Djilasism without Djilas *is nothing else but sheer bluffing.*" In the indictment itself, only this is given: "*Talk of social democracy, Yugoslav self-government, is nothing other than sheer bluffing.*"

Not only is it illogical to accuse someone with a part of a sentence, but it is also illogical to quote only one part of an entire text. Only a complete text can convey the true point of an article, the general drift of its ideas and its aim.

It is understandable that as long as there is only one political party that may act legally and that possesses a monopoly of all the information media, the realization of economic liberalization will be impossible. This has been proven by our own press, which, particularly in the last few months, has carried a wealth of material confirming my assertions. If the market laws and the play of economic factors really operated without the interference of Party controls, that is, if business enterprises were truly self-administrative, then what our press tells us simply could not be. *Nin* [a Belgrade weekly] of September 11, 1966, published a discussion on "The League of Communists Today and Tomorrow" in which a member of the Central Committee of the League, Dr. Dragan Milojevic, said the following:

That this is so has been shown to us from our experience with the policy of integration. We started off with some clear ideas, looking at economics as a whole and at its development in the world and in our own country; we came to the conclusion that integration is a positive thing. However, we started by applying it incorrectly. We started with forced integration of enterprises without sufficient further economic analysis. Remarks were made about this procedure and about this policy. The remarks were made not only by the persons who study these matters, such as economists and technicians, but by other individuals and by entire groups of working people. Not only was no consideration given to these remarks but they were also frequently hushed up. The League of Communists was even very active in fighting against these criticisms, operating always with the conviction that integration is a good thing. Quite a long time had to pass for them to see that these criticisms were justified and that even decentralization was helpful. A clearer attitude was adopted only at the Eighth Congress, and more detailed and categorical discussion of this topic took place still later at the Third Plenary Session when it was decided that the opinion of experts in these matters was not to be disparaged. I hold that we were dealing here with a conservatism which was dearly paid for.

N. Burzana, in his article "The All-Powerful Committees" in *Borba* of August 13, 1966, writes: "The intervention and direct interference by committees in these integrating processes are especially frequent. This was precisely the reason for the failure of many economically justified cases of integration—they were not appealing to certain committees (or, more accurately, to some individuals in these committees). They often paid no attention to the disposition of the unions of working people and of organs of self-government, or to the economic soundness of integration. In other words, local interests often came before general interests whether in forcing non-economic integration or in putting the brakes on economic integration."

I personally know the situation in the publishing establishment, which now cannot prosper without government subsidy. This situation could very easily be changed, were it not for the ideological restrictions on the publishing of certain books. *Doctor Zhivago,* for example, was first published some years after Pasternak received the Nobel Prize, when the public's interest in the novel had lessened considerably. And it does not need to be pointed out that Milovan Djilas's *The New Class* and the books of the condemned Soviet writers, Andrei Sinyavsky and Yuli Daniel, could sell in enormous numbers.

I will give only a few quotations from our press which illuminate the question of self-government. Here are the words of Dr. Vladimir Bakaric in the August 14, 1966, *Vjesnik:* "Now it has come out that it was possible to maintain a certain attitude against the autonomous tendencies in the central organization because similar conditions were to be found in the establishment itself."

The statement "Most likely you agree that by means of its power the League of Communists has up to now dictated to a large extent what decisions were to be taken by autonomous bodies" gets the following reply from Mika Tripalo, political secretary of the Town Council of the Zagreb League of Communists: "If by the League of Communists you mean the committees, then this is right."

Krste Crvenkovski, political secretary of the Central Committee of the Macedonia League of Communists, writes in *Vjesnik* of August 21, 1966: "The primary organs of the League of Communists in various organizations have not always been, nor are they now, the leaders of a decisive struggle for self-management and for consistent application of the Socialist principle of distribution according to the work accomplished. They have often supported certain definitely techno-bureaucratic positions or interests, be it in organizations of working people or communes. Actually, one can speak of a real and not fictitious contradiction between clearly expressed Socialist thought, at least in its basic premises, and an inadequate, inefficient, non-revolutionary practice coming from some organizations of the League."

Latinka Perovic, a member of the Central Committee of the Serbian League of Communists and president of the Commission for the Ideological Training of Members of the League of Communists, writes in *Nin* of September 11, 1966: "I think that the League of Communists has in ideological matters as well acted from a position of authority, even though in a more complex political struggle it ought to have used more force of argument and persuasion to show the untenability of contrary opinions."

Perovic expressed this opinion in a discussion published by *Nin* to clarify the following statement in a lead editorial: "How can we determine the real place of the League of Communists in society under the new conditions, or, in other words, *how can we remove* the mechanism of self-government and direct democracy *from the shadow* of such a powerful and influential political organization."

In the previously quoted *Borba* article, "The All-Powerful Committees," we find: "A series of examples clearly shows that many committees had the wrong attitude, the wrong starting premise in their actions. They actually very often acted from a position of authority: they would give orders, intervene directly in the policy of the local administrative organs and the autonomous bodies in enterprises, bypass members, issue mandatory punishment, lock themselves behind tapestried doors, usurp all rights for taking decisions. . . . Acting this way from a position of authority, the committees naturally underrated working people and their social, socialist and Communist consciousness, in spite of their numerous declarations in favor of the working class and its autonomy. Bypassing the interests and the rights of workers, thrusting upon them their own policy, they inevitably began, perhaps unconsciously, to reduce the system of self-government and the democratization of society to a mere formality of procedure. Party membership dropped, became passive, feeling neglected and powerless to fight against bureaucracy. To destroy this reputation of the omnipotence of these committees—symbols of power in the minds of the people—the Communists of Belgrade and Palilula counties even suggested changing the word 'committee' to something else."

The article "How Sound Is the Reputation of the Red Booklet," in *Vjesnik* of August 10, 1966, contains the following statement: "The reputation of the League of Communists has declined because some of its members behave as if they were the only ones invited to decide on the future of our collective. They consider their functions as their monopoly. . . . Some Communists, on the other hand, are very active but more as the protagonists of power. They identify themselves with authority, directorships, and the 'upper echelon' in enterprises, institutions, communes, and state bodies, considering these functions their own monopoly. As if by some agreement, all the participants (in this discussion) were of the opinion that these 'trumpeters' organize the scenery and lead the performance in most of the organizations of working people." This article is especially significant because it was written on the basis of an inquiry among working people themselves.

Again, in *Nin* of August 28, 1966, we find this passage: "How can we eliminate monopoly by individuals over Party consciousness, patriotism, and socialism? Why must some people be the arbiters on every occasion and in every situation? When will the Communists step down from this platform of authoritative, very often formalistic and unobjective appraisal of other people's conduct, without public control of their own work and behavior? Why have many functions become a 'hereditary right' in the hands of some individuals? Why does a group of ten or fifteen persons hold, year after year, a monopoly over membership in workers' councils, the steering committee, the syndicate in various enterprises? Is it not bureaucracy, for instance, when a Workers' Council takes important decisions behind closed doors or when someone always goes around displaying the banner of self-government and in reality, with the help of various official and informal groups, carries through what he wishes? . . . The Brioni Plenary Session accomplished much but it was only a beginning; the roots of bureaucracy are very deep."

Our press is overflowing with these and similar comments, which are even stronger than mine. I could give ten more quotations, but I think those mentioned should suffice. I will conclude by citing two short letters from groups of workers to the editorial office of *Vjesnik:* "We are turning to you because we do not know whose duty it is to help us. Our Workers' Council and the primary organization of the League of Communists have not got the power to do so. For it appears to us that not a word from the Fourth Plenary Session has so far reached our leadership. With us the self-management of the workers has not functioned in the past nor does it function now" (*Vjesnik,* September 14, 1966). A letter from another group of workers, using almost the same wording, appeared in yesterday's *Vjesnik* (September 21, 1966). But if someone had expressed himself this way before the Fourth Plenary Session he would undoubtedly have come to grief.

Since our Constitution says nothing about a one-party system, this monopolizing of power by the League of Communists is naturally in contradiction to the intentions of the Constitution and the laws. Yet the indictment incriminates me for this sentence: *"It is clear to all that today in Yugoslavia it is precisely the League of Communists which departs from the Constitution and breaks the laws, insofar as it attempts, with all the means at its disposal, to maintain this unnatural monopoly over the socio-political life of the country."*

I really do not know whether the charges of false information and assertions are meant to imply that the League's monopoly is not unnatural, or that the League is not breaking the law. As is obvious, the incriminating sentence says that the League of Communists is violating the Constitution if it tries to maintain its monopoly, which is a qualified statement. Our Constitution, in ten places, specifies the freedom for social and political activities through organizations and associations which citizens themselves create. Articles 39 and 40 of *The Principles of the Constitution* specifically state that freedom of opinion and association is guaranteed, as is freedom of the press and other forms of information, freedom to speak freely and discuss publicly, freedom to assemble and hold public gatherings.

The Constitution especially emphasizes that every citizen must conform to *The Principles of the Constitution* (Article 63), and that all arbitrariness on the part of anyone which damages and restricts the rights of a person is punishable (Article 66). *The Principles of the Constitution* mention the League of Communists only to say that because of the exigencies of historical development, it became the organized leading force of the working class and working people in the building of socialism. However, the leading and ideologically directing factors are in no case also monopolistic, as is confirmed by the qualifications appended to Articles 39 and 40. These articles declare unconstitutional only that activity which is anti-socialist, but nowhere in the constitution is socialism identified with the League of Communists.

Moreover, *The Principles of the Constitution* come out directly against monopoly by anyone. Chapter 2 states: "Every form of directing production and other social activi-

ties, and every form of distribution which, through bureaucratic arbitrariness and privileges based on monopolistic positions or through selfish private ownership and particularism,
degrades social relations based on this condition of man, is
contrary to both the general and the particular interests of
men and to the social, economic, and political system confirmed by this Constitution." Article 33 states that all citizens
are equal before the law in their rights and duties, while
Article 70 says that "freedom and rights guaranteed by the
Constitution cannot be taken away or limited. These freedoms and rights are realized on the basis of the Constitution
itself."

All this makes it perfectly evident that the Constitution
does not give the League of Communists any monopolistic
rights over socio-political activities. No one, according to our
new Constitution, has the right to any ideological or political
monopoly whatever.

Although I did not explicitly say this but implied it in a
qualified sentence, I do not mind its becoming a statement.
Reading the latest declarations by our government leaders, it
is not difficult to discern that the League of Communists is
trying to hold on to its monopoly. Krste Crvenkovski, while
attacking me directly, emphasizes this: "It should be realized
once and for all that Yugoslavia is going forward with determination along its marked road of transforming its society
into a non-party democracy. . . . It is ridiculous and sad to
raise so much dust in the West when it is known that our
Constitution proclaims a non-party, direct democracy as the
direction of our development and that all anti-Socialist
activities are forbidden" (*Vjesnik*, August 21, 1966) .

I think that in these cases we are dealing either with a
conscious or with an unconscious mystification of the public.
In our Constitution not a single word is to be found about a
non-party system, but just the contrary. Article 40 guarantees

the freedom of political association. A non-party society as an object of development exists in the Program of the League of Communists of Yugoslavia; but as the basic law for the citizens of Yugoslavia, undoubtedly the State Constitution itself is more important. As far as I am concerned, I salute the League's wish to wither away, and the sooner the better; but as long as one single monopolistic political organization exists, the striving for democracy will always go in the direction of demands for the establishment of constitutional rights —that is, for the destruction of monopoly. On the same occasion Crvenkovski said: "Certainly, the League of Communists will, for a certain period of time, have to retain certain elements of a primary political organization. . . . Comrade Tito has clearly pointed out that we will march on consciously for the further *strengthening* of the part played by the League of Communists in Yugoslavia—but as an ideological and political directing force which will be acting through organs of self-government."

The President of the Republic says: "The role of the League of Communists is not declining, as is being said abroad and by our class-enemies at home. On the contrary, its role *grows and will continue to grow.* It will have to grow as long as the consciousness of our ordinary citizens has not been elevated to that point where it will no longer be necessary for the Communists to guide them. The withering away is a long process, and it does not mean the withering away of the Communist ideology but rather the growth of the consciousness of the citizens. The withering away of the role of the Communists as an organization is accompanied by the strengthening of the consciousness of the whole social structure, and thus it will be less necessary for the League of Communists to be the teacher. But now we must be teachers" (*Vjesnik,* September 5, 1966). However, our Constitution gives no one the right to take on himself the role of teacher and to treat the rest of the citizens as nonrational pupils. It is self-evident that without political democracy there cannot be a democracy of ideas, and the teaching role of the League of Communists manifests itself in a totalitarianism of ideas. Totalitarianism is precisely the monopoly of an ideology without considering whether or not it is by itself positive.

That it is impossible simultaneously to execute economic reform and retain a monopoly of organized ideas by the League of Communists is confirmed by a statement of the President of the Republic in the speech referred to above: "Now we raise the issue of collaboration between Communists in enterprises and those outside of them. At this juncture the Party cells will have to meet to prevent antagonism between producers and consumers and so that consumers at these meetings, naturally through the Communists, will be informed about the problems of producers."

Naturally, it is impossible to liberalize the economy, which is the intention of the economic reforms, if the policy of various enterprises is dictated by the League of Communists and not by economic laws. The fact that the Socialist Union of Working People has not been an independent organization but only a satellite of the League of Communists was confirmed by a statement of Latinka Perovic's in his September 11 article in *Nin:* "The most important aspect of all this is that socio-political organizations, including the Socialist Union, are not to be treated as transmitting agents of the League of Communists, which heretofore was usually the practice."

In *Nin* of September 18, 1966, in the continuation of the discussion entitled "How to Separate from the Authorities," Dr. Stojanovic writes: "Although at the Fourth Congress it was said that they are not transmitting agents, they are *de facto* that to this day."

Now, after the Fourth Plenary Session, who can guarantee

that the previous practice will not be repeated? As long as the monopoly of information is exclusively in the League's hands there will not be any guarantee that the Fifth, Sixth, or Seventh Plenary Sessions will not declare that, say, Veljko Vlakhovic, Edward Kardelj, or Mika Tripalo is a new Rankovic. This is confirmed by a Marxist from Belgrade, Dr. Mihajlo Markovic, who in *Nin* of September 4, 1966, writes: "I think that we are beginning to forget that theoretically we adopted very important ideas at the Fourth Congress about the place and role of the League of Communists. Now we say again that the League of Communists should be changed from an executive power into a power of ideas. But this is an old story and an old thesis. . . ." This shows that when we speak today of the withering away of the League of Communists we do not necessarily mean this will happen.

The September 11 *Nin* carries an article by the same author entitled "Our Analyses of Bureaucracy Are Superficial," in which he says that in no case must we confuse self-government at the level of workers' units—that is, direct democracy—with the necessity for *indirect democracy* at the level of the whole state, where the League of Communists still has the only word. Speaking about the conservative forces, he goes on: "Very often the slogan of these forces is to reduce democracy to 'direct democracy,' with which we certainly made a great breakthrough. But it is impossible to remain only at that stage, for not a single contemporary society is a polis; there is no society in which all citizens assemble into one parliament or some other body where key decisions are made. Such decisions will inevitably continue to be made in representative bodies, which in our system should more and more strive to be self-governing. I believe that much can be accomplished in this direction in next year's elections."

The indictment accuses me of denying the independence

of Yugoslavia. Of course, again the quoted sentence is distorted and only its second part is inserted into the incriminating document. The beginning of the sentence reads as follows: "Still the difference between the Soviet type of open centralization and the fact that Yugoslavia relies relatively heavily on the West for material aid . . ." This relative dependence for material aid is known to us all and in no case means that I have denied the political independence of our country. In the text of my Draft, from which this quotation was taken, I explain what I mean. There I say that today when "Yugoslavia is, to a certain extent, concerned about world public opinion and the preservation of her reputation as a nation of 'liberal socialism' where law is respected—because of material aid and economic integration with Western markets—today it is possible, through legal means and within the framework of the Constitution, to found an independent magazine of opposition as a nucleus for future sociopolitical organizations. Naturally, it would be illusory even to attempt this without the moral support of world public opinion."

I do not know if it is necessary to speak of how much the help from the West means to us, how much the standards in our country depend on this help, and consequently the very prestige of the Yugoslav authorities themselves. (From 1946 to 1962, economic aid from the United States, without credits, loans, technical aid, etc., amounted to $1.7 billion while military aid amounted to $693.9 million. This is from the United States alone.)

The indictment also accuses me of *"calling all the dissatisfied persons, all the most reactionary elements in the country, to meet and organize. Among these dissatisfied persons he counts as most important the main advocates of nationalism in Croatia and Serbia."*

These allegations are based on a quotation from my Draft

which consists of one entire paragraph. Regrettably, out of six sentences, only the first and third are quoted fully, so the whole meaning of the passage is lost. In my Draft I expressed the opinion that a magazine independent of the League would be supported, as I put it, by the potentially democratic forces: "Inside the Framework of the League of Communists, particularly among the younger members and intellectuals, there exists great sympathy for that *potential force* which I will call *democratic* and about which I will speak."

In its entirety, the passage mutilated by the indictment reads as follows: "The primary potentially antagonistic forces in Yugoslavia are still unorganized. Among these, in the first place, are the democratic elements inclined toward all kinds of liberalization, who are drawn more by the Western European social and economic systems than by Eastern 'socialism,' *and are particularly attracted to the Scandinavian countries.* These elements differ in many ways in their conceptions and tendencies, but are uniform in their wish for the creation of a positive social force which would be able to place itself in opposition to a totalitarian dictatorship at the moment when Tito abandons power. *Today there are very few of the old-line opposition capitalistic elements.* We are concerned primarily with *the technological and cultural intelligentsia, religious people of all faiths, those in the highest cultural strata who are ideologically opposed to Marxism, the sympathizers of Christian individualism in Slovenia,* those who sympathize with the nationalist tendencies of the Croatian people in Croatia and the Serbian people in Serbia, *the supporters of Djilas, and with great numbers of the young in the League of Communists.* All these forces could, at any given moment, unite under the banner *'Djilas—Djilasism.'* "

The prosecution removed all that is italicized from this passage and thus distorted the meaning. I do not understand why the prosecution thinks that I count on the Croatian and

Serbian nationalists as the main potential readers of the magazine, in spite of the fact that I mentioned them only at the end of my list of readers. Also, it is not clear to me what the indictment considers as false statement in my assumptions regarding the potential opposition elements in our country.

In the summary of the indictment I am accused of "calling, rallying, and organizing" the most reactionary elements in the country, the Croatian and Serbian nationalists among others. At the same time the indictment asserts that the citizens of Zadar and our press grasped the truth and exposed me and my work, and that they condemned this work as hostile. But the citizens of Zadar, that is, the local organization of the Socialist Union of Workers, Zadar I, proclaimed that I was fomenting national hatred. That is also asserted by our press, especially by the *Narodni list* and *Slobodna Dalmacija* [newspapers in Zadar and Split, respectively] of August 6, 1966. In short, am I fomenting national hatred, as asserted by our press and repeated in the indictment, or am I uniting the nationalists as is asserted in the very same indictment?

The President of the Republic himself acknowledges that "there are still people in some republics who think that somehow a day will come when we will separate from one another. This is a very bold statement on my part but I am telling you that it is correct" (*Slobodna Dalmacija*, August 23, 1966).

Therefore, to deny the existence of the nationalist question in our country is absurd.

However, we should certainly distinguish the nationalists from the chauvinists. It is impossible to put the nationalistic democratic elements and the chauvinistic extremists in the same basket. Thus in Croatia, it is difficult to lump together the Ustasi and the sympathizers of the Croatian Peasant Party; in Serbia, the Cetniks and the democratic republicans;

in Slovenia, the White Guard with the Christian Socialists, who, in coalition with the Communists, have since 1941 taken part in the national liberation struggle. To describe as reactionary the sympathizers of nationalistic tendencies in Croatia and Serbia is non-dialectical. Whether a thing is reactionary or progressive depends on the given historical moment; so much so that nothing by itself is either reactionary or progressive. It is not necessary to document the great liberating significance of so many nationalistic movements in the world. And whether a certain potential social current at a given moment is aiming toward democracy should be discussed ideologically in magazines and not in a court.

We must not forget that the Yugoslav Constitution guarantees absolute freedom in the expression of all nationalist feelings, including the right of separation. For nationality is an undeniable, existing entity, conditioned historically, culturally, and economically, which, with its own characteristics, contributes to the variety and richness of the entire human community. Accordingly, all leveling and obliterating of national characteristics is essentially reactionary, for the human race is a symphony and not a chant in unison. Chauvinists are not defined in connection with their own people but by their hostilities to other nationalities; nationalistic tendencies are constructive while chauvinistic tendencies are destructive.

Even if I were to campaign publicly, through legal means, for the separation of a Yugoslav nation (since my parents are Russian, I cannot imagine which one it would be), *my campaign would not be unlawful and unconstitutional*. It would be illegal and unconstitutional if I advocated separation with illegal means, that is, by force. But as is clear in my Draft, the intention of the magazine was just the opposite: the unification of those potential forces which at this moment can contribute substantially toward democratization in our society. The indictment reproaches me for trying to unite all those who are dissatisfied. But there is nothing unconstitutional in this. As a matter of fact, the Constitution guarantees to all the dissatisfied who wish to do so, the opportunity to organize and carry out through legal channels the struggle for the realization of their ideas. Since when are the dissatisfied a priori also reactionaries?—which is what is implied in the indictment. The mere fact that I have spoken at the same time about both the Croatian and the Serbian nationalists excludes the possibility of my fomenting national hatred.

In my Draft I contended that "the 'national question' is not to be and cannot be solved by the disintegration of the federal union, but only by a social-political plan and by the democratization of the entire system. . . ." On the same page I further say: "And very often the appearance of a national question is only the wrong projection of social discontent. . . ."

And in the incriminated article "Djilas and Yugoslavia Today," I said this about the nationalities question: "As a reaction against the unnatural absence of political life in the country, we see today the appearance of national extremism, religious fanaticism, narrow-minded clericalism, etc. . . . All this is evident today in Yugoslavia as well as in the U.S.S.R. No police measures can stop it. The only remedy for the creation of a healthy society is in political freedom."

It is evident, in the Zadar Declaration of the Organizing Committee of August 9, 1966, that my friends who espoused the intentions of my Draft adopted an identical attitude toward our nationalities question. Obviously the Draft itself was in no manner a call for public rallying but only an analysis of current conditions, an analysis which may be wrong (I do not consider it wrong), yet one which cannot under any circumstances be characterized as a means of "spreading false information or an assertion aimed at inciting citizens."

Regarding the second point of the indictment, my conditional punishment of last year was only a formality, since the court has freed me from the charges for which *Delo* was proscribed. I have lodged a complaint with the Federal Court for the protection of legality, but with no result so far. *Moscow Summer* was translated and published in many languages while I was still in prison last year. It was also translated into Polish, among other languages, by permission of the American magazine *The New Leader,* without my being asked for permission.

In the autumn of last year I negotiated with the Polish publishing house Kultura in France for the publication of a book with my articles entitled *Russian Themes.* I signed a contract with this house without stating precisely what was to be in the collection. At that time I could not foresee that *Moscow Summer* would be included, because I had sent a great number of old and new articles to Kultura and *Moscow Summer* had already been translated into Polish. The final composition of the collection became known to me only in March of this year, in a letter from the director of Kultura, Jerzy Giedroycz. I then requested that on all accounts the page for which I was tried last year be taken out of the text. This was carried out in the book *Russian Themes.*

The indictment is basing its allegations on a contract which I signed with the Ost Institut of Bern, imputing that I have given the Institut the world copyright for all my writing except *Moscow Summer,* which will, as was stated in the contract, be included in *Russian Themes* in Polish. Since at the time of the signing of the contract precisely what was to be published in *Russian Themes* was not yet agreed upon, I did not raise questions about the wording. However, a few months later I signed a new contract with the Ost

Institut which annuls all previous contracts (the contracts can be found in the evidence before the court), and in the last contract it is clearly stated that we are dealing with two books—*Moscow Summer* and *Russian Themes*. Now translations are being prepared for the several editions of the book *Russian Themes* in its final form—that is, without *Moscow Summer*.

I do not think that it is possible to forbid the publishing of an entire book if those parts for which I was tried, and for which an issue of a magazine carrying a section of the book was proscribed, are removed.

I must admit that in a certain sense I was glad this discussion came about. Unfortunately, since there is no independent press in Yugoslavia, the courts are the only place where both sides can be heard, and not just the prosecution. *The Principles of the Constitution* proclaim that all forms of public administration, including the political hierarchy, are guaranteed to the people through the control of constitutional legality by the courts. Article 136 of the Constitution reads: "The Courts in the execution of their functions are independent and pass judgment in accordance with the Constitution and the Laws."

Regrettably, then, this discussion is my only public defense, as I was unable to defend myself through our press, which published the resolution of the Socialist Union of Workers in Zadar charging that I was "spreading national hatred" and "receiving money and orders from our enemy"—a serious libel. If there had been any truth in what the Zadar group said about me, I would have been tried for "spreading national hatred" and "receiving money and orders from our enemies." (The Socialist Union of Workers, Zadar I, regrettably did not state precisely which enemy they were alluding to.) Both these incriminations constitute heavy criminal activities, and it is inconceivable to me that the prosecution is not charging me with them since it at the same time alleges in its introduction: "Our home press and the citizens of Zadar have perceived and discovered who and what the accused man is and what his activities are."

It is evident that this trial is not based on my articles, because a full *investigation* of them *was completed* in the spring of this year, whereas I was arrested two days before the Founding Assembly in Zadar. The public explanation for the arrest was that I would continue to spread, at the Founding Assembly, the lies begun in my articles; the present charges were brought against me after it became clear that my arrest alone did not frighten my collaborators from founding an independent socialist magazine. In fact, they went on to register the protocol of the magazine and continued to work on it. All this despite the fact that we are on the eve of reforming our courts—as the Parliament reported to the Republics—on the premise that "the Law Courts and entire judicial system form one of the *basic conditions in a democratic society*" (*Borba*, September 14, 1966).

Although it was cognizant of the real situation, this court, or rather the prosecution, did not try to uphold the law and to protect me from this obviously libelous campaign in our press; instead, it in many ways upheld that campaign. *Although Article 207, paragraph 3 of the Criminal Code strongly forbids the misuse and the passing on to outside persons of documents confiscated in the course of criminal investigation, some of my manuscripts confiscated by the authorities of this court were illegally used in the press campaign against me.* Such was the case of my "Draft of a Program for the Founding Assembly in Zadar," from which sentences and parts of sentences (as in the indictment) were maliciously deleted. This was obviously done with the court's consent, for only the Court of Zadar had possession of that manuscript after my manuscripts were confiscated on July 28, 1966.

It is precisely because I cannot defend myself through the

medium that attacked me, the press, and because the prosecution has shown no desire to protect me from libel, that I can only now answer the incredible assertions of our press. I am entitled to do this because the indictment asserts that the press has discovered who and what I am, and that the Zadar Socialist Union of Workers is right in demanding my punishment. The witch hunt in the press was executed with typically Stalinist methods—by charging the political adversary with all imaginable crimes, and primarily the crime of being an enemy agent in the pay of international reactionaries. At the assembly of the Zadar Socialist Union of Workers which condemned me, the citizens were presented with the claim that I received the unbelievably large sum of 70 million dinars from "our enemy." That the assertions for which I am tried today are absolutely truthful will be proven by tomorrow's Yugoslav press. There will not be a single word about the fact that I was *libeled* by the Socialist Union of Workers, Zadar I, for spreading national hatred and receiving money and orders from our enemy—libel, as proven by today's trial.

If anyone is to be tried for spreading false information and assertions in order to incite the citizens, it should be those members of the press who initiated the campaign against me and those people who deceived the members of the Zadar Socialist Union of Workers.

I deny the prosecution's allegation that I wrote my articles for the purpose of weakening the citizens' confidence in the building of a socialist socio-economic system. It is precisely my confidence that the Constitution and the law are respected in our society that inspired me to write these articles and to think about founding an independent socialist magazine.

In spite of the greatest effort, I did not succeed in grasping why it states in the summary of the indictment that I assert "that it is the socialist intellectuals who have a hostile attitude toward our socialist system." Nor do I think that anyone can say I was spreading false information through the press. Those few copies which came into the hands of a few friends, and which I occasionally sent to the administration of our newspapers, can in no case be construed as going to the press, for, according to the law, the press is defined as only that which spreads information to the public.

I cannot agree that those of my incriminating articles published in the West were featured in reactionary papers and magazines.

I have never written a letter to "Freedom House,"[2] a constant claim in our press.

I have shown that everything I wrote in my articles has lately been printed in our press. How is it that when certain things are written by Bakaric or Tripalo or Crvenkovski they are evaluated as constructive criticism, while those same things written by Mihajlov become criminal acts? This means that it is not so much a question of what is said, but of who says it and when he speaks. In this we can discern the spirit of all totalitarianism. If a one-party system and socialism are synonymous, then I am certainly guilty. Should this be the case, however, it ought to be written into the Constitution, to avoid future misunderstandings. I personally think that a multi-party system can achieve a true renaissance precisely in a socialist society—in a socialist society it is impossible for great concentrations of capital to influence the development of political thought. This is a very crucial difference between the multi-party system under socialism and the same system under capitalism. That is why I am convinced that today the conservative forces are those which

[2] In June 1966 Freedom House, New York, held a press conference to announce Mihajlov's plans to publish an opposition journal. Moral, not financial, support was asked for. [Ed.]

try to maintain a one-party system and the monopoly of one ideology.

This trial certainly shows that it is still impossible to speak here of a struggle of ideas. *All that was said today is material for a polemic of ideas and not for a courtroom.* At the same time this case shows that there is no freedom of ideas without political freedom, and that it is impossible to have only one organized social force and, at the same time, several opinions.

Economic liberalization alone (which economic reform is expected to produce) is no guarantee against a Stalinist revival if it is not accompanied by political democratization. Let us recall a well-known case in the history of the socialist countries: the extreme economic liberalization of the New Economic Policy in Soviet Russia which stabilized the Russian economy at the time. Immediately thereafter, the most virulent Stalinism erupted, destroying that economic liberalization because the New Economic Policy was not accompanied by political liberalization and the Party maintained its monopoly over authority. But political liberalization is not possible as long as the Constitution is not respected, as long as it is mere empty words and paper. Let us recall the Stalin Constitution of 1936, an unusually humane document. But because Stalin as head of the Party had a monopoly of authority, 1936 is notorious in Russian history as a year of wide-scale purges and mass deportations to concentration camps.

Already in 1953 we find the following in *Borba:*

In my opinion the judiciary must . . . be freed of the recent Party intervention in its work; otherwise it cannot avoid (however good its intentions) undermining democracy insofar as it continues to conform in its work to political and ideological standards, or even to local criteria. The judiciary must become an organ of the state and the law—which means the people—not an organ of political interest or opinion from the Party ranks.

. . . How long shall we use ideological instead of legal arguments? How long will decisions be based on dialectical and historical materialism instead of the law? [Milovan Djilas, *Borba*, December 31, 1953.]

[1966]